Nurturing Attachments

of related interest

**A Practical Guide to Using Attachment Theory and Research
with Children and Young People**
Steve Farnfield
ISBN 978 1 84310 100 0

Understanding Looked After Children
Psychology for Foster Care
Jeune Guishard-Pine, Suzanne McCall and Lloyd Hamilton
Foreword by Andrew Wiener
ISBN 978 1 84310 370 7

New Families, Old Scripts
A Guide to the Language of Trauma and Attachment in Adoptive Families
Caroline Archer and Christine Gordon
ISBN 978 1 84310 258 8

Trauma, Attachment and Family Permanence
Fear Can Stop You Loving
Edited by Caroline Archer
Foreword by Daniel A. Hughes
ISBN 978 1 84310 021 8

First Steps in Parenting the Child who Hurts
Tiddlers and Toddlers
Second edition
Caroline Archer
ISBN 978 1 85302 801 4

Next Steps in Parenting the Child Who Hurts
Tykes and Teens
Caroline Archer
ISBN 978 1 85302 802 1

**A Safe Place for Caleb: An Interactive Book for Kids, Teens and Adults
with Issues of Attachment, Grief, Loss or Early Trauma**
Kathleen A. Chara and Paul J. Chara, Jr.
Illustrated by J.M. Berns
ISBN 978 1 84310 799 6

Understanding Attachment and Attachment Disorders
Theory, Evidence and Practice
Vivien Prior and Danya Glaser
ISBN 978 1 84310 245 8

Nurturing Attachments

Supporting Children who are Fostered or Adopted

Kim S. Golding

Jessica Kingsley Publishers
London and Philadelphia

First published in 2008
by Jessica Kingsley Publishers
116 Pentonville Road
London N1 9JB, UK
and
400 Market Street, Suite 400
Philadelphia, PA 19106, USA

www.jkp.com

Library of Congress Cataloging in Publication Data
Golding, Kim S.
  Nurturing attachments : supporting children who are fostered or adopted / Kim S.
Golding.
     p. cm.
  Includes bibliographical references and index.
  ISBN 978-1-84310-614-2 (alk. paper)
  1. Foster children. 2. Foster parents. 3. Attachment behavior in children. 4. Adopted
children—Family relationships. 5. Foster home care. I. Title.
  HV881.G65 2008
  362.73'3—dc22
                                                                    2007024884

British Library Cataloguing in Publication Data
A CIP catalogue record for this book is available from the British Library

ISBN 978 1 84310 614 2

Printed and bound in Great Britain by
Athenaeum Press, Gateshead, Tyne and Wear

I would like to dedicate this book to all the foster and adoptive families that I have worked with.

Contents

Part 2: A Model for Parenting the Child with Difficulties in Attachment Relationships: Providing a Secure Base

List of Figures

Acknowledgements

Academic acknowledgements

In writing this book I have drawn upon knowledge of attachment theory and interventions, which I have gained over the years through the work of a range of notable theorists, researchers and attachment therapists. As my understanding of their work has been integrated into my pre-existing knowledge it is not always easy to separate out what I have learnt from whom. This means that ideas are not always attributed to the originator, and for this I apologize.

I would therefore like to acknowledge and thank: Caroline Archer, Kate Cairns, Patricia Crittenden, Richard Delaney, Mary Dozier, Vera Fahlberg, Peter Fonagy, Danya Glaser, David Howe, Beverley James, Ann Jernberg and Phyllis Booth, Gillian Schofield, Allan Schore, Dan Siegel, Dan Stern, and in particular Dan Hughes – whose work has provided me with a framework for the parenting model used within this book.

Not forgetting the originators of attachment theory: John Bowlby with Mary Ainsworth, Mary Main and colleagues.

Personal acknowledgements

In 1999 I made a decision to return to clinical psychology after a break of a number of years spent enjoying my young children. The job I returned to led me into a whole new world without which this book would not have been written. Thank you to all those who believed in the Primary Care and Support Project (PCSP), and had the vision to make it happen.

I would especially like to thank Kathy Smith and Claire Burgess who always supported my own vision; Jenni Stephens who quietly gave me confidence; and Julie Elliott who, as PCSP became Integrated Service for Looked After Children (ISL), continued to believe in us, and what we were doing. I must also thank all the foster carers who showed me what I didn't know and led me to attachment theory.

The 'Fostering Attachments' group was a logical development of our support service for carers. It continues to develop and grow. I must thank Wendy Picken who helped me to develop the initial group and Lisa Cogley, Vicki Wood and Debbie Kavanagh who continue to support me in the running of the group. Thanks also go to the adoptive parents who have helped me extend the reach of the group further.

Of course this would not be possible without the support of other team members, Margaret Webby, Nick Price, Annie Wise, Jo Thompson, Lyn Speake, Debra Turner and Michelle Hudspith.

Further afield I would also like to thank the members of the national network of Clinical Psychologists working with Looked After and Adopted Children (CPLAAC), who have always been so supportive of me and whose input has helped me to further develop my ideas. Thanks especially to Julie Hudson, Frances Gulliford, Jackie Lees, Helen Rostill and Miriam Silver.

Even further afield I must acknowledge a debt of gratitude to Dan Hughes whose sensitive support and responsiveness has given me a secure base from which I have had the confidence to explore.

There are of course a range of people who have supported me in the writing of this book. My family: Alex, Deborah and Chris, who have everlasting patience with me. Thanks are also due to Chris for the stress thermometer, volcano and brain drawings. My mum, who never complains when I bring work on my visits. My sister Cheryl and her family Paul, Charlotte, Sophie and Olivia, for always being there for me. My friend, Jane Foulkes, our discussions have always been thought provoking.

Finally, thanks to all those who read and helpfully commented on earlier drafts of this book. Foster carers, adoptive parents and a young person: Caroline, Helen, Sue, Lyn, Jacqueline, Richard, Debbie, Marie and Chantelle.

And my colleagues: Wendy, Margaret, Emma, Rachel, Lisa, Jane and Nick.

Introduction

There are only two lasting bequests we can hope to give our children; one is roots, the other, wings.

Reverend Henry Ward Beecher (1813–1887)

If you are caring for, or working with, an adopted or foster child who has difficulties in attachment you will know that finding roots and using wings can be very hard for these children. As they struggle to achieve a secure attachment they find it difficult to feel safe enough to take root within the family, to use the family as a secure base. This in turn makes finding their wings, moving away from the family, a much more challenging undertaking. Neither the need for attachment nor for exploration is being successfully met. You will need to find special ways of parenting the children, which will help them to experience a more secure attachment increasing resilience and contributing to emotional health. I hope that this book will give you some ideas and thus contribute to your special task of parenting or supporting your child.

Over the years I have worked with a range of foster carers and adoptive parents trying to meet the emotional needs of their children. Often I meet these parents at a time when they feel like they are failing. They are demoralized in the face of the continuing difficulties of their children. We begin to explore together the problems being presented, and in particular we start to understand these difficulties from the perspective of attachment theory. We experience sadness as we revisit the depth of adversity many of the children have experienced. We experience concern at the trauma involved in leaving a birth family and adjusting to a new family. We experience worry for a child removed at birth following difficult prenatal conditions, with the additional trauma of separation from a short-term foster family. With understanding about how this early experience has impacted on the children, however, comes a reduced sense of failure and some ideas about the way forward. We all have a renewed optimism that we can make a difference to the lives of the children.

I have come to believe that the narrative of attachment theory is an important one because it provides a way of understanding the children that does not
position difficulties firmly within the child nor the parents. Instead it leads to a
focus on relationship, the importance of what happens between the parents and
the child. Parents are left aware of the extent of difficulty the children experience within relationships, but also with a sense that they can help by offering a
new and very different relationship experience. The attachment narrative therefore points to a way forward.

I have also been privileged to continue to support many of these parents.
Together we have explored their parenting experience. We combine their exper-
tise about their children, and my knowledge and psychological understanding.
We find ways of providing nurture and support, helping the children to feel
more secure and thus to develop resilience, improved emotional health and
capacity for relationship. The journeys we travel together are not easy ones,
progress can be slow and setbacks are common but we usually manage to see the
road ahead.

It is out of this work that the 'Fostering Attachments' training group, and
this book, have emerged. Drawing upon the knowledge of many professionals
within this field, combined with the wisdom of the adoptive parents and foster
carers, I have developed the 'house model of parenting'. This model of
parenting, firmly based on attachment theory, provides a coherent set of ideas
for parenting the children in a way that fosters security of attachment and therefore resilience and emotional growth.

In writing this book I have tried not to write a 'how to parent' book but
instead to offer a framework for parenting. It is my hope that this can be used in
a way that allows parents to continue being innovative and creative in their
approach. Practical suggestions are offered but importantly these are grounded
in theory so that readers can develop a deeper understanding about what they
are trying to achieve, and can be flexible in the way they use and adapt the ideas
being discussed. For the less theory minded there is a path through the book
that provides a more practical focus.

Neither is this book a 'how to fix it' book. Whilst attachment experience
can increase risk or resilience to later difficulties it does not directly cause these.
Developmental or behavioural difficulties arise from a multitude of causes and
are influenced by a range of factors including life experiences built upon genetic
make-up, temperament, prenatal and birth experience, as well as attachment
experience. This book aims to help you provide as good an attachment experience as you can for your child, helping her to develop confidence in herself and
others. This is likely to increase her resilience and emotional well-being but, as
with all children, other difficulties or problems are likely to arise. Children need
our continuing and sensitive support throughout childhood, into adulthood
and beyond.

The book is divided into three parts. This takes you through an understanding of attachment theory, patterns of attachment and implications for parenting. This leads into the house model of parenting, providing guidance on how to help your child experience the family as a secure base. This in turn provides a context within which you can build a relationship with your child and manage her behaviour. In this way your child's confidence and ability to manage her own behaviour increases.

This book can be read chapter by chapter. This will provide you with the theory integrated with practical ideas for parenting. Alternatively you can follow the theory and the practice separately.

To focus on the *parenting ideas* read Chapter 1, which provides a brief overview of the theory, and then move to Chapters 4, 5 and 6 to consider the implications of the theory for the difficulties the children may face and for the parenting approach adopted. You can then read through Parts 2 and 3, but omitting the additional theory which appears in Chapters 10 and 13.

If you would like to read the *theory* first I would suggest reading Chapters 1 to 3, and the additional theory at the end of Chapters 10 and 13.

I have tried to keep psychological jargon to a minimum, but inevitably in a field that integrates so much across disciplines many psychological terms are used. I explain these as they first appear, but have also included a glossary to refer to at any time. Words defined in the glossary appear in italics in the text.

I have also included a further reading list for those of you who, like me, get hooked on thinking about attachment theory. The reading list includes a range of books that I have personally found useful. Many of these books provided me with inspiration when developing my ideas for this book; some have been published whilst I have been writing.

To avoid clumsiness I have alternated gender throughout the book. Adoptive parents and foster carers of course can be mothers or fathers and children can be boys or girls. Additionally I have used the general term 'parents' to refer to both foster carers and adoptive parents.

I hope you enjoy reading this book, but more importantly that it helps you find your own inspiration so that, whether you are parenting or supporting children living in foster or adoptive homes, you can find this an enriching and rewarding experience, to the ultimate benefit of yourself and the children and young people.

Throughout the book the ideas and thoughts expressed are illustrated by the experience of four children and their families. Whilst these children and families are entirely fictional some of the episodes described are based on the real experience of parents and children I have known.

Let me introduce you to the children.

Catherine

Catherine's mother, Fiona, lived with her own parents until she was five years old, but after this drifted through a series of foster homes until she was 16 years old. She then moved into a bed-sit. Following a series of casual relationships Fiona became pregnant with Catherine, unsure herself who the father was. Since that time she has drifted in and out of a relationship with Mark.

When Catherine was born Fiona was 17 years old and Mark was 20. Mark drank heavily and could be physically violent towards Fiona. Sometimes Fiona moved into a women's refuge taking Catherine with her, but she always returned to Mark after a few months.

Even though Fiona had a lot of support from her social worker the level of neglect Catherine experienced remained high. Eventually, when Catherine was two years old, she was voluntarily accommodated and moved into foster care. Fiona did attend some parenting classes and regularly attended contact sessions with her daughter. Rehabilitation home was attempted, but this failed when it was discovered that Fiona and Mark were going out and leaving Catherine alone in the flat. Catherine moved into another foster home.

Fiona and Mark moved away and only made occasional contact to see how Catherine was doing. A plan for adoption was made. Jenny and Martin formally adopted Catherine when she was three-and-a-half years old. Over the next few years they found Catherine to be a quiet, withdrawn child who liked to play by herself. She could be spiteful, for example towards their young niece when she came to play. She was wary of Martin for a considerable time but did develop a relationship of sorts with Jenny.

Jenny is concerned that this relationship hasn't deepened over time, as she would have expected. Sometimes she feels like she is just looking after her for someone else. Jenny gets particularly frustrated when Catherine is reluctant to let her help. As Catherine's level of self-care and ability to look after her belongings are poor this can cause a lot of tension between them.

There are no concerns about Catherine expressed at school. She copes with the schoolwork, working at an average level. She is quiet in class and has few friends.

Zoë

Zoë is the youngest child of five children born to Karen and Damien. This was a chaotic household with little routine or boundaries. The older children tended to look after the younger ones. They all looked unkempt with clothes not quite fitting and faces unwashed. There was little food in the house and the children would beg food from neighbours. Karen and Damien often went out and left the children to sort themselves out.

Karen did appear to enjoy Zoë, although she continued to treat her as the baby of the family and appropriate stimulation was lacking.

When Zoë was 18 months old Damien left and shortly after this Karen began a relationship with Dave. Dave had recently come out of prison following a conviction for sexual abuse of a niece. His name was put on the sex offenders' register. Despite the concerns expressed by her social worker Karen continued to allow Dave to live with them and therefore a decision was made to remove the children on an emergency protection order. A care order was eventually granted and the four older children were placed in two foster homes.

It was decided that Zoë would need more individual attention and stimulation. Jenny and Martin, who had adopted Catherine, were at this time wondering about adding to their family. They were not sure how five-year-old Catherine would cope with a sister and thought they might offer some short-term care to foster children instead. Zoë was placed with them on a temporary basis. This temporary placement dragged on as assessments were carried out with Karen and an aunt who had stepped forward to offer a home to Zoë. Neither was thought to be suitable.

Jenny and Martin applied to adopt Zoë who was now two and a half, but there were plans to reunite Zoë with her two youngest siblings. Zoë moved to live with them; unfortunately the foster carers found it difficult to cope with the three children together. Belatedly Zoë was moved back with Jenny and Martin and they eventually adopted her when she was four years old.

Whilst Jenny and Martin very much love Zoë they also find her hard work. She does not like Jenny to be out of her sight and will even follow her to the toilet. She constantly chatters, asking endless questions but rarely waits for an answer. She will display prolonged temper tantrums, especially when she can't have what she wants, when she wants it. She can also be very demanding, wanting help to be dressed, fed, and generally looked after.

At school the teachers quickly become exasperated by Zoë's constant need for their attention. She also finds it difficult to get on with the other children, quickly becoming frustrated if they do not do what she wants. She will sometimes bite or hit them when they don't fit in with her plans.

Marcus

Marcus's mother, Tessa, lived for much of her teenage life in a children's home following the death of her mother in a car crash. Her father had by this time gone to live in Jamaica. In the children's home Tessa met Richie, who shared her African Caribbean heritage. Richie introduced Tessa to Rastafarianism, although he was more interested in dreadlocks and reggae than the more spiritual elements.

When Tessa became pregnant her social worker helped them to move into a sheltered flat where support would be on hand if they needed it. Richie is a difficult young man. He is easily provoked to violence and not willing to engage with anyone who might help him. He found Marcus difficult and would often resort to hitting him if he didn't 'behave'.

When Marcus was two-and-a-half years old they had a second child, Bob, named after Richie's favourite reggae singer Bob Marley. By this time both parents were becoming involved with drugs and their parenting became more and more erratic. Social workers were trying to support them, but they struggled with Richie's temper and Tessa's difficulty in doing anything not sanctioned by Richie.

Sadly, when he was five months old, Bob died, apparently a cot death. Marcus was in the room with him at the time. With increasing concerns for his safety, Marcus was removed into foster care.

As he grew older Marcus's behaviour became increasingly challenging and unpredictable. He would never do what others wanted him to do, and could be verbally aggressive. He enjoyed drawing, but his drawings always appeared the same, featuring violence and bloodshed.

His first foster placement broke down after nine months because of concerns that Marcus might seriously hurt their pet dog, whom he had tried to suffocate on a number of occasions. He had three more placements before being placed, at the age of six years, with Rita and Frank, very experienced foster carers, whose own children are now adults. As they are also African Caribbean it is hoped they will be able to help Marcus develop a sense of his family's heritage.

Marcus finds it very difficult to stay still or concentrate on anything for very long. He can become excited or angry very easily and then becomes difficult to manage.

Marcus attends a school for children with emotional and behavioural difficulties. He finds it difficult to manage even in the smaller classes at this school and he has had periods of exclusion because of the level of violence he displays towards the other children.

Luke

Luke is the third of Tina's children. Tina has learning difficulties and struggles to understand or meet the needs of her children. All the children have different fathers. Gary, Luke's father, has not lived with them since Luke was 18 months old.

Tina managed to provide some positive parenting experience for her older children, supported by her health visitor, and aided by her current partners. The birth of Luke however precipitated a difficult period for Tina, which was increased because of the erratic presence of Gary and his final departure. Luke therefore was severely neglected as a small child. Later it was suspected that Luke had been left for very long periods alone in his cot or strapped into a buggy. Support services offered practical help and the family did stay together during Luke's preschool years.

When Luke was five years old Tina became involved with an older man who was well known as a drug dealer. Tina quickly became dependent upon him, and the children's needs were further neglected. By this time Tina's eldest son was living with his father.

A decision was made to remove Luke and his sister. They were placed in separate foster placements. Luke went to live with Jackie, a single foster carer. Luke continued to have supervised contact with Tina and his siblings. Whilst he appeared to look forward to these visits, they also unsettled him.

Luke struggles at school with learning and with friendships. The further up the school he goes, the wider the gap between himself and his peers. Luke finds this very stressful and his behaviour at school can be quite challenging. When he was eight he was given a statement of special educational needs because of learning difficulties and emotional and behavioural problems. The additional support this provides helps Luke to make some progress although he remains a very vulnerable child in school.

Part I

Attachment Theory

Overview of Attachment Theory

Attachment theory is a theory of child development that focuses on the influence of early relationships on children. The theory suggests that the child's subsequent development and capacity to form relationships will be influenced by this early experience. This theory therefore has important implications for children growing up in substitute care. Children who live in foster or adoptive homes all share a disruption of their early relationships, a loss of or separation from their biological families. Additionally most of these children and young people will have experienced inadequate parenting early in their lives, and many will have had to cope with multiple placements following removal from their family.

Catherine, Zoë, Marcus and Luke have all experienced difficult early home lives with neglect of their emotional and physical needs, inconsistent or unavailable parenting and, for Marcus in particular, the fear of hurt and pain from at least one of his parents.

They were all removed from these families and Catherine, Zoë and Marcus experienced multiple placements before being able to settle in a more permanent home.

The legacy of these early years is still very apparent in the difficulties they display in developing relationships with their foster or adoptive parents.

Attachment theory can guide our understanding of the effects of early abuse, neglect, separation and loss on the child's ability to form healthy *attachments* with new parents. It can help you to make sense of some of your child's subsequent behaviour. In particular the way that your child relates to you can be heavily influenced by the way he learnt to relate to birth parents. You can find yourselves caught up in interactions that are not your own. In fact a child can hold so tightly to these ways of relating that you find yourself pushed into taking the role of abusive or neglectful parent despite your usual ways of relating to children or the ways that you want to relate to this child.

Understanding the processes that you are being subjected to and the way that this influences the developing attachment relationship can help you to resist responding to your child as he is anticipating. Instead you can gently lead or guide him into different ways of relating. He will then be able to experience a more *secure attachment* relationship than previously.

What is attachment theory?

Attachment theory was first proposed by John Bowlby (Bowlby 1973, 1980, 1982, 1998) and expanded with the work of Mary Main (Main and Solomon 1986) and Mary Ainsworth (Ainsworth *et al.* 1978). It is a theory of child development. It focuses on how children develop within relationships, and the impact that this has for later social and emotional development. This in turn impacts on *cognitive* development: the way the child learns about and understands the world.

The theory suggests that the earliest years of a child's life are critical for later development. Infants are born biologically predisposed to form relationships from which they can experience security and comfort. This means that the human infant has evolved to instinctively form relationships. Very early in life the baby is already attending to the human face and voice, and is particularly interested in the voice and face of mum and very soon of dad too. This very early instinctive interest in other humans indicates the importance of relationships for a child's ability to feel secure and for subsequent development. Babies are born able to elicit interest and care from other people. As they grow older these care-eliciting behaviours become more sophisticated and more purposeful.

Thus between six and nine months children will develop a range of 'attachment' behaviours that they can use to keep the parent close. In this way the child is using the parent as a *secure base*, as a way of increasing feelings of security when in a situation that might arouse feelings of insecurity. For example, a stranger entering the room, an unusual or loud noise or other worrying event in the child's surroundings might cause the infant concern, leading to behaviour such as crying. The child therefore expresses distress, bringing the parent close to provide comfort. This in turn reduces feelings of insecurity; the child is soothed and feels calm again. These same behaviours can be triggered by behaviours of the parent, for example if the parent threatens to leave or is rejecting of the child.

These attachment behaviours are complemented by explorative behaviours when the child is feeling safe. These behaviours are also instinctive. The child is biologically predisposed both to seek care and comfort and to explore and learn in the world. The child is born to develop relationships and to enjoy novelty and experience.

Bowlby (1998) further suggested that the early experience of attachment relationships leads to the development of a *cognitive* model (*internal working model*) of these relationships which influences and is modified by later relationships. This means that the child's early experience leads to the development of a memory or template for how relationships work. Children learn about themselves and about how others are likely to respond based on their early experience. Later experience may lead to changes to this model but these changes will not replace what has been learnt from this early experience. In effect the child develops a range of models of how relationships might work, early experience remaining very important within these models.

Why are attachment relationships important?

The very earliest years of a child's life provide experiences that are critical for the child's later development and ability to make close relationships. The experience of first relationships provides the foundation stones for the child's subsequent development. Later experience will also influence the developmental pathway that the child travels, but the early experience provides the starting point.

When children experience warm, sensitive and responsive parenting or early care they will develop a *secure attachment*. This provides children with the opportunity to develop positive expectations about future relationships; to develop trust in others. The children also use this relationship to learn about themselves. Experience that allows a child to develop positive feelings (e.g. 'I am somebody that people like', 'I am somebody who is successful') leads to appropriate independence and *autonomy*. The child develops self-reliance. Bowlby (1998) suggests that securely attached children with positive expectations of self and others will approach the world with confidence. Thus when faced with potentially alarming situations these children will tackle them effectively or will seek help to do this.

For Catherine, Zoë, Marcus and Luke, sensitive, warm and responsive parenting in their early years was in short supply.

If Catherine woke in the night and heard Mark fighting with Fiona there was no-one there to comfort her. If Fiona did come she was more likely to be angry with Catherine for making a noise than comforting. Catherine became used to experiencing stress but did not learn that others could help her to manage this. She learnt to stay alert to what was going on around her and to keep her feelings of distress to herself.

Zoë, too, might wake in the night to the sounds of people downstairs being loud and often drunk. She did cry out because this might bring some comfort. Sometimes one of her sisters would come and maybe put a bottle of milk in her mouth; on occasions mum came up and would hold and cuddle her. Zoë could

...ver reliably predict when someone would be there or when she would be left alone. She therefore learnt to cry loud, in the hope that this would attract someone's attention.

When Marcus woke in the night he felt scared. He did not want his parents to come to him however as that would be even more scary. He tried to manage by himself. He would get out of bed and crawl underneath it, dragging a blanket with him. In the darkness and shelter this provided he experienced some reduction in his anxiety.

Luke rarely woke in the night. As an infant the level of neglect he experienced meant that he did not expect attention. An undemanding child, Luke spent a lot of time sleeping.

What happens when attachment relationships are insecure, unavailable or frightening?

When an attachment figure is insensitive, neglecting or rejecting an insecure attachment develops. The child finds it difficult to rely on the parent to help him feel safe and secure. He learns to behave in ways that increase the chance that the parent will be there when needed. Attachment behaviour is behaviour that lets the parent know that the child is feeling insecure, worried or distressed. Instead of displaying this attachment behaviour in a straightforward way as in a *secure attachment* relationship the child distorts the display of behaviour.

Like Catherine, children may minimize attachment behaviour to maintain closeness to parents who are already rejecting. Thus they appear less emotionally distressed or worried than they feel. This is expressed through passive and withdrawn behaviour with little display of emotional distress. The children act as if they do not need the parent. This is called an *avoidant attachment*.

Alternatively, as Zoë demonstrates, children may maximize attachment behaviour to elicit care from inconsistent parents. Thus they appear more emotionally distressed or worried than they feel. This is expressed through demanding and clingy behaviour. Additionally these children will resist being soothed. Once they have the parent's attention they do not want to appear comforted in case the parent becomes unavailable again. This is called an *ambivalent-resistant attachment*.

In both cases these behaviours are organized to increase the chance that parents will be responsive when needed. The children adapt their behaviour to suit the particular parenting environment that they find themselves in.

More seriously a *disorganized-controlling attachment* relationship develops when, for children like Marcus, parents are frightened or frightening to the child. Parents can be frightening to children because of behaviour directed towards them, e.g. hitting the child; because of a lack of behaviour, e.g. not protecting the child; or because of behaviours that the child is witness to, e.g. a father hitting a mother.

The child will also be frightened if the parent is frightened. For example, a parent may have been mistreated during childhood or may have experienced an unresolved loss of their own parent. Aspects of parenting their own children trigger the unresolved feelings they have about their childhood. The parent appears frightened and this is frightening to the child.

Situations in which a parent is frightening or frightened are very difficult for a young child because the behaviour of the parent activates the child's attachment system. The child feels frightened and therefore instinctively wants to behave in ways that will elicit care and comfort; but the source of potential comfort is also the source of the fear. The child is left with an irresolvable dilemma and does not know how to behave. The child is unable to organize his behaviour at times of stress to receive emotional support because the parent is both the source of fear and the potential for safety.

This state is highly stressful and damaging for children. Therefore as they become older they find ways to solve this dilemma. They develop ways of behaving that are less reliant on the parent. Additionally they increase feelings of safety by increasing the degree to which they feel in control. They cannot trust the parent to keep them safe and so they become controlling in their behaviour and they take control of the relationship. Rather than the attachment being disorganized, the children develop highly organized but controlling ways of interacting with parents that build upon the early patterns of avoidant or ambivalent relating.

The children who have an *avoidant attachment* to their parents become even more self-reliant, compliant or even caretaking. They look after the parents who are not able to look after them.

The children who have an ambivalent attachment to their parents become very coercive in their interactions. They use aggression and anger alternating with appeasement and displays of helplessness to control the degree to which the parent is attending to them.

A small proportion of children who have had no experience of early attachment relationships, either because of severe neglect as in Luke's case, or impoverished institutionalized care, will demonstrate a failure to develop selective attachments. This difficulty has developed because of a lack of relationships. These children have not learnt to relate to a caregiver as special, compared to other adults, because they have not had experience of such a person. These children can be *disinhibited*. They appear indiscriminately friendly, but are unable to engage in mutually satisfying, genuine relationships. They relate to everyone but at a superficial level. Alternatively the children can become extremely *inhibited*. When distressed they inhibit all signs of this and fail to approach anyone for comfort.

These patterns of attachment will be explored in greater depth in Chapter 3.

What happens as the child grows older?

Interactions between parent and child often tend to reinforce the early attachment patterns. Patterns of relating in families develop that are stable over time. Additionally these early attachment relationships act as a guide for the child in later relationships. Children have expectations about how other people will relate to them based on their early experience. Children therefore approach these relationships in ways that are in line with these expectations. Children also have expectations about the type of person they are. If children's experience is that they are not very likeable they will approach other people in a way that conveys this feeling about themselves.

Thus Catherine behaves with Jenny and Martin as if she does not expect them to be available and responsive. She makes few demands on them, plays on her own, and if upset makes little fuss. Catherine will give them a cuddle when they initiate it, but she rarely cuddles them spontaneously. It is difficult to know how Catherine is feeling or what she wants. A few months after she had come to live with them Martin took Catherine to the dentist. He was amazed to be told that she had a nasty abscess at the back of her mouth; she had given no sign of discomfort.

Zoë on the other hand makes sure she has their attention all the time. She does not like to have Jenny out of her sight, because she fears that she will not come back. She expects inconsistency from Jenny and Martin and therefore works very hard to make sure that they don't stop noticing her. When Zoë hurts herself the whole household knows it; in fact even when not hurt she will act as if she is. On one occasion when Zoë was in the garden she smeared her finger with blackberry juice and then asked for a plaster! Zoë wants cuddles from Jenny all the time but especially when Jenny is seeing to Catherine or is attending to other things. She does not expect attention to come automatically.

As he did when he was little, Marcus takes control of his own care. He coerces Rita and Frank to care for him on his terms. He always makes sure he is in control. He remains very vigilant to where they are and what they are doing and will behave in ways that makes sure they are meeting his needs. He will tell Rita where to sit and instruct Frank in how to put the milk on the cereal. He will refuse to wear clothes they have put out for him, and becomes angry if they do not let him have the TV on. For Rita and Frank it feels like walking on 'eggshells' as they wait for the next outburst.

Luke appears to settle in with Jackie easily; he is initially compliant and uncomplaining. However, this gradually changes as Luke becomes more secure in the household. At times he can still be undemanding but he passively resists Jackie's attempts to care for him. At other times he can become much more difficult, being fussy and hard to please. Luke does not know what to expect of Jackie; his experience of being parented is so limited that he appears confused and uncertain with her. Sometimes he will be loving with her, but this feels quite superficial; he can be equally loving with her neighbour, the local shopkeeper and even the postman!

The quality of the early *attachment* therefore has two important influences on children as they grow and develop.

    1. It influences how the child relates to other people.

As we can see with the examples of Catherine, Zoë, Marcus and Luke their expectations of their family are very much linked with their early experience.

Catherine learnt that parents are unresponsive and not available. She has few expectations.

    Zoë learnt to demand attention, expecting inconsistency and unpredictability.

    Marcus found parents scary; by feeling in control he reduces the anxiety he experiences when relating to parents.

    Luke expects little of parents but looks for attention indiscriminately from the range of people he meets during the day.

    2. It influences how the child feels about self.

When children are not getting their needs met reliably they tend to make sense of this in terms of themselves. They feel bad, naughty, not good enough.

Catherine has developed a sense of not being good enough to be cared for. This has also extended into school. She is reluctant to show the teacher her work for fear of disapproval.

    Zoë works so hard at getting attention that she knows she is a nuisance. When her parents or teachers get frustrated with her this just confirms that she is naughty and that she won't get attention when she needs it.

    Marcus feels very weak and ineffectual and this is frightening. The weak get hurt. He therefore acts as if he is powerful and tyrannical, especially with his 'soft' foster parents. Marcus then feels strong and bad as he 'rules the roost'.

    Luke has a very underdeveloped sense of self; he appears to be testing out who he is, appearing unpredictable and insecure.

2

Attachment Theory: Caregiving and its Impact on Attachment and Exploration

Chapter 1 provides an overview of attachment theory. In the next two chapters this theory will be explored in greater depth.

Characteristics of the attachment relationship

We all form *affectional bonds* with a range of people during our lives. These are people for whom we feel affection and whose company we like to be in.

The attachment bond is a special kind of *affectional bond* that forms when one person experiences security and comfort from another. This is the bond that forms between a child and an adult who is in a caring role to that child. Most typically this is a parent or substitute carer.

When a child forms an attachment bond with an adult it indicates that the child is forming a relationship within which she needs to feel safe and secure. The child actively seeks the adult for such safety.

The child can form an *attachment* with a number of adults. One of these will be the primary attachment figure. If children are feeling especially vulnerable (distressed, hungry, tired or ill) they will prefer the primary attachment figure to the other secondary attachment figures.

An attachment relationship is characterized by a range of attachment behaviours. The goal of these behaviours is to seek protection. The child wants to stay close to the attachment figure in response to real or perceived stress or danger. The child therefore behaves in a way that ensures that this happens.

These attachment behaviours are:

- *Proximity-seeking*: The young child will attempt to remain within the protective range of the attachment figure. This protective range is reduced in a strange situation, but extends when the child is in familiar surroundings. At times of threat the young child will seek physical contact with the adult. Thus the child seeks proximity to the attachment figure in order to feel safe and secure.

- *Secure base effect*: The presence of an attachment figure fosters security in the child. This results in reduced attention to attachment considerations and in confident exploration and play. The parent is therefore acting as a *secure base* for the child.

- *Separation protest*: Threat to the continued accessibility of the attachment figure gives rise to protest and to active attempts to ward off the separation. If separation does occur the young child will vocally protest leading to *proximity-seeking* behaviour.

These behaviours therefore make up what is termed the *attachment behavioural system*: a group of behaviours that are displayed when children experience a need to be reassured or comforted by their attachment figure.

Attachment and exploratory behaviour

The *attachment behavioural system* interplays with an *exploratory behavioural system*. This system represents a group of behaviours that are displayed when the child is curious about something novel or interesting in the environment. Something draws the child's attention and she is motivated to explore. Whereas the attachment system focuses attention onto issues of safety and security and the availability of the attachment figure, the exploratory system focuses attention outwards, motivating the child to explore and learn about the world. The system activated by the highest intensity – in other words the need that is strongest within the child – will determine the behaviour the child displays.

Novelty in the environment will activate an exploratory system leaving the attachment system at a low intensity. If the child strays too far from the attachment figure or if a threat is introduced into the environment, the attachment system is activated at a higher level and the child returns to the parent. This decreases the intensity of the attachment system again and the exploratory system is again activated.

This is easy to visualize if the scenario of a young child in a waiting room is considered. When the child and parent first enter the room the child remains close to the parent. The attachment system is activated at a higher intensity in this unfamiliar environment. However, as the child surveys the room and the parent, acting as secure base, is unconcerned the child begins to feel comfortable. The intensity of activation of the attachment system is reduced. The child notices the presence of a box of toys and books. This activates the exploratory system at higher intensity and the child moves off to investigate. At some point a stranger will enter the room. This presents a threat to the child and the attachment system is again activated at higher intensity. The child seeks proximity to the parent, all thought of further exploring temporarily abandoned.

Thus a balance between the systems at a particular time determines what the child will do. This balance is affected by the quality of care the child is experiencing.

Children will selectively attach to a number of familiar adults, using these adults as a *secure base* from which to seek security and to facilitate play. They will attach to a primary attachment figure who is first in line to provide safety and comfort, and a number of secondary attachment figures. Children may preferentially seek out different familiar adults for play and exploration. It is not uncommon for the mother to be the main caregiver and the father to be the one who provides most opportunities for play and exploration, although of course these roles can be swapped around, and one parent can meet both needs.

The waiting room example demonstrates the triggering of the attachment system by occurrences within the environment. Anything threatening, frightening or confusing that occurs will trigger the attachment system, leading to a weakening of the exploratory system and an increase in attachment behaviours.

However, the attachment system can also be triggered at higher intensity because of events within the child. For example, if the child is feeling unwell, hurt, tired or hungry she is likely to demonstrate less interest in exploring and more concern with staying close to the parent.

Similarly if the parent signals the possibility of separation (e.g. preparation for going out), or is emotionally unavailable or actively rejecting of the child, this too will trigger the attachment system, reducing the likelihood of exploration.

Dimensions of caregiving

So far we have been considering the attachment relationship from the point of view of the child. We have thought about the behaviours the child displays and the ways in which the child uses the adult to increase feelings of security. Now we will think about the characteristics of the caregiver.

All infants, providing they experience some consistency of carer, will selectively attach to the small number of adults caring for them. Only in the case of severe neglect will a child fail to develop selective attachments. The quality of the care that children receive will however determine the security of these attachments and therefore the behaviours that the children display. The type of caregiving provided will lead to varying levels of confidence in the availability of the parent. When children feel confident they will behave in very straightforward ways signalling clearly: 'now I need you' and 'now I need to play and explore'. When confidence is low the behaviours become less straightforward as the children attempt to increase the likelihood that the parent will be there when needed.

Sensitive-responsive caregiving

The degree to which a parent is sensitive depends upon the extent to which he monitors the child's needs and responds to these predictably and consistently. Mary Ainsworth and colleagues (Ainsworth *et al.* 1978) describe how a sensitive parent will notice his infant's signals (acceptance), will interpret the signal correctly (co-operation) and will respond promptly and appropriately (accessibility).

Insensitive-unresponsive caregiving

An insensitive parent will not notice the signals (rejection), or will misinterpret them (interference), or will respond slowly, inappropriately or not at all (ignoring).

Sensitive and insensitive caring are part of a continuum depending on the degree to which parents are accepting or rejecting, co-operative or interfering, and accessible or inaccessible. This does not mean that parents have to be sensitive all the time. We all have bad days or times when we are preoccupied or distracted. The sensitive parent attends to the child's needs enough of the time to help the child feel secure. It would take a superhuman effort to do this all the time.

- Acceptance – rejection.
  The extent to which the parent accepts the child and the emotional state being signalled; the accepting parent will consider the child's perspective. If the child is upset because of a minor hurt, the parent may think that it is no big deal, but will accept that it is for the child who is now in need of a bit of loving attention.

- Co-operation – interference.
  The co-operative parent listens to or observes what the child is communicating. 'I don't think that is a serious hurt but as you think it is I will take it seriously.' The interfering parent will tell the child what to feel. 'Don't be silly, that doesn't hurt. Now go and play.'

- Accessibility – ignoring.
  The accessible parent is emotionally available to the child, meeting the needs that are being signalled. Availability and nurturing is dependent upon what the child is communicating. If the parent ignores the child's communications, and instead tells the child what to feel, he is inaccessible to meet the child's needs as they are expressed.

Sensitive parenting: The infant cries. The mother approaches and comforts the infant. She notices that the infant is squirming and looks uncomfortable. She changes the baby and soothes her until she is calm.

Insensitive parenting: The infant cries. After a while the mother approaches, looking cross. She picks up the infant and then puts her down again, telling her there is nothing wrong with her as she has just been fed. The mother walks away, thinking that her child always tries to stop her getting on with making tea.

It is important to remember that sensitive parenting is about being able to notice and understand the signals the child is giving so that her needs can be met. It is equally insensitive to ignore a child's need for comfort as it is to provide comfort when this is not needed. A disinterested and rejecting parent is being insensitive, but so is a fussy, overprotective parent. Sometimes a child will be very poor at signalling needs, perhaps because of a disability; this makes it difficult for the parent to meet these needs, and again this would be described as insensitive. Insensitive is not a judgement of the parent but a description of what is occurring between parent and child.

It might be helpful to think about this for Catherine, Zoë, Marcus and Luke.

Catherine's experience was of a highly insensitive parent. Fiona was young, and had received little nurturing herself. She quickly became overwhelmed by the needs of her young infant. When Catherine cried or needed her this would increase the anxiety that Fiona experienced. She did not know how to respond to this need and would therefore be highly insensitive. She might ignore Catherine, hoping that she would quieten by herself. Alternatively she might attend to Catherine but with a roughness that was frightening to her. She became convinced that Catherine was just crying to annoy her. Fiona needed Catherine to be quiet and placid; only then could she enjoy giving her a cuddle and feel secure in her infant's love for her. When Catherine expressed her own needs however it felt like she was getting at Fiona. She would become distant and hostile, perceiving this neediness as a lack of love for her, and as betraying her lack of parenting skills.

Karen had grown up herself in a large, chaotic family. She was used to no routine and unpredictability. She liked the kids but was too tired to meet all their demands. It suited her to let the older ones attend to the younger ones. When she felt like it she would pick Zoë up for a cuddle; if Zoë complied she liked her and enjoyed having her as a baby. If Zoë was fretful she would become cross however and think she was horrid. When the children were very demanding she would give them sweets to keep them quiet. There was, however, little food in the cupboards. Sometimes the older children would go to a neighbour to beg some tea. If there was enough they would bring Zoë back crisps, or other equally unsuitable food.

Tessa was frightened. When her infant needed her it stirred unconscious memories of being hurt by her own mother. She couldn't think about Marcus's needs because of her own preoccupation with this early trauma. She was also in fear of Richie and her fear increased if Marcus was demanding or needy. Her own level of fear made her highly insensitive to Marcus. She needed to keep Richie happy and needed Marcus to help her with this. As her stress increased would feel more and more out of control. As she became agitated she would try harder to control Marcus. She would threaten him or hit him to get him to do what she wanted. At other times she would put him in the bedroom, leaving him there for hours.

Tina had limited understanding of Luke. Her level of learning difficulty made it difficult for her to think about Luke's needs or to understand what he was signalling. She would try to do what the health visitor suggested, but quickly became overwhelmed if Luke didn't respond as she had been taught to expect. She would often leave him alone for long periods. She did not understand his need for stimulation nor know what to expect of him at different ages. Tina easily became overwhelmed and then would switch off. Luke therefore experienced little in the way of an emotional connection with Tina.

Sensitive parenting also requires that parents adjust to the changing needs of their growing children. The balance between attachment and exploration changes throughout childhood. Parents need to adjust their parenting as their children mature. Parents who encourage closeness when the child wants to explore and parents who encourage exploration when the child needs closeness are equally insensitive. Parents therefore need to understand the changing needs of their children and respond appropriately.

How attachment behaviour changes through childhood

The first three months

Babies are born predisposed to respond to others. At birth, babies are already born with abilities that ensure that they will be interested in other people. For example, they prefer to look at faces, they recognize the sound of voices.

As they mature, babies respond in ways that increase the likelihood that contact with people will continue. They calm when picked up; they smile when people talk to them. Therefore babies are born able to elicit interest and nurture from others. At this stage the parent has to maintain proximity and protect the infant, but the infant is already behaving in ways that ensure that this will happen. If the infant reliably interacts with parents who are well attuned to the infant's behaviour then stable patterns of interaction will become established. For example:

- The infant cries because of hunger and the parent responds by feeding her.
- The infant cries because of discomfort and the parent responds by changing her.
- The infant is alert and interested and the parent responds by playing with her.

- The infant is tired and the parent calms and allows her to sleep.

At this stage babies are unselective. They will respond in the same way to any human who can meet their needs reliably.

Three months to six months

As infants mature they develop the ability to actively seek attention rather than to passively respond to it. They also begin to discriminate between people, starting to show preference for some over others. This is the beginning of the development of the attachment bond. Parents can see this happening over the first six months. Babies change from being comfortable to be held and looked after by anyone, to being fussy about who is doing the holding and caring, showing more selectiveness about who will hold, feed and soothe them. During this period infants become less able to be comforted by all but a few familiar adults.

Six months to two years

Between six and nine months the development of the *attachment* to the parents is consolidated. The child is said to have formed selective attachments to a few familiar adults. Equally the young child will be wary of unfamiliar adults, only demonstrating sociability if reassured that an attachment figure is able to continue to provide a *secure base*. In our waiting room scenario, when the stranger enters, the child will move closer to the parent and will actively scrutinize the stranger. Only following this period of scrutiny and with the continued physical presence of the parent will the child become sociable, perhaps smiling at the stranger or taking an offered toy.

Between six months and two years the attachment system is very evident with clear *separation protest* and *proximity-seeking*. The infant will protest when separated and make active attempts to maintain proximity to the attachment figure. Separation distress is harder to relieve, and comfort by a stranger can lead to an increase in distress.

This is also the time when the child is becoming increasingly mobile and able to move away from the parent at will. Thus the exploratory system is also evident. The child is comfortable with moving away from the parent to explore, to play and to learn.

The child is therefore able to use the parent as a *secure base*, to gain comfort from the parent when needed and to move away and explore and learn in the world, secure in the availability of the parent if danger threatens.

Two years to four years

During this stage of development the child is learning to become more autonomous and self-reliant. She will be increasingly comfortable with moving further away from the parent in order to explore the environment. At this stage children are not yet able to keep themselves safe and thus attachment behaviour remains easily activated.

Toddlers will actively monitor parents to ensure that they are attending to them. They will also use attachment behaviour to regain this attention if lost. This is sometimes called 'attention-seeking' behaviour but represents a need for continuing attention and is therefore better described as 'attention-needing' behaviour.

As children mature they are increasingly confident, able to explore a wider world and to relate to a variety of people. The child however remains very vigilant to the availability of the parents and can still be reliant on their physical presence as a *secure base*. This is the stage at which the child and parent go together to toddler group. The child learns to play and interact with others with the continued presence of an attachment figure.

Children grow and develop further. Now distress at a brief separation reduces and they are increasingly able to tolerate longer periods of separation. Reunion no longer always requires bodily contact. This coincides with children having improved language and motor skills. They can use language and actions to both plan for and anticipate periods of separation and to reconnect with the parent when they come together again. Thus somewhere between two and four years children will be able to manage a period of time apart from an attachment figure, for example attending a playgroup session.

School age

As children go to school there are significant changes taking place in the degree to which they are autonomous and able to function in the world separate from attachment figures. Under normal circumstances a child now only needs periodic assurance of the parent's presence for security. Attachment needs do not disappear but become attenuated or weakened.

Adolescence

It is during adolescence that attachment needs again begin to predominate. Paradoxically as young people seek to become more independent of parents attachment security becomes even more important.

Young people are beginning to move away from hierarchical attachments, where parents offer security, towards friendships where they give and receive care and support. In the meantime the exploration of sexuality and the search for a romantic relationship influences the continuing need for *affectional bonds*.

By the end of adolescence successful young people will have moved from being receivers of care from their parents to being young adults who can enjoy reciprocal friendships, intimate relationships and have the potential to be competent caregivers.

The transition to increased *autonomy* and reduced reliance on parents is a stressful one requiring the support of parents for its successful completion. Thus *autonomy* is most easily established from a base of secure relationships that will endure beyond adolescence. Adolescents can explore living independently from parents because they know that they can turn to their parents when they need to. Insecure attachment relationships lead to difficulties as the young person attempts to re-negotiate a relationship with parents. This can lead to a high activation of the attachment system at the same time as the young person is attempting to become more independent of parents.

The internal working model

By adulthood young people have experienced a range of attachment needs. The way these have been supported will influence their continuing relationships. The attachment relationships that they have previously experienced are stored mentally as *internal working models*. These are like templates, stored as a memory in the brain, of what has been experienced. The memory guides future expectations of self and of others. They don't know what will happen in the future or what will happen when they make new relationships, but they do know what has happened in the past. Past memory therefore creates an expectation, which will influence how young people react to future experience.

These models begin to develop in early childhood. As children mature the models become more complex. Initially they allow infants to anticipate what parents are likely to do next. Later children can use the model to make simple plans, e.g. how to get proximity to the parent, where to look for him. By the time children reach the school years they can use the working models to feel secure even when the parent is not physically present.

In adolescence young people extend their range of relationships. The multiple models of relationships experienced in childhood now develop into an integrated strategy for approaching attachment relationships. This pattern predicts behaviour in romantic relationships and eventually as parents themselves.

These *internal working models* therefore reflect children's experience of relationships, leading to a complementary working model of the self and of the emotional availability of others.

For example:

- Positive *internal working model*: A child might hold a positive model that views the self as loveable and effective and others as available, loving, interested and responsive.

gative *internal working model*: A child might hold a negative model of
self as unloveable, uninteresting, unvalued and ineffective and others
as unavailable, neglectful, rejecting, unresponsive and hostile.

As can be seen from this example the model of self and of others is linked. Taken
together they represent both sides of the relationships that the child has experienced.

This impacts on children's feelings of:

- *self-esteem* – the degree to which children feel positive or negative about
  themselves

- *self-efficacy* – the degree to which children feel able to make things
  happen

- *social understanding* – the degree to which children understand social experience, can make friends and can co-operate with others

and their ability to experience:

- *empathy* – to understand how another person is feeling

- *autonomy* – the capacity to be appropriately independent and self-reliant.

The internal working model as a stable model

Internal working models are used by children to make predictions about future
experiences; they guide their expectations of what to expect of themselves and
of others. The models tend to be stable. The presence of the model tends to bias
the child's perception of events. Thus if a normally sensitive parent demonstrates some insensitivity this does not disrupt the child's expectation of sensitivity. Of course the reverse is also true: occasional sensitivity from a predominantly insensitive parent will still result in a model of parents as unresponsive.

Following on from these predictions the model will then guide how the
child acts and thinks. This becomes habitual over time, and thus less accessible
to consciousness. It is like driving a car. Initially this takes a lot of thought and
concentration; with practice however it becomes automatic. Thus the child
develops habitual ways of relating to others guided by expectations of self and

Catherine, Zoë, Marcus and Luke have all made predictions of their foster or
adoptive parents based on their early experience and this is beginning to have
an effect on the parenting they are receiving.

Catherine expects not to have her needs met; she hides her feelings rather
than risk overwhelming Jenny and Martin. They in turn are beginning to respond
to this. It is easier to let Catherine do things herself than battle over it and be-
sides they are worn out with Zoë. Catherine's ability to go and keep herself
occupied is a blessing. Without meaning to they are reinforcing Catherine's
avoidant behaviour. On the rare occasion when Catherine does get angry at

them they are surprised and reactive – 'not you as well, Catherine, I don't know if I can cope with both of you.' Catherine learns once again that her own needs are overwhelming to her parents.

Zoë on the other hand is difficult to ignore. It is exasperating but they try to be patient with her. They give her a lot of attention and reassurance, but even this is not enough. Sometimes they just want to scream at her to go away and let them have some peace. Fearing that they might shout at her when feeling this frustrated they take themselves away for a time whilst they recoup their strength. Zoë's expectation of inconsistency is being met and she redoubles her efforts not to let them out of her sight.

Rita and Frank are having an even harder time. They seem to move from one outburst to another; they tiptoe around Marcus waiting for the next demand, the next defiant 'no'. They try to give each other breaks. Frank takes Marcus to the garden centre with him whilst Rita catches up on the washing. Rita tries to occupy Marcus with a game whilst Frank catches up in the garden. They are spending less and less time with each other. Sometimes Rita feels so exasperated that she comes close to hitting Marcus, and Frank did push him away rather harshly when Marcus had him pinned against a wall. As Marcus senses these times of near loss of control he is reminded of the scary parenting of his past. He redoubles his efforts to stay in control.

Luke does not know what to expect of a mother and Jackie can feel quite ineffectual with him. Whilst he does need her, she sometimes thinks that he would be equally happy with anyone who passed by. Jackie finds the lack of a real relationship difficult. She cares for Luke, but she doesn't feel like his mother. Coupled with this he is becoming very active and impulsive; Jackie has to keep a close eye on him all the time. This combination of activity and lack of relationship is hard for Jackie; she feels like she is keeping him safe without really meeting his emotional needs.

others. The automatic nature of these patterns of relating mean that they tend to be stable over time; we see children relating to new people in the way they related to their early parents.

The internal working model as a changing model

When there is a more consistent and dramatic change in a relationship this can lead to change in the *internal working model*. For example, if a mother becomes ill or very stressed leading to a consistent change in the way she relates to the child the working model can be reconstructed. Fortunately the converse is also true: a sustained increase in sensitivity and responsiveness in the mother can also lead

Jenny and Martin, Rita and Frank, and Jackie are all beginning to match the pattern their children are expecting. They all experience dissatisfaction with this however.

Jenny and Martin are disturbed at the lack of closeness they experience with Catherine. They feel quite rejected by her at times and this is hurtful.

With Zoë, Jenny and Martin want to find a way to help her feel secure so that she can relax with them and not have to work so hard at maintaining their attention.

Rita and Frank need a way out of the negative cycle they are slipping into. They want to be kind, attentive parents to Marcus but are finding this hard when they are so tyrannized by him.

Jackie feels that she is floundering with Luke; she wants to offer him sensitive, nurturing care but finds it difficult to predict what he needs. She frequently feels she is managing his behaviour without having an impact on him.

These parents need to find ways of gently challenging the internal working models of the children. They need to find a way to provide consistent, predictable care within which they can be nurturing and emotionally responsive to the needs of the children. In this way the children can begin to relax and start to behave in a more spontaneous way with them. They need to help the children develop an alternative working model of the way parents behave.

to a reconstruction of the *internal working model*. However, to continue with the driving analogy, it is easier to learn good driving habits initially than to change bad habits later. It takes a lot of practice and effort to get rid of a bad habit and replace it with a different pattern.

The internal working model as parents change

As we have seen, when children have a change of caregiver the *internal working model* will influence their expectations of these new parents, the way they behave in order to feel secure with them and their ability to manage separation from them. Children will often act as if they expect these parents to be like their previous ones. The parents can find themselves influenced by this behaviour and in turn come to resemble the previous parents.

However, parents will also have expectations of themselves and the children. The children will be encouraged to think about themselves and others in different ways.

Children therefore both retain the old construction of the working model whilst also reconstructing this in the light of new information. In effect children will hold multiple models of how relationships work.

It is important to note that old models don't go away; children have had the experience of parents as insensitive and unresponsive. They know relationships can be like this, but they also now have experience that not all relationships are like this.

The Adoption and Attachment study, in London (Hodges *et al.* 2003), aims to track the way attachment representations in *internal working models* change over time for adopted children. This research suggests that the negative view of self that children learn early in life is the most difficult to change. Even after two years of living in a different family, children continue to hold negative predictions about parents and family, although they now have positive predictions as well. Thus children may hold conflicting models about how families work. They may know that parents hurt children, but they now also know that parents love and take care of children.

This is the challenge that faces Jenny and Martin, Rita and Frank, and Jackie. They need to find an alternative way of parenting the children, but to do this they will need a lot of patience and perseverance. Nothing will change quickly, and they will find themselves slipping back into the child's way of doing things quite frequently. They will need all the support they can find, not only from each other but also from friends, family and professionals.

3

Attachment Theory: Patterns of Attachment

We have so far explored the relationship between the child and parent from both the child's perspective and from the parent's perspective. We have also considered how this experience of relationship becomes a model to guide future relationships. We are now going to explore some of the stable patterns of behaviour that develop between child and parent depending upon the ways they respond to each other. These patterns of attachment have been explored and described by a number of researchers over the years.

Mary Ainsworth developed an experimental study called 'The Strange Situation' to demonstrate the organized patterns of attachment, based on the way children respond with their parents when they are taken to an unfamiliar room and left for a short time with a stranger and then on their own (Ainsworth *et al.* 1978). Some children did not fit easily into the secure, ambivalent or avoidant pattern of relating with their parents. This led Mary Main and Judith Solomon (1986) to describe the disorganized pattern of relating that arises when children experience damaging parenting.

Patricia Crittenden has explored the development of these different patterns of relating through childhood and into adulthood, focusing especially on the way children can become increasingly controlling in their attachment styles when under stress (Crittenden, Landini and Claussen 2001).

These patterns of attachment were briefly considered in Chapter 1 but will now be considered in more depth. Figure 3.1 provides an overview of the different patterns.

The secure attachment pattern

Secure attachments develop when children experience sensitive and responsive care. These children use the parent as a *secure base*, developing patterns of behaviour that combine active exploration with comfort-seeking from the parent. This allows them to go out into their wider environment confident that they

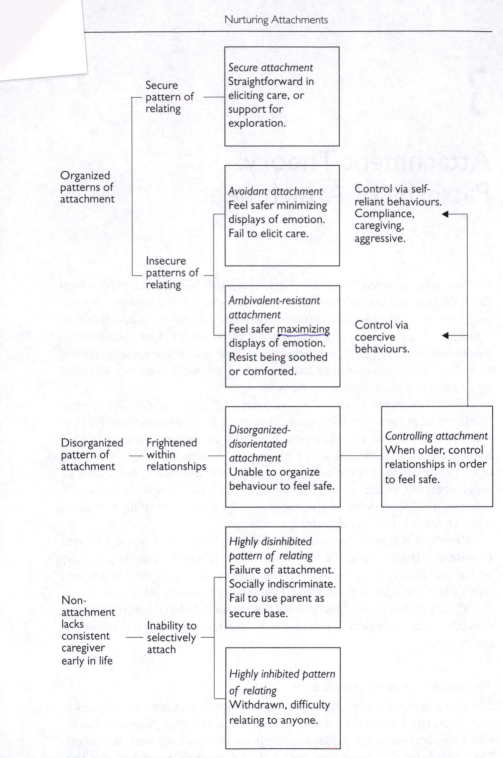

Figure 3.1 Patterns of attachment

will, if needed, be watched, supported and helped. When they need protection or comfort they will return to the parent. This is represented visually in Figure 3.2.

These children base their prediction of danger or insecurity on what they know, their prior experience. 'Last time mum took me to this building we met this strange lady who put a needle in my arm. I don't think I am very happy coming here again.' They also use how they are feeling to determine how close to mum they want to be. 'I don't feel too comfortable here, I think I'll keep close to you.' In this way when faced with potentially alarming situations children will tackle them effectively. They will look to the parent for support when their feelings of insecurity reach a certain level; at other times they will demonstrate self-reliance and independence. Therefore a *secure attachment* allows a child to develop self-reliance balanced with the ability to seek and gain help from others.

Secure attachment therefore requires sensitive parenting. It can be a bit daunting to think about the concept of sensitive parenting. It can feel like an impossible task. All parents can think of times when they are insensitive or unresponsive. They are in the middle of cooking tea, have just had a row with their partner or are preoccupied with other issues. Fortunately this is quite normal. Children need sensitive, responsive parents some of the time but not all of the time. Children need good-enough parenting rather than superhuman parenting. A reasonable sensitivity and the capacity to reassure the child following a period of insensitivity will help the child to feel securely attached.

The experience of a *secure attachment* relationship will impact positively on the development of the child. The *internal working model* of these children is that they are loveable, effective in relationships, and of interest to others. The child anticipates that others will be caring, protective and available.

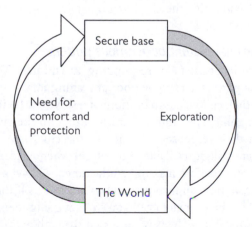

Figure 3.2 The secure attachment pattern

The older child can draw on the full range of *cognitive* and emotional information to make sense of the social world. These children have a good understanding of their own and others' feelings. This has led to a sense of self-efficacy,
self-confidence and social competence. They are able to make friends and mix
well with their peers. They demonstrate self-reliance but when they need to they
trust others and they will approach them for help. They can resolve conflicts,
problem-solve and cope with stress and frustration. They are able to experience
empathy for others, leading to the development of moral behaviour.

This can lead to success in school. The child copes with the learning tasks,
enjoying achievement and managing mistakes, whilst being able to draw upon
the teacher for support as needed.

As adolescents these young people are confident in their developing independence, and changing relationships.

As adults they will value relationships and be able to offer security to their
children. They are likely to be consistent, responsive and predictable parents.

We will next explore how this development is different when the child's
early experience is of a parent who is insensitive or unresponsive to a significant
degree. In considering this it is important to remember the degree of insecurity a
child experiences can vary between parents and over time. The extent of insecurity will determine the degree of impact on development. Experience of
insecure parenting is a risk factor for developmental difficulty, but the final
outcome will depend on a range of factors including both early and later experience, as well as genetic and constitutional factors.

The organized insecure attachment patterns
Where an attachment figure is predominantly insensitive, unresponsive and
unavailable an insecure attachment will develop. This is reflected in the organi-
zation of the behaviour that the child demonstrates.

Insecure ambivalent-resistant attachment pattern
Some parents are inconsistent in responding to children. Thus their care is
insensitive. These parents tend to be poor at reading infant signals. The attention they give to their child tends to be more in response to their own needs than
to those of their child. They find it hard to attune to the child and they are
unpredictable in their responses. This leaves the child very uncertain about
whether the parent will be available and helpful when needed.

These children therefore maximize attachment behaviour to ensure that
they do receive care from an inconsistent parent. It is as if they think 'I don't
know if you will be there when I need you so I am going to make sure that you
are there for me all the time.' This is expressed through demanding and clingy
behaviour. The children display a lot of emotional distress even to minor events.

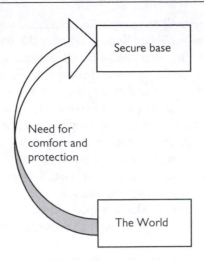

Figure 3.3 The ambivalent-resistant attachment pattern

They are also resistant to being soothed and comforted. They remain distressed. They fear that if they do calm, the parent will then leave them alone once more. They won't know when the parent will be available again.

These children rely on their feelings to guide their behaviour. If they feel anxious they will anticipate danger and the attachment system will be activated, i.e. they predict future danger based on how they feel rather than what they think.

This pattern is represented visually in Figure 3.3. This shows that the children are very focused on checking out that they will get comfort and protection, and this is at the expense of exploration.

When young, these children hyper-activate their attachment behaviour. They approach angrily, are fretful, demonstrating crying, whining and clingy behaviour. Their need for attention is often seen as 'attention-seeking'. Being dependent and needy for attention these children reduce their exploration. When they do get attention they fear the withdrawal of the parent thus they become resistant to being soothed. These children show high dependency. They feel helpless, with low self-efficacy; they don't expect to be successful at making things happen. They also demonstrate poor social competence; they don't expect friendships to go well.

The *internal working model* reflects this. The model of self is unloveable, of little worth and ineffective. The model of other is unreliable, unavailable, not interested.

As they grow older the children remain preoccupied with their relationship with their parents and with others. They remain alert and vigilant to what others are doing and to their moment-by-moment availability. This leads to the development of enmeshed and entangled relationships. In order to keep others involved with them they will demonstrate *coercive behaviour* alternating between aggressive and helpless behaviour as they regulate the parents' attention. The children will be demanding, angry and difficult to please. As parents' frustration and anger build in response to these behaviours the children switch and becomes coy and helpless. The parents are now drawn to look after the children, to meet their helplessness; as the parents become solicitous, the children switch again. In this way the children are able to keep parents attending to them. If the parents become used to the levels of anger shown, and begin to ignore them, the children are likely to escalate these angry displays. The children become more confrontational and will even take risks, or court danger, in order to maintain attention onto themselves. If these behaviours don't serve to keep fear at bay the children will escalate these emotional displays through *obsessive behaviours*. For example, a child might become obsessively interested in where the parent is and what the parent is doing.

For these children emotional states are transparent as emotion drives their behaviour. Despite the degree of feelings on display children are not able to talk about these. They continue to act out their feelings, displaying these non-verbally. The children tend to view the world in black and white. The parent is all-good whilst attending to them and all-bad in response to the withdrawal of this attention.

Zoë reflects this attachment style. Her moment-to-moment behaviour is driven by how she is feeling. Her anxiety increases whenever it appears that Jenny or Martin will not be attending to her. Thus when Jenny is cooking tea Zoë becomes more demanding and difficult. Similarly when Martin is trying to talk to his neighbour about some local events in the community, Zoë pushes herself into the middle of the two of them and prevents them talking.

Jenny is trying to help Catherine to bake some cakes. She has settled Zoë down with some magazines, allowing her the safety scissors to cut out some of the pictures. Zoë needs Jenny's help. She can't cut the pictures out; she becomes upset when she cuts a lady's head off. Jenny does her best to help both Catherine and Zoë, but Zoë's anxiety increases, as she does not have Jenny's full attention. She starts to try to cut herself instead of the magazine; when she can't make much of an impression on her finger she resorts to cutting her hair. Jenny removes the scissors and gets out the drawing things instead. Zoë draws for a short time and then looks around the kitchen. She starts opening the drawers, and when that doesn't have an effect she reaches up for the kettle. Jenny becomes cross with her and sends her from the room. Now Zoë becomes upset, crying in a heartfelt way. With relief Jenny puts the cakes in the oven and goes to calm down her now distraught child. As she picks her up and comforts her, Zoë clings to her like a limpet. 'I'm sorry mummy,' she whispers as she snuggles in.

As these children grow older their preoccupation with the parent relationship extends to include other significant relationships. They find it difficult to maintain friendships however because of their tendency to be clingy and possessive, over-sensitive to signs of rejection. They look to their friends to support them but tend not to reciprocate this; they don't view themselves as a source of support. The children are looking for something but are not able to give in turn.

Their hyper-attention to their attachment and relationship needs means that the children demonstrate poor concentration and distractibility to other things. Whilst they are hyper-vigilant to what other people are doing, this is at the expense of a focus on other aspects of the environment. This impacts on their ability to benefit from education. They are overly focused on their relationship with the teacher at the expense of the learning tasks they are meant to be engaging with.

As adolescents these young people continue to have little confidence that their parents will be reliable. Their behaviour can be intense and angry. They remained preoccupied with their dependency upon the parent and therefore struggle with the conflict between wanting to stay close and learning to be independent.

These young people will remain preoccupied, but experience low satisfaction, with relationships as adults. They can be jealous, possessive and coercive. With a low capacity for self-reflexivity ambivalent feelings are dealt with by *splitting*. Thus they oscillate between viewing others as all-good or all-bad. Feelings are still not thought through but continue to be acted out.

As parents they will be uncertain and ambivalent. Still looking to have their own needs met they will be inconsistent and neglectful. They need to keep their child close and look for acceptance from her but will be insensitive to her cues and needs. They will alternate between viewing her as wonderful and horrid, but find it difficult to just accept her.

Insecure avoidant attachment pattern

Some parents find it difficult to care for their children when the child is emotionally expressing this need. They therefore tend to back off at the time the child is expressing 'I need you close'. Children quickly learn that this is what happens and will adjust their behaviour in order to prevent this 'backing off'. Thus the children minimize attachment behaviour to maintain closeness to parents who otherwise would be rejecting. This is expressed through passive and withdrawn behaviour with little display of emotional distress. The child anticipates that 'if I show you how I feel, you will move further away'. These children rely on knowledge and ignore feelings to guide behaviour, i.e. they predict danger and insecurity based on what has happened in the past. This pattern is represented visually in Figure 3.4. This shows that the children act as

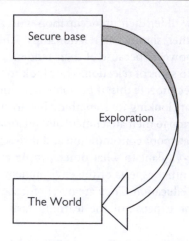

Figure 3.4 The avoidant attachment pattern

if they do not need the parent, focusing attention outwards onto the wider environment instead.

Children who have developed an *avoidant attachment pattern* of relating to others will have experienced parents as resentful, rejecting, intrusive and controlling. They will have found that their parents were consistently unresponsive to their negative emotion and distress. These children learn to deactivate their attachment behaviour. They inhibit emotional expression, becoming undemanding and compliant and/or self-sufficient. The children have learnt that emotional displays lead to reduced availability so they learn not to show how they are feeling.

The *internal working model* is of the self as unloveable and of little worth; for some, achievement might lead to some sense of accomplishment, but they will fear not achieving. The model of others is that they are not available, intrusive, interfering, controlling and consistently unresponsive. They may expect others to be hostile and rejecting.

As these children mature they continue to minimize the expression of negative affect. At its extreme these children can appear socially facile, always smiling, or playing the clown. These behaviours hide the negative feelings of sadness, anger or anxiety that they might be feeling. Alternatively they can appear *inhibited* and withdrawn. If these behaviours do not allow the children to feel safe they will escalate the avoidance of emotion through *compulsive behaviours*. For example, they may compulsively try to help or take care of the parent.

Catherine has a strongly developed avoidant style of relating to Jenny and Martin. She is very vigilant to what they expect of her and tries to meet these expectations. In addition she is wary of displaying her own emotional needs. She tries to keep her feelings locked tightly away, denying that she is sad, upset or cross. When feelings do threaten to surface Catherine becomes very anxious. This is displayed through angry, threatening behaviour often directed towards Jenny and Martin.

Catherine is approaching her sixth birthday and as a treat Jenny is taking her out. The local town is having its annual parade. Jenny is sure that Catherine has not seen anything like it before and anticipates that this will be a fun experience. Catherine is quiet in the car so Jenny fills her in about what to expect. She enthuses about the parade, telling Catherine of the trips she took to see it when she was a child. They arrive and park the car and Jenny helps Catherine out. Momentarily she looks reluctant but then she grasps Jenny's hand and with a big smile asks what they are going to see first. Catherine enjoys looking at the decorated town and willingly has an ice cream. Jenny offers her one ride and Catherine chooses the merry-go-round, the very ride Jenny enjoyed most as a child. It is nearly time for the parade so Jenny finds a good spot where they will see everything as it passes. Jenny is transfixed as she happily points out all the different floats and describes the themes the characters represent. Catherine holds on to Jenny's hand and keeps smiling. It is only as they approach the car to return home that Catherine's big smile deserts her. They are walking through the car park when a large, brown bear suddenly appears from between the cars. Startled, Catherine screams and suddenly all control leaves her as she pulls free of Jenny's hand and runs. Fearing that she might run into the road Jenny runs after her and grabs her. 'It's okay, Catherine, it is only someone dressed up, like in the parade. He won't hurt you.' It is only then that Jenny realizes how scared Catherine is. She asks Catherine if she has been scared of the dressed-up characters all day. Catherine nods tearfully. Jenny is dumbfounded; Catherine had appeared to be enjoying herself, but now Jenny realizes that she was only doing it for her. Her apprehension and anxiety hidden from view, she smiled at the floats and chose the ride that Jenny enjoyed. If the brown bear had not stepped out when it did, Jenny would never have known how difficult this day had been for Catherine.

Through childhood these children can become increasingly self-reliant and independent. They can be achievement-oriented, as this has gained approval from their parents. *Cognitive* development is therefore enhanced but the integration of cognition with emotion is limited. The children learn to think about situations but are very poor at interpreting the way they or others are feeling. The children appear emotionally self-sufficient with distress being denied or not communicated. However, they are not managing their emotion but ignoring it.

Children who have developed avoidant patterns of relating to others will be able to make friends but they shy away from intimacy. Sometimes friendships are spoilt by their need to be controlling of the relationship and their belief that they will not be liked. They lack self-confidence and self-worth.

Self-reliance combined with low self-confidence can also be apparent in the classroom. The children resist developing a supportive relationship with the teacher, but lack confidence in their own ability as well.

During adolescence the tendency to disengage from relationships deprives the young people of the support needed to develop independence and *autonomy*. They remain cut-off from their feelings, especially negative feelings such as fear, anger, hurt or loneliness. Often past relationships are idealized, and past difficulties minimized. This means that they will not be able to manage conflict or difficulty within current relationships.

As adults they will continue to avoid intimacy and become very task-oriented. Emotions will be intellectualized, thus they can appear cold and detached. Thought and knowledge is seen as more reliable than feelings.

As parents they will find that their baby's distress and neediness makes them feel anxious. Thus they deactivate their caregiving in response to negative emotion from the child. They feel uncomfortable in the parent role, dismissing or devaluing the infant's attachment needs.

The disorganized/controlling attachment pattern

Sometimes a parent is not just insensitive to a child but is actually frightening. This is much more difficult for the child to adjust to. Infants and young children feel fearful and helpless. They experience confusion. Distress and arousal remain high and unregulated. No behavioural strategy reduces the danger the children find themselves in nor brings care and comfort. The parents may be actively behaving in a way that is frightening. They might hurt the child,

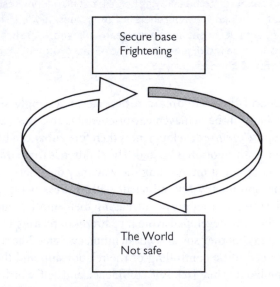

Figure 3.5 The disorganized attachment pattern

neglect the child or expose the child to situations that are scary. Alternatively children can be scared because they experience the parents as frightened. A frightened parent is not likely to be a parent who can keep you safe.

A disorganized attachment pattern therefore develops when parents are frightened or frightening to the child. The frightening/frightened behaviour of the parent activates the child's attachment system. This motivates him to seek protection and comfort, but the source of this is the very same person who is being frightening. The child is unable to organize his behaviour at times of stress in order to receive emotional support because the parent is both the source of fear and the potential for safety. For the young child times of fear or stress lead to disorganized behaviour. This behaviour is bizarre or ineffective, as the child expresses 'I don't know what to do here'. Thus children may freeze, may flap their hands or may approach the parent whilst actively looking in the other direction. This is represented visually in Figure 3.5. The children are neither able to effectively seek comfort and protection, nor are they comfortable exploring the world.

This pattern overlays more organized patterns of behaviour that the child displays when the danger is lessened. The child can show any of the organized patterns. The disorganized pattern represents behaviour when the organized behaviours fail.

Disorganized or organized? The move to controlling behaviours

An absence of strategy to deal with dangerous situations is intolerable. Therefore as the child matures he adopts strategies that bring some measure of safety. These strategies are organized around control. The child has an *internal working model* of himself as unworthy of care, as powerful and as bad. The model of others is that they are frightening and unavailable. The child becomes fearful, angry and violent. By becoming controlling, these children avoid intimacy and they attain some measure of predictability. The parent is left feeling manipulated, ineffectual and in a relationship that doesn't feel genuine.

For these children relationships cause distress with little provocation. They experience violent anger coupled with anxious dependence. Strong feelings are experienced as overwhelming, and children are left unable to understand, distinguish or control emotions in themselves or others. They are anxious and afraid whilst violence and aggression alternate with apathy and despair. These children dislike being touched or held. They find it difficult to make or to keep friends.

Marcus finds relationships very stressful; feeling close to Rita and Frank reminds him of how scared he was with Tessa and Richie. He tries to keep them both at arm's length and finds that refusal and defiance are good ways to do this. Occasionally Rita or Frank penetrate this defence and Marcus finds himself feeling affection for them. This makes him scared and he becomes very angry. He will do something hurtful to ensure that the close feelings disappear. He can be especially aggressive toward Rita whose kindness he interprets as weakness. He is a little more compliant with Frank, believing him to be the stronger of the two.

Rita has taken seven-year-old Marcus out to buy him some new clothes. Marcus is sullen and disinterested. He refuses to try anything on and Rita resorts to holding clothes against him and guessing which ones he will like. Rita stays calm and patient, and she makes sure that she doesn't spend too much time in the clothes shops. Pleased that they have found some clothes, she says they will go back via the toyshop. Marcus is immediately taken with a Power Ranger toy and asks Rita for it. Rita is worried about the level of violence in Marcus's play and suggests something else instead. Marcus storms out of the shop and starts kicking the pillar just outside. Rita goes up to him. She knows not to reach out and touch him but instead talks to him calmly. She tells him that she knows how cross he feels, and how hard it is not to get what you want, but that she would like to buy him the fire engine as he has been so good about the clothes shopping. Marcus is torn between staying angry with Rita or going with her to get the toy. He continues to kick out but it is more half hearted now. Rita walks towards the shop, knowing that Marcus will now follow. After a short hesitation Marcus goes with her to buy the toy. He holds the engine all the way home. Rita is pleased at how well the trip has gone and they have a peaceful evening.

The next day however is a different matter. Marcus wakes up in a foul mood and does his best to provoke Rita all day long. He calls her names, refuses to eat her cooking and will not remove his shoes when he comes in from the garden. The final straw comes after Marcus has gone to bed; Rita finds that her jewellery box has been ransacked and her favourite necklace taken. Marcus has carefully pulled it to pieces and placed the bits on her bed – he has certainly paid her back for the nice time they had yesterday.

Patricia Crittenden has developed a model called the dynamic-maturational model, which explores the way the different patterns of behaviour develop over time. Her model is very helpful in understanding the way that children develop their controlling behaviours around avoidant and/or ambivalent patterns of relating to others (Crittenden *et al.* 2001).

Some children develop these controlling behaviours around avoidant patterns of attachment. Thus children who experience parents as overwhelmed or angry by their displays of emotion will as infants learn to minimize displays of negative emotion. At this stage they are able to inhibit what they feel but cannot yet pretend that they are feeling something different. As the infant matures into toddlerhood they become more sophisticated in the behaviour they display. In particular they can become compulsively self-reliant. 'You are frightening to me so I will not need you.'

At this stage these children can both inhibit negative emotion in order to ward off the parent's rejection of them, but they can also pretend to be feeling something different. In other words they display a falsely positive emotion, which suggests that they are happy and content, in order to elicit attention and approval from their parent. The true feelings of anger, fear or need for comfort are not displayed as the child has learnt that displaying these leads to rejection. These children are often very compliant and can even learn to be caregiving, looking after the parent rather than seeking care for themselves.

As they mature these children will continue to be very compliant when with the frightening parent. 'When I am with you I will do my best not to annoy you. You are powerful and I will look after myself by not getting into trouble with you.' However, the child is also learning how to treat people who appear weak. 'I will show you how powerful I am; look how frightening I can be.'

Other children develop controlling behaviours around more ambivalent styles of relating to others. They become very coercive in their interactions, becoming obsessively concerned about the parent's availability, and using behaviours that keep the parent focused onto them. Thus they may be very non-compliant, aggressive or engage in risky behaviour. The parent has to attend but is also likely to get more and more frustrated and cross with the child. The child monitors this rising anger and at some point, when uncomfortable with the level of anger the parent is displaying, switches to a more compliant, appeasing behaviour. Through childhood and into adolescence, the children can become more obsessed about maintaining the adult attention onto them-selves. They experience anger and can become revengeful against the source of their anger. They can be quite punitive towards the parent who is not providing them with all the attention they are demanding. This is alternated with frankly seductive behaviour as they endeavour to display their helplessness and need for rescue to a, by now, angry parent. At all these different levels the child is behaving in response to how he feels and in a way that maintains parent attention on to him.

Children with a strong need to control others can be highly anxious or fearful at school. They need to maintain their feeling of being in control both with peers and the teaching staff. This makes them provocative, bullying and difficult. High levels of anger and aggression can serve the dual purpose of masking the anxiety whilst allowing them to dominate others.

The frightening experience of parents in childhood means that the adoles-cent will find the possibility of deriving security from others as threatening. Expressions of warmth and care from others are experienced as frightening. The attachment system tends to be *inhibited*. Shunning close relationships the young person does not develop an ability to reflect on mental states, leading to difficul-ties in empathizing and rigid, inflexible ways of relating to others.

For these young people the level of disturbance is likely to remain high as adults and they will have difficulty meeting the needs of their own children as parents. Often they will look to their child to fulfil their own needs, and they may replicate the frightening caregiving of their own experience.

Non-attachment

Emotional neglect of a child early in life means that there is an absence of an attachment figure at the very time that the child should be learning how to selectively attach to caregivers. A small proportion of children have had no experience of early attachment relationships. The child is left with severe difficulties in forming relationships. These children have experienced such extreme neglect of their needs that the attachment system does not operate and the child does not develop attachment behaviours. This can be seen in children who have had very little contact with adults. They may have spent large periods of time left in their buggy or cot, locked into a separate room or brought up in an impoverished institution with too few carers caring for too many children. These children will demonstrate a failure to develop selective attachments. They do not understand how to form a relationship within which they can elicit care and protection. These children can be disinhibited in their behaviour. They appear indiscriminately friendly, craving attention from whoever is around. They are however unable to engage in mutually satisfying relationships. Alternatively they can be *inhibited* and extremely withdrawn, appearing passive and lethargic with little interest in other people.

Luke lacked early maternal care, and this has left him uncertain about what to expect and how to relate to people. He finds it difficult to realize that Jackie is special and can provide him with something that other people can't. He can be very demanding and attention-needing, but this will be directed at whoever is around.

At six, Luke is still not properly toilet trained. He will wet or soil his pants but appears not to notice. Jackie finds it particularly disturbing when he wets his bed; he does this whilst fully awake and seems to enjoy the feeling of the wet bedclothes around him.

Luke eats voraciously, whatever is put in front of him. He also tries to secrete food in his bedroom, hiding it in unlikely places. He especially likes biscuits, crisps and sweets. Jackie has to hide such foods to prevent Luke constantly helping himself.

Luke's impulsivity can lead to situations that are very alarming to those trying to care for him. For example, when Jackie was a little late arriving at school she found Luke trying to get into the car of one of the other mothers. Jackie fears that Luke would go with anyone that held out a hand at the right time.

4

Difficulties in Development:
The Impact of Loss and Trauma

A child's development arises out of her genetic potential; this genetic program-ming determines what will develop and when. The environment however influences the realization of this potential, making it more or less likely that optimal development will occur. John Bowlby (1998) suggests that there is the possibility to proceed along a range of *developmental pathways*; at each stage of development this pathway is influenced by an interaction between the child's current state of development and the environment being experienced. Much like branches forming out of the trunk of a tree there are a greater array of potential pathways early in a child's life, with the number reducing as the child grows. As the child moves along one branch, some branches are lost to her, whilst the number of junctions ahead lessens.

Development is determined by constitutional factors (for example, genetic endowment, temperament and intelligence) and also by experience. This expe-rience goes beyond the parenting received. School, friendship and leisure, for example, will all exert an influence, but parenting starts at the trunk of the tree. Attachment experience will be an important factor in determining the *develop-mental pathway* a child travels along.

This chapter will explore the way the early attachment relationships and experience of separation and loss can impact on the development of the child. Traumatized children entering foster and adoptive homes will need very special parenting to allow them to recover from their early traumatic experience of attachment, separation and loss, thus opening up new *developmental pathways*.

The attachment relationship and development
In order to fully understand the impact of loss and trauma on a child's develop-ment it is helpful to understand the impact of caregiving on the way a child comes to understand emotion and to make sense of the world.

The attachment relationship and emotional development

Children with *secure attachments* will have experienced an attuned relationship with a parent. *Attunement* allows the child to experience the parent as understanding, supporting and when appropriate enjoying the emotions or feelings that she is experiencing.

During infancy children will have experienced emotion as being overwhelming. The children are not able to regulate this emotion and are reliant on the parents doing this for them. When babies are distressed and hungry the parents will pick them up and soothe and comfort them. As the babies calm, their emotion is regulated, and the parent can then attend to their need for food.

Toddlers will start to learn to regulate their own emotion. Initially they will need the support of their parent through a process of *emotional co-regulation* as they gradually learn to manage feelings themselves. The experience of *attunement* with another is therefore essential to help toddlers to understand and manage the feelings they experience.

At times *attunement* is broken because children have to be disciplined or because the parents are temporarily unresponsive and insensitive. Following these times the parents will re-establish *attunement* through *interactive repair*. They demonstrate to the child their continuing love and availability. This reassures her that the relationship has survived the loss of *attunement*.

This experience of *attunement* and *interactive repair* therefore helps children to develop capacity for *emotional regulation*.

Children who do not have sufficient experience with an attuned and sensitive parent will be less successful in developing *emotional regulation* abilities. Emotional arousal is poorly understood or managed. Children will therefore show higher levels of dysregulated or dissociated behaviour as either the emotion overwhelms them or they attempt to manage it by cutting off from it. In neither case is the child able to regulate emotion without support.

The attachment relationship and cognitive development

The attachment relationship also provides an opportunity to help children understand themselves and other people they interact with. As parents help children to make sense of their experience the children develop a sense of psychological self; their minds learn to make sense of experience. Infants are born needing to understand and to feel understood. This understanding develops through childhood further helping the child to understand and regulate emotion.

In particular a sensitive relationship provides children with experiences that help them to *perspective-take* (the ability to understand how something looks from the perspective of other people).

In order to do this they need to be aware of the mental states of others, to understand that people can experience a different feeling and have a different understanding from their own.

These are the processes of:

Tom

- *Reflective function* (the ability to understand the feelings of others)
- *Mentalization* (the ability to predict the responses of others).

The parent provides children with opportunities to develop these abilities through their conversations with them.

> For example, imagine a child with his mother at a bus stop. At the same stop is a lady looking visibly upset and hunting for something in her bag. The child, curious, asks why the lady is upset. The mother replies that maybe the lady has lost her purse and that is why she is upset. During this dialogue the child learns that it is okay to be curious about other people, that other people can have thoughts and feelings that we don't know about, and that we can make guesses about these thoughts and feelings. This help us to understand other people, to predict their behaviour and to have empathy for them.

These experiences, within the attachment relationship, provide children with learning that helps them to further make sense of emotion. They learn to:

- remain regulated when experiencing stress or insecurity
- explore, understand and express emotion
- think about things from their own and other perspectives.

This in turn allows:

- the development of *empathy*
- the development of *social understanding*
- the foundation for moral development.

A child who is not helped to make sense of herself or other people will be at a disadvantage. In particular she will struggle within social relationships as she struggles to understand or empathize with the other person.

The impact of attachment difficulties on development

The experience of trauma early in life and within the family compromises the child's first emotional bond. This will have a significant impact on her emotional, social and *cognitive* development.

Often emotional functioning is very young as the children have not satisfactorily learnt to use parents as a *secure base*, allowing them to both go out and explore and to return and receive nurturing in response to their moment-by-moment needs. The children might be left uncomfortable with sep-aration or uncomfortable with closeness and often a combination of the two.

This can be masked behind apparent *pseudomaturity*, appearing more mature than they actually are, or apparent immaturity, a reluctance to give up infantile behaviours.

Immature emotional functioning combined with an internal model of self as unloveable and unworthy means that friendship formation is difficult. The child can appear socially immature and may not trust the friendship that is on offer or may act in hostile, controlling, independent or highly needy ways, leading potential friends to withdraw.

Marcus appears tough, and dismissive of the care of Rita and Frank, but under-neath he is insecure and yearning for love and nurturing. These needs are fright-ening for him and so he hides them under a veil of power and control. He appears mature in many ways, declining the help of Rita and Frank, and manag-ing many things on his own. His immaturity is betrayed however by his choice of play and of TV, when few are watching.

He also has many fears; he doesn't like sleeping in a dark room and despite his apparent independence he does not like it when Rita goes out.

At school Marcus is aggressive and confrontational. His hyper-vigilance to his environment makes attention to schoolwork difficult. He also finds it very difficult to sit still for any length of time.

Many things increase his anxiety and then he becomes aggressive, being verbally abusive to teachers and physically abusive to the other children. He does not have friends; his bullying attitude means that most of the other chil-dren are afraid of him. He frequently accuses the other children of being racist, believing that their shunning of him is connected to his difference; he does not understand that they find him difficult because of his aggression towards them.

Children with attachment difficulties may be of average intelligence and yet they fail to apply this intelligence on a day-to-day level. This is because early experience of poor parenting means that they don't get the necessary experi-ence for good *cognitive* development. This especially impacts on *cognitive* abilities involving learning from others. Kate Cairns and Angela Stanway (2004) point out that whilst the children may develop the ability to complete quite complex *cognitive* tasks they continue to fail to learn from observing cause and effect: 'if I do this then this happens'.

In addition, as Peter Fonagy and colleagues (2002) highlight, when young children do not have experience of a parent who can help them make sense of their experience, they will lack capacity for *reflective function*. They will react to how they feel or to what they are expecting but they will not be able to step outside of this immediate experience and think about what they are doing or how others are responding. The children will lack the ability to make sense of their own inner feelings or to be able to predict what another person might be feeling: difficulties in *mentalization*. This all contributes to difficulties in relationship as children fail to make sense of the behaviour of others or how this relates to their own behaviour.

Moving into foster and adoptive homes

Difficulties in attachment may be apparent when children move into foster or adoptive homes. 'Attachment difficulties' is a term that is used to describe the detrimental impact of children's early experience on the way they form later relationships, especially those within intimate caring relationships. Children develop strategies to enable them to feel safe and secure within insensitive parent–child relationships. These strategies are more complex the more insensitive the parenting they experience.

When the children move into new homes they initially behave with their new parent as they did within their original family, by signalling their emotional and attachment needs in a distorted way. This makes it difficult for the new parent to provide sensitive care. The children who have previously developed avoidant patterns of attachment may act as if they do not need nurture when feeling distressed, whilst the children who have previously developed ambivalent patterns of relating may seek nurture and comfort even when distress is low. The children are organizing their behaviour around what they expect of the parent rather than around the actual availability of the parent.

If the parenting style of the foster carer or adoptive parent is markedly different to the child's experience this will create a mismatch. The child's behaviour is no longer matched to the experience of being parented. Change will occur over time. Daniel Stern (1985) uses the metaphor of a dance to explain this. The dancers are not co-ordinated and therefore a change is needed to bring them back into step again. If the parents lead the dance they will help their child to find the right steps. However, Mary Dozier (2003) has demonstrated how it is often the child who leads the dance; in this case the foster carer or adoptive parent adjusts to match the child's expectations instead of the other way around. This perpetuates the pattern of relating that the child learnt within her first attachment experience. To help children achieve a more secure pattern of relating within new attachment relationships they need to experience therapeutic parenting. Mary Dozier describes this as parenting that provides a 'gentle challenge', encouraging children to change their expectations of parents and to develop new, more healthy patterns of relating.

Children with ambivalent patterns of relating need to experience the parent as consistent and reliable. Over time this will help them to reduce their vigilance and preoccupation with the availability of the parent. They will learn to move away with a confidence that the parent will be there for them when needed.

Children with avoidant patterns of relating need to experience the parent as nurturing and responsive. Over time this will help them to relax some of the more avoidant strategies of relating they have previously learnt and start to trust the parent, accepting nurture and comfort. In my experience, as some of these children experience an increase in safety they can become very needy of the parent's time and attention, demonstrating this through displays of more ambivalent-type behaviours. All the unmet need of their past is now accessible and the child craves the time and attention of the parent. A longer period is needed to allow the children to develop trust in the reliability of the parent and for the child to display a pattern of relating that appears more secure.

When children present severe attachment difficulties their expectations are that parenting will be frightening. These children organize their behaviour around the need to feel in control. This helps them to feel less afraid and helpless as they hide their need for comfort and concentrate instead on controlling the relationship. These children need support to find the experience of being parented as less stressful and frightening. Only then will they be able to relax the control and enter into more reciprocal relationships.

The term 'attachment disorder', sometimes called 'reactive attachment disorder', describes children whose early experience provided them with little opportunity for an attachment relationship. A lack of a consistent caregiver means that the child cannot make a selective attachment to a parent. When these children move into a family they do not know how to form meaningful relationships. Their behaviour is indiscriminate. This means that they are often indiscriminately but superficially friendly with strangers and family alike. It is a disturbance in the capacity to develop an attachment relationship that distinguishes these children from children with attachment difficulty. These children need help to learn how to form and use close relationships. This can be a challenging task. Michael Rutter and his colleagues have followed a group of children adopted following a period of care in an impoverished institution (Rutter *et al.* 2007). These studies have shown that when the children experienced institutionalization for more than six months these *disinhibited behaviours* can persist into adolescence. This is in contrast to children who have experience of selective attachment but who show mild disinhibition of behaviour. Typically these *disinhibited behaviours* reduce over time in their adoptive homes.

Supporting children with the experience of loss and separation

Helping children change their expectations of 'parents' is not the only challenge that foster carers and adoptive parents face. They also need to support the children with their experience of loss of earlier caregivers. When children move away from their family of origin they experience a loss, even though their early experience has been detrimental to them. Some researchers, such as Nancy Verrier (1993), suggest that children experience this loss even when separated from their family as a very young baby; at the least the nine-month connection with mum is severed. Thus children moving into foster or adoptive homes will be distressed and will need support to recover from this sense of loss.

David Brodzinsky and colleagues point out the importance of this support being life-long (Brodzinsky, Schechter and Henig 1993). Children will need to revisit their sense of who they are as an adopted or fostered child as they mature and pass through different developmental stages. As young children they will gain their understanding from the story their parents tell them. With maturity the children start to develop their own story. They will also now develop a more complex understanding. Thus they may understand that they are special to their parents, but this understanding will come alongside knowledge that they were originally born to another family where they appeared not to be special or wanted. With adolescence and the search for self-understanding the young people may want to learn more about their origins. A psychological or even a tangible search for who they are and where they started may occur. Life-story work is often symbolized as a book providing the facts about the child's own history. This work is however much more complex and evolving than this. The children will need to develop a narrative about self that is added to and embellished as they grow and understand at an increasingly mature level.

Thus for all children living in foster and adoptive homes there is likely to be a sense of loss, connected to their early attachment experience, that will impact on their developing relationships. Parents will need to be sensitive to and supportive of these feelings. Even children removed from their mother at birth can be affected by early experience. Often the mother experienced a high level of stress during pregnancy. The stress hormones released in the mother affect the developing baby. The mother may have used substances, alcohol, drugs and tobacco, that affect development within the womb. These children will need particularly sensitive early care if they are to recover from this early experience, and for some children the effects of this will never entirely go. For example, children with foetal alcohol syndrome are left with impairments that impact on their development detrimentally.

Helping children recover from the trauma of early adverse parenting

Children with difficulties in attachment will have experienced early parenting, and the loss of parents, as traumatic. Trauma is experience that is overwhelming and threatening. In the face of this experience the child feels fearful or helpless. This leads to stress resulting in the production of stress hormones. These hormones help the person to cope with the stress. Too high a level of stress hormone for too long a time however is damaging. The way the body reacts to experience, and corresponding development within the brain, are affected by such traumatic experience. Experience of adverse parenting means that the young child experiences is ongoing, with little relief. Van der Kolk describes the quite complex effects of developmental trauma on a child particular the impact on her physiology. Suffice it to say that the experi- of prolonged trauma impacts on the way the child thinks, feels and behaves as well as on physiological development in the brain and throughout the body.

Traumatic experience of parenting includes abuse, neglect and exposure to frightening events such as domestic violence or parental use of alcohol and drugs. Children also experience trauma when their parents are frightened. A frightened parent is not going to be able to keep his child safe. Although the child may not be directly affected by the frightening event, this lack of security in the parent will be stressful. Additionally sometimes the parent is frightened by the parenting task itself. The neediness of the child in front of him can trigger early memories of not having his own needs met. The parent becomes dysregulated by his early experience and is not available to the child. This can be especially frightening to a young, dependent child.

Clearly in these situations the child is doubly affected. She encounters the traumatic experience; in addition the parent is not able to provide her with the experiences of a safe environment needed to recover from trauma. This means that children experiencing adverse parenting have an increased likelihood of developing post-traumatic stress reactions.

Recovery from trauma is helped when the child experiences a safe environment, *secure attachment* relationships, friendships and the ability to express the experience through words or play. These conditions provide the child with resilience to the trauma.

Signs that the child is experiencing a trauma reaction can include:

- Being unable to stop thinking about the trauma.
- Vivid feelings that the trauma is happening all over again. These vivid memories, which feel like you are back in the original event, are sometimes called flashbacks.
- Difficulty sleeping at nights.
- Bad dreams.
- Becoming frightened or upset when reminded of the trauma.
- Feeling angry or irritable.
- Not wanting to think or talk about what happened.
- Being reluctant to go out or be with others.
- Hyper-vigilance (being over-attentive to what is going on around them) and hyper-arousal (being very on edge and quick to react).
- Extreme emotional reactions to further feelings of stress. Quick to anger or overly fearful.

When a child feels this degree of trauma on a day-to-day basis she needs a lot of help from you. Your child will need:

- To feel safe. This is the first priority for children who are traumatized. Until they start to feel safe they will not be able to benefit from anything else.

- Your stability and support. Clearly until children experience stability, and parenting that is continuously available, they will not be able to feel safe. Your child needs to know that you, or someone equally trusted, are going to be there when she gets up in the morning, as she returns from school in the afternoon, and whenever she needs support.

- Structure, predictability and nurture. A high level of structure and predictability will lead to a sense of continuity and stability. High levels of nurturing will help your child to feel loved and cared for and will provide reassurance of your availability.

- Opportunities to talk about experiences. Sometimes children will want to talk about what has happened to them. Some children will talk to anyone they meet about this. These children need gently re-directing to the parent as the appropriate person to talk to. Other children will be much more reticent about talking to anyone. They may feel that this is disloyal to their birth parents; or they may prefer to deal with their experience by not thinking about it. In these cases you need to remain available and open to your child, allowing her to talk about what she is comfortable with and helping her to know that you are available when she does want to talk.

- Your child may use play and drawing to help her to understand past experience. Often children do not want to talk about the symbolism they have used to reflect on past experience. It is enough to have just played or drawn it out. Linking this to their past experience may be too difficult for them. If your child appears very stuck in the same play or drawing you might help by giving her an alternative ending, e.g. 'That doll must be very scared; maybe the mummy doll will come and give her a cuddle.'

- Safe place visualization. Your child can be helped to visualize a place, real or imaginary, in which she feels safe and comfortable. When feeling fearful or worried she can visualize being in this place. A safe place visualization exercise is included at the end of this chapter.

Angela Hobday (2001) uses the concept of timeholes to help parents under-stand and manage the trauma reactions of their children. A timehole is a metaphor to explain the behavioural response that children display in response to an experience from their past rather than in the present. These types of responses are characterized by sudden mood changes. The child displays extreme negative behaviour that appears to be inappropriate to the present situation. The child may demonstrate *regression*, extreme emotion or a blocking of emotion. This can include an intense sense of fear, anger or distress. Your child can be helped to manage these timeholes. It is important that you avoid getting angry and being pulled into the timehole with her. Instead provide reassurance that she is safe; make clear that you are not the abuser and will not behave in the same way as the abuser. Reassure her that you will love and care for her. Afterwards time can be spent helping her to understand what happened and to express the feelings she experienced through talking and writing. Children often like to use the language of timeholes themselves. For example, you can talk to your child about falling in, stepping around or being pulled out of a timehole.

Exercise 4.1: Safe place visualization
Here is an example of a safe place visualization. This will need adapting for children of different ages; speak the instructions in a way that the child will understand.

Before you start the exercise spend a few moments thinking with your child about her safe place. Is it outdoors or indoors? If in a room what else is in there? If outside where is she? Does she want to stand, sit or lie down? What can she hear? What can she see? What can she touch? Are there other people around or is she on her own? Your child might want to draw the scene or write a description of it. You can use these details to help you visualize this scene for her.

When ready ask your child to get into a comfortable position sitting or lying down, but arms and legs unfolded.

Suggest that she lets her body relax and focuses on her breathing.

Talk your child through the relaxation process, adjusting the language used here to suit your child:

'As you are lying there notice your breathing. Breathe quietly and easily. Breathe in for the count of three, hold for a moment and then breathe out for the count of three. Nice and relaxed.'

Continue talking in this way whilst your child gets into a gentle rhythm.
Comment to your child:

'As you breathe in notice the relaxation spreading through the right side of your body.

As you breathe out notice the relaxation spreading through the left side of your body.

As you notice the relaxation spreading you will feel more and more relaxed.

Enjoy the feeling of relaxation spreading through your body.'

Let your child breathe gently for a while and then begin the visualization

> 'You are feeling relaxed and comfortable. As you enjoy the feeling of relaxation notice that you are standing at the top of a small flight of steps. In a moment I will ask you to walk down these steps. As you walk down them you will feel more and more relaxed.
>
> Okay, slowly start walking down the steps. With each step you take, you are feeling more and more relaxed. Enjoy the feeling of relaxation as you walk down the steps.'

Pause or repeat to allow your child to reach the bottom.

> 'You reach the bottom of the steps and notice a door in front of you. In a moment I will ask you to open the door and walk inside. As you do you will feel more relaxed, safe and comfortable.
>
> Okay, now open the door and walk through. Notice how relaxed and comfortable you are as you walk through. This is your special place. In here you are safe. Enjoy feeling safe as you explore your special place.
>
> You find yourself in...'

Describe the scene as your child described it before starting the exercise. Make it as real as possible by describing details that can be seen, heard and touched. Allow your child to spend a little time here enjoying the feeling of safety that she is experiencing.

> 'Okay, now it is time to leave your place. In a moment I will ask you to walk back to the door. As you do so you will continue to feel relaxed and safe. You will bring this feeling of relaxation back with you.
>
> Okay, now move back towards the door. As you walk towards the door you are feeling relaxed and comfortable.
>
> You reach the door, feeling relaxed. Go back through the door and up the steps once more. With each step you take, you are feeling relaxed and comfortable. [Pause or repeat whilst your child visualizes climbing the stairs.] Reach the top of the steps feeling relaxed and comfortable. Enjoy the feeling of relaxation and comfort that you are experiencing.
>
> In a moment I will ask you to open your eyes. As you do so you will notice your surroundings once more. You will continue to feel relaxed and comfortable as you get used to being aware of where you are again.
>
> Okay, in your own time open your eyes and get used to being aware of being in this room with me.'

5

Parenting Children with Difficulties Experiencing Relationships as Secure

This chapter will explore the task of parenting children with difficulties in attachment. Ordinary sensitive parenting may not be sufficient to help these children learn to feel safe and secure within foster and adoptive families. The difficult issue of when to request therapy will also be discussed. To what extent can therapy outside of the home facilitate developmental recovery? How can therapeutic work with the child complement the therapeutic parenting that he is now experiencing?

How can an understanding of attachment theory influence parenting?

Attachment theory provides a framework within which we can understand the children and the behaviours that they are displaying. This understanding is useful by itself. Understanding why children behave in the way they do can reduce feelings of frustration, guilt and blame. Knowing that this behaviour links to past experience can leave you feeling less that it is your fault or that you are getting it wrong with this child. This in turn helps you to accept your child and the difficulties he displays and provides a greater sense of *empathy* for how hard relationships are for him. Feeling understood and experiencing *empathy* is the starting point from which children develop trust and new ways of relating to people.

> Jenny and Martin are feeling worn out with caring for Catherine and Zoë.
> After four years Catherine still remains distant despite all their attempts to help her develop a deeper, trusting relationship with them. Her ready smiles hide away all that she is feeling and sometimes when they hold her it is as if they are holding a cardboard cutout rather than a real child.

On the other hand, although nearly five years old, Zoë continues to be clingy and needy. No matter whether they maintain attention on her or encourage her to need them less she remains petulant and difficult.

Jenny and Martin feel like they are failing these children. They wonder if they are the right parents for them. Jenny feels that Martin does not understand how difficult it is to manage Zoë's constant demands whilst Martin is concerned by how frustrated Jenny is getting with Catherine. They are beginning to argue over how they should be managing the children and both are feeling guilty about the way things are turning out. As time has gone by they have forgotten how difficult the early lives of Catherine and Zoë were and instead feel that they are to blame for the children's continuing difficulties in relating to them.

Jenny and Martin need help and some time apart from the children to reflect on what is happening. It is important for them to re-visit the early lives of the children and to think about how this has impacted on the way they are now. They might find it useful to learn about attachment theory, and to think about the way the children relate to them in relation to the patterns of attachment that can develop.

As they have a deeper understanding of the influence of early relationships on later behaviour they will begin to understand Catherine's deep mistrust of them and their availability to her. They will also learn that Zoë's behaviour stems from a fear of abandonment; if she does not keep them attending to her they might literally forget her and she will be left alone again.

With this understanding will come some acceptance and empathy for the way the children are. Their feelings of frustration will reduce and they will no longer feel guilty about their own parenting but will start planning together how they might move forward and help these children to move on from the trauma of their past and start to relate to them in a different way.

They are starting out on a difficult journey but they are now more hopeful. There will be obstacles along the way and times when they feel like they are going backwards instead of forwards but now they at least understand the journey they need to make with the girls. They will celebrate small steps and minor successes, and they will accept continuing difficulties. They will continue to experience frustration and some guilt at times, but they now recognize this as a need for 'time out'. Time to think about what is happening, to make use of support available to them, time to rebuild their emotional strength. An understanding of attachment theory has helped them to make sense of their current experience and to understand the context that has led to this.

Attachment theory can also provide guidance for parenting your child. The aim of parenting children with attachment difficulties is to help them experience increased safety and security with parents: to learn to use the parents as a *secure base*, from whom they can leave and return to. They have had to develop strategies, certain patterns of relating, which increase their feelings of safety. Alternative experience of being parented helps children to start to trust in parent availability. The children will not forget the early strategies that they developed but they can be helped to use these strategies more reflectively and flexibly, and to develop new ways of relating. This will allow them to 'earn' security. They will learn to be able to rely on their parent and in turn they will have greater confidence in themselves.

This chapter will introduce you to some initial ideas for parenting children with attachment difficulties; the next chapter will then explore the parenting needs of children with different attachment patterns. This will provide you with a framework for parenting. This framework will be explored in depth in the remainder of the book as we work through the house model of parenting.

How can we increase feelings of safety for the child?

The environment

Children need to experience a decrease in stress and an increase in support. This will help them to feel more secure and to develop increased resilience. They additionally need to experience the world as more predictable and reliable. Home and school environments need to be set up in a way that decreases the stress children feel and increases the support available to them.

> Jackie has been working hard at providing Luke with a very predictable and responsive environment. She wants to make it clear to Luke that if he needs her she will be there. She hopes that in time Luke will learn to direct his needs for parenting more firmly at her.
>
> This is very demanding on Jackie but she works hard at being available and nurturing. She develops a consistent routine to the day. Luke is up early in the morning and Jackie uses the time to linger over the washing and dressing routine; helping Luke to experience being taken care of. They breakfast together and then walk to school. At the end of the school day they walk home via the park. Whatever the weather Luke needs time to run around and let off steam after the tension of school.
>
> Jackie also builds in regular 'mum' times. At these times she will hold and rock Luke and engage him in very young play. For example, she might sing a lullaby to him or read him a simple story. She discovers that he loves nursery rhymes and teaches him the actions. At first these periods of 'mum' time are short. Luke can only stay with her for brief episodes before he has to run around the room, but gradually he responds to the routine and the activities and he is able to be calm and relaxed, often for the only time in the day.
>
> Jackie also keeps Luke close by to her, spending a lot of time playing with him or letting him watch her as she gets on with some housework. She finds that Luke is responsive to this attention and availability, although he remains very active and impulsive at other times.

relationship

Children need to experience parents as emotionally available, sensitive and responsive. A more *secure attachment* will only arise within the context of stable, long-term relationships with warm, loving and consistent caregivers.

Vera Fahlberg (1994) suggests that the arousal-relaxation and positive interaction cycles, used consistently, can help children to learn to trust parents.

AROUSAL–RELAXATION CYCLE

This cycle (see Figure 5.1) replicates the early experience an infant has with a sensitive parent. It can provide your child with a sense of predictability, consistency and reliability. This cycle relies on you noticing when your child is experiencing high arousal levels, often because he is distressed or uncomfortable in some way, although this can also be because of the level of excitement being experienced. He will display this increased arousal through a range of behaviours that can be quite challenging. If you can provide support and *empathy* this will help him to modulate high arousal and to experience a sense of relief and relaxation. It is this experience of co-regulation of high arousal that will help your child to experience a *secure attachment*.

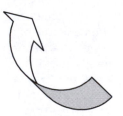

Child experiences discomfort, leading to an increase in arousal

Child experiences relief and relaxation

Child experiences increased trust and security

Child displays increased arousal through behaviour

Parent supports, empathizes and nurtures.
Child is open to experience attachment security

Figure 5.1 Arousal–relaxation cycle (Adapted from Fahlberg (1994). 'A Child's Journey Through Placement'. Copyright © BAAF. Reproduced with kind permission.)

As Rita and Frank begin to understand that Marcus's aggression is an indication of his feelings of distress and fear they plan to deal with it in a different way. Instead of becoming angry back, or trying to find ways of showing Marcus how naughty he is being, they will see the increased aggression as reflecting an increase in stress. They will look for ways to reduce the stress he is experiencing. They will increase the amount of empathy they are providing, showing understanding for the difficult feelings that are underlying the increase in aggressive behaviour.

One Saturday Marcus has come in from playing out. He is clearly uptight and he appears on edge. Frank decides to make him a drink in the hope that this will help him calm down. He hands a glass of blackcurrant squash to Marcus. Marcus takes it and throws it down, shouting that he wants orange. Frank ignores the spilt drink and comments instead on what a hard time Marcus has had this morning. He wonders aloud if he has found the children playing out difficult today. Marcus angrily turns away but Frank notices a slight relaxing of the shoulders. He continues talking, commenting on how difficult it can be when kids start picking on you.

Marcus looks at him and says, 'I hate Adam, he never lets me join in.'

Frank continues with the empathy. 'It sure sounds like Adam was mean to you today. I bet you would have loved to join in as well.'

'Yeh, I hate him. I'm good at football. I could have won too!'

Frank agrees. 'Yes, remember how you ran rings around me when we went to the park? You sure ran fast that day.'

Marcus smiles, remembering, but then his feelings from the day surface again. 'I still hate Adam. I'm going to knock him out tomorrow.'

Frank empathizes but this time talking more quietly. 'Yes, it's very difficult when you are left out. It feels like nobody in the world likes you. I bet you do feel like hitting him, showing him how strong you are, but I wonder if it would help really.'

Marcus gives a deep sigh and then says to Frank, 'If I clear up that spill will you make me another drink?'

'Sure thing, kiddo. Would you like blackcurrant or orange?'

Marcus looks up from where he is now wiping the spilled juice and gives a sheepish smile: 'Blackcurrant please.'

POSITIVE INTERACTION CYCLE

Finding ways to provide positive experiences for children who find it hard to feel a sense of fun in life and to feel positive about themselves can be quite challenging. It is however well worth the effort. As your child responds positively self-worth and *self-esteem* will increase. Your child will feel more positive about himself and more valued by you (see Figure 5.2).

Parent provides child with experiences of a fun and loving relationship

Child responds positively

Child experiences increase in self-worth and self-esteem

Child may initially resist these experiences, or feel overwhelmed by them

Parent supports child, providing empathy for feelings and encouragement to participate more fully

Figure 5.2 Positive interaction cycle (Adapted from Fahlberg (1994). 'A Child's Journey Through Placement'. Copyright © BAAF. Reproduced with kind permission.)

Jenny and Martin have noticed how Catherine likes to make pots out of play-doh. She will spend ages moulding it into just the right shape, before squashing it all back down again. They wonder if she would enjoy clay modelling, making a pot that she can keep. They decide to take her to the Saturday morning clay session at the arts studio. Catherine is nervous to start with, and is reluctant to touch the clay. Marianne, the class instructor, notices her reluctance and comes over to her. She shows Martin and Catherine how to squash the clay down and roll it into different shapes. With no pressure to make anything in particular she soon has them rolling out shapes, squashing it down again and then making a different shape. Soon Catherine is absorbed. She starts to mould a pot as she does with her play-doh. She is about to squash it down when Martin puts a hand on her arm. 'Hey Catherine, that is a great pot. Would you like to keep that one to put your pencils in?' Catherine eyes him suspiciously but then agrees. The following week they return so that Catherine can paint her pot before it is fired. She chooses to paint it with coloured stripes like a rainbow. Catherine is very proud when she brings her rainbow pot home. She sits it on her desk in her bedroom and fills it with her pens and pencils.

ATTUNEMENT/INTERACTIVE REPAIR

A third cycle has developed out of the observations of Allan Schore (1994) (see Figure 5.3). He describes the natural cycle of *attunement* and *interactive repair* that occurs between the parent and young child. With increasing mobility children need parents to keep them safe and to teach appropriate behaviour for different situations. This process is called socialization.

When you demonstrate disapproval toward your child a state of mis-attunement is created between you, and he experiences the emotion of *shame*. You then help him to manage this increase in negative arousal through a process of co-regulation. You establish re-attunement with your child who once again experiences feeling loved and cared for. Your relationship has been repaired.

Attunement
Child feels connection to carer
Child feels loved, of value
Child experiences empathy

Breaking of attunement
Discipline, breaking of
connection

Interactive repair
Child feels supported
Child learns self-regulation

Figure 5.3 Attunement and interactive repair cycle

Jenny and Zoë are busy making a collage together. Jenny has been collecting up all the pictures that Zoë has been cutting out and is showing her how they can stick them all on a piece of card. Zoë is very absorbed in this task when the phone rings. Jenny suggests that Zoë stick the next two pictures on whilst she gets the phone. As Jenny is talking she can see Zoë through the doorway. Zoë sticks the next picture on her collage and then calls out to Jenny. Jenny signals to her to wait a moment, but Zoë is looking uncomfortable. Looking at Jenny she picks up the pot of glue and tips it over. Jenny hurriedly finishes the call and angrily points out what Zoë has done. Zoë looks aghast and quickly shouts out: 'I didn't do it, it wasn't me.' Jenny is about to retort that of course it was her, she saw her do it, when she remembers what she has learnt about a child's feeling of shame when they do something wrong. She bends down so that she is at eye-level to Zoë and says: 'We were having such a good time making the collage, I bet you felt really cross when the phone rang.' Zoë hides her face, burying it into Jenny's jumper. 'Now we are going to have to spend the rest of our time clearing up the mess instead of finishing the collage, what a pity.' Zoë is crying now and gently Jenny cuddles her and wipes her eyes. 'I'm sorry mummy, I didn't mean to spill the glue.' Jenny cuddles her for a while longer and then says: 'I think you spilled the glue to show me how much you wanted me to come back to you, but now we have a big mess to clean up. No more collage today.' As she gets two cloths and gives one to Zoë, Jenny says: 'You are very special to me and I will always come back to you.'

These cycles can provide a parenting approach that helps your child to experience his strong feelings being supported. Your child can find out that relationships can be positive and fun and that he can learn to tolerate feelings of *shame*; that relationships can survive things going wrong.

Therapeutic help

Many children living in adoptive or foster homes appear so troubled that those caring for them feel that therapy will be necessary. However, this often arises from a misunderstanding of what therapy is and what it can do. Children are seen as not happy and therapy is seen as a way of helping them to be happier. Children are seen as behaving badly and therapy is seen as a way of helping them to behave better. This is understandable. A definition of therapeutic is to provide a cure or treatment. This view of therapy however rests on a medical model of helping people with psychological problems; the difficulty is viewed as being within the child and therefore treatment can be used with the child to make it better. People's psychological difficulties are however more complex than this; problems emerge out of a complex range of factors that interact. For this reason a range of therapies have emerged aimed at helping the child, the family or the school. These interventions may involve working with the child, but often the focus is on the environments within which the child lives.

Marcus has a problem in that he gets very angry. This is a problem for him because when he gets angry he then feels bad. Marcus is left feeling that he is the naughtiest boy in the world. This is a problem for Rita, Frank and for his teachers. They have to manage Marcus when he is being angry and aggressive; they sometimes get hurt by him and they have to stop him hurting other children.

Rita and Frank would like Marcus to get help. They hope that therapy would help Marcus to stop being angry so often. Marcus does not want to talk to anyone. He does not think he has a problem; when he is angry he always sees it as being someone else's problem. 'Mum wouldn't let me watch television', 'Jack took my pencil', 'The work was too difficult'. Marcus cannot think about anger as being his problem because that would increase his feeling of being bad; it would increase his negative self-esteem. By blaming others he is able to defend against this feeling of badness.

There are also a number of reasons why Marcus gets angry.

Sometimes he becomes overwhelmed by frustration or stress. He cannot regulate this level of stress and thus he becomes angry.

Sometimes Marcus feels close to Rita and Frank; he starts to enjoy being with them. Even after three years this is frightening for Marcus; being close to 'parents' leads to hurt and fear. Marcus needs to put some distance between himself and his foster parents; he uses anger to do this.

Sometimes Marcus feels very sad. He cannot cope with feeling sad; when he was little, feeling sad did not lead to comfort. Marcus has learnt that he can stop the feelings of sadness by being angry.

Marcus believes other people don't like him; he is oversensitive to signs of dislike in others. He thinks that he is disliked because he is Afro-Caribbean, or because his hair is different, or because he lives in foster care. Deep down Marcus cannot believe that he can be liked because he never experienced this from his own parents. When he is told no; when he notices Rita or Frank looking tense; when he is asked why he has done something, Marcus experiences rejection; this frightens him and he gets angry.

Marcus's anger can also be understood in terms of his past experience. His early relationships did not provide him with the experience necessary to develop good emotional regulation abilities.

He also learnt to interact with other people based on these past relationships. His experience of being moved from his birth family and multiple placements has left him prone to feeling rejected.

Rita and Frank can unwittingly contribute to Marcus's difficulties with anger. They try to remain calm with him, but there are times when they feel very frustrated with him. On days when he is being particularly provocative and defiant they can end up 'losing it'. They shout at him and threaten him. Marcus is reminded of his early life; he suspects it is only a matter of time until he is hurt or abandoned again. His pattern of relating with them is reinforced.

Marcus's anger occurs for a multitude of reasons. This is not just his problem and 'therapy' for Marcus is unlikely to make a lot of difference.

If the reasons that children have problems are complex then therapeutic interventions will also need to be complex. Individual therapy for children sets up an expectation that children can be 'made better', can be helped to adjust to the social environments that they interact with. This type of therapy does not look at the other side of this and consider how social environments can be adjusted to help children feel more secure and comfortable. Family therapy can provide help to the family environment, but this may not take into account the alternate family experience that the children have experienced prior to entering this family. Behavioural therapies can be used to help children modify their behaviour; but these may not take into account core deficits they have in managing their emotion or in living within relationships. Finding therapeutic help is therefore a difficult and frustrating process.

Marcus's feelings of anger are difficult for everyone. Marcus does not understand why he gets angry and therefore it is hard for him to take responsibility. It
is hard to live with Marcus without getting frustrated and angry. Rita and Frank
are willing to try to parent Marcus in a way that helps him feel less angry, but
they are only human and he can drive them to distraction. The school teacher
knows that Marcus finds the structure of school and the need to interact with
the other children difficult but there is only a certain amount of time that he can
spend helping Marcus.

They all want Marcus to get help, but it is unlikely that individual help for
Marcus would make a substantial difference without some changes within the
home and school environment.

Lastly, the severity of difficulty that Marcus experienced when he was
young is likely to have left him with neurodevelopmental difficulties – in particular, difficulties regulating emotion and problems in making sense of his experience. This will slow down his capacity to benefit from help being provided.

Marcus will need time, patience and long-term relationships so that he can
learn to feel better about himself, experience more confidence in others and
can develop the capacity to manage his feelings, and to express these in a more
socially appropriate way.

Children with complex difficulties therefore need long-term help that is also
extended to their parents and the other people caring for them. There is no
quick fix, but there is a need for a high level of support for parent, teacher and
child. What are needed are a range of flexible intervention packages that can use
any from the whole spectrum of interventions, combined in a way that meets the
needs of individual children or young people, their family and their community.

A starting point for helping a child needs to attend to how safe he is feeling
within the range of environments he encounters. This means helping the child
to develop positive relationships, from which he can elicit care and comfort
when needed. The parents, teachers and other adults supporting the child in his
day-to-day life need to find ways to provide a safe environment. They need to
demonstrate their availability and nurturing care despite any difficult behaviour
being demonstrated. This means being able to offer an attuned relationship
with opportunities to repair this relationship when it meets difficulty. The adults
need to remain regulated especially when the child is distressed and
dysregulated. Alongside this co-regulation experience the adults offer the child
empathy for what he is feeling and help to make sense of his experience. As the
child develops the capacity for self-regulation and learns to understand himself
and those around him he will be able to tolerate more stressful environments.
Alongside this the child will experience more day-to-day success leading to the
development of a more positive self-identity and improved self-esteem.

Thus helping a child begins with relationships from which the child can elicit support, care and comfort. As Beverly James (1994) suggests, such a protective and supportive environment will allow children to commit to relationships within which they can heal from past hurts and say goodbye to lost relationships. The child will experience adults as containing and nurturing, allowing the child to feel safe, to develop resilience and to grow emotionally.

It is the parenting provided for the child that provides a therapeutic environment. This is the starting point for recovery and needs to be in place before therapist-directed therapy is likely to be useful. As the child experiences a healthy parenting environment he will develop the capacity to relate to a wider range of peers and adults. This replicates early attachment experience; the infant feels secure with the parent and with maturity will use this security to explore the world and develop other relationships. As children experience success and supportive relationships they will be more ready to develop an understanding of their past experience and the impact this has had on them; to develop a *coherent narrative* about who they are and where they have come from. At this point some children may benefit from the help of a therapist perhaps using play, artwork or narrative work to help them explore themselves and their current and past experiences.

As the children learn to trust adults to protect them and develop security in the relationships they encounter, they will be able to address issues from their past and current experience without being overwhelmed by them.

If you are a parent struggling with a child with difficulties this may sound unhelpful and burdensome. You are not managing to help your child feel safe and secure, and yet you are being told that until he is feeling safe and secure then therapy will not be helpful. You do need help and support. A therapist can help you reflect on your parenting and the family environment and help you to find ways to increase feelings of security for your child. This help might come through group work, providing you with the valuable support of other parents as well. Alternatively you might be able to find a therapist who will work with you and your child together. The focus of this therapy will be on helping your child to feel more secure with you. An adoption/fostering-sensitive family therapist might be able to work with the whole family to find ways of relating with each other that make you all feel more comfortable and secure. Finally, a therapist might give you opportunities to 'offload', to share the burden. This will give you opportunities to emotionally re-charge, and help you keep going in the face of what is likely to be slow change.

6

Parenting and Patterns of Attachment

If helping your child starts with parenting then it is important to think about how your parenting can be tailored to the particular needs of your child. Thinking about parenting in terms of the patterns of attachment that children develop from their early relationships can be helpful.

Children need to experience parenting that replicates good infant–parent interactions. These need to be sensitive, responsive, empathic and attuned. However, there is an added complexity because of the children's past experience of being parented. This means that they will have learnt to distort the way that they express needs.

Parenting has to be sensitive and responsive to both the expressed and the hidden emotional needs. You therefore need to be able to accurately interpret your child's need for nurturance. This is despite sometimes difficult and alienating behaviours, as she expects you to be unavailable, unpredictable or rejecting. Mary Dozier (2003) suggests that these expectations need to be gently challenged with available, predictable and accepting care.

This parenting task is made difficult because as children continue to respond to their past experience they may:

- Experience increased anxiety at the possibility of a close, intimate relationship. This triggers their learnt attachment behaviours of avoidance, clinginess or control, as described below.

- Avoid intimacy and dependence, or become clingy and overly dependent.

- Act in a way that elicits hurt and rejection.

- Cling to premature *autonomy*, appearing more independent than they should do for their age, or to infantile behaviours, appearing emotionally young and dependent for their age.

- Become very manipulative and controlling, thus preventing the parent from providing security or nurturance.

All of these different ways of behaving can present a challenge. They each in their own way make it difficult for you to be sensitive and responsive to your child. The starting point needs to be an acceptance of why she is displaying particular behaviours. From this stance of acceptance you can then lead her in to new ways of relating to you. Your acceptance and understanding will build trust. Trust builds your child's confidence to try out different ways of relating.

Parenting the child with an ambivalent attachment pattern of relating

The child who brings an ambivalent style of relating into the new home expresses the need for continuing attention from the parent very clearly. 'Stay close to me. Where are you going?' Often these children will follow the parent, even to the bathroom. They also find it difficult if the parent is trying to talk to someone else, and they can keep up a constant chatter just to make sure that the parent keeps attending to them. Thus the children's expressed need is for:

- Reassurance of the availability of the parent. They fear psychological abandonment, the parent not noticing them or being attentive to them, and thus they seek reassurance all the time.

- Predictability and consistency. Insecurity increases with changes of routine, at times of transition or when others behave inconsistently.

- Structure and routine. High levels of structure and routine help the children to feel more secure.

- Co-regulation of emotion that is expressed. The children are quickly overwhelmed by their feelings. They need help to manage these feelings, otherwise the feelings control them.

The children also have hidden needs. These are emotional needs that they hide away because they conflict with the expressed needs.

- Support to be apart – the children need help to learn to be apart and to feel secure that the parent will be there when needed.

- Support to be able to trust their knowledge of the world and not just to rely on their feelings. The children need to learn that they can trust that the parents will do as they say.

Zoë has learnt to relate to Jenny and Martin with this ambivalent pattern. Her early experience taught her that parents can become unavailable at any time, and that she is not very effective in getting their attention at these times. Zoë has learnt to fear psychological abandonment. She keeps Jenny in her sight at all times; she reminds her that she is there through constant talking, through a variety of challenging behaviours and through clinginess and dependence. She learnt with Karen that 'mums' are more likely to offer nurture to babies than to older children. Zoë clings to 'baby' behaviours; she does not want to be a big girl.

This is a demanding task, especially for Jenny who is the primary focus of Zoë's anxiety. No matter how much she meets Zoë's need for attention it is never enough. Zoë's needs are bottomless. Some days Jenny just can't remain calm and sensitive with Zoë. She gets snappy and irritable. This increases Zoë's feelings of insecurity and she becomes clingier. It feels like every step forward leads to two back.

The task for Jenny, supported by Martin, is to provide a very structured and predictable routine for Zoë. She needs clear reminders and support at times of change such as when she is going to school; and reassurance, perhaps with a tangible reminder, that she will be re-united with Jenny again when they are apart. A note in her lunch box, a piece of Jenny's scarf sewn into the inside of her school jumper, and some idea of what Jenny will be doing during the day all help Zoë to manage school more easily.

Jenny and Martin will offer Zoë a high level of reassurance of their support for her. She needs to know they are predictably available to her, but they will also provide a gentle challenge to this. They will build in brief periods when Zoë has to wait a little, gradually increasing the time as she manages these periods. She will receive quiet praise for coping. When Zoë appears very insecure however they will be there, demonstrating that when she needs them most they will respond. Zoë will receive empathy for how hard and scary it is wondering if they will be there when she needs them. They will also need to notice when Zoë is becoming emotionally aroused, stepping in and co-regulating this emotion with her. Thus they might spend time with her, talk quietly to her, change the activity, or give her a cuddle until the emotion subsides.

They will also help Zoë to understand cause and effect so that she is not only relying on her feelings to guide her behaviour. When Zoë falls and needs a plaster Martin points out to her: 'You cried when you fell; I bet that hurt. I heard you and came; now I am cleaning it up and putting a plaster on.' Jenny reminds her: 'Zoë, when I was on the phone to grandma last week you tipped all the cutlery out of the drawer. I guess you were really cross that I was being so long, but then I had to wash all the cutlery and we couldn't finish the puzzle. Today, I talked to grandma for ten minutes; now we have time to do some drawing before lunch.'

Zoë will be helped to do more for herself; this too will be in small steps. When she wants to be dressed by Jenny they will do it together; when she wants to be fed they will take it in turns. Very gradually Zoë will be supported to do more for herself. To help with this Zoë will have a regular 'mum' time each evening whilst Martin helps Catherine with her homework. For 15 minutes Zoë can experience what it would be like to be Jenny's baby. She enjoys being cuddled, and for a while wants to be fed with a bottle during these times. Lately she has preferred to cuddle into Jenny whilst Jenny reads her a story. All the time nny lets her know that this is how she would have looked after her as a baby. Zoë's trust in Jenny increases as she experiences this special nurturing time.

Jenny and Martin know they need some time for themselves. They have made an arrangement with their friends who have also adopted two children. They are going to baby-sit for each other on alternate Friday nights. They are going to make Zoë a visual calendar to remind her when it is Friday so their going out isn't unexpected.

Some days are going to be bad; Jenny and Martin will be irritable or tired. Some days Zoë's demands are just too much. It is important they don't feel guilty or too despondent on these days. They might find it helpful to go to a support group with other adoptive parents; this will remind them that they are not the only ones who have difficult days with the children. They can reassure Zoë that all is well once they are feeling a bit emotionally stronger again. 'Zoë, we had a difficult day yesterday. Mummy was worried about a letter she had to write and I think you felt very wobbly in your tummy when I was cross. I love you and will always be here for you.' On good days they will celebrate their successes. 'Zoë, you did so well getting ready for bed by yourself. Shall we have the special biscuits for supper?'

Parenting the child with an avoidant attachment pattern of relating

The child who brings an avoidant style of relating into the new home expresses the need for self-reliance very clearly. 'I don't need you; I can do it by myself; I am not hurt.' These children appear to manage very well and therefore can cause little concern, but parents often report that they feel there is something missing in the relationship, and that underneath they don't feel their child is happy. Thus the children's expressed need is:

- to be left alone, to get on with it themselves.

The conflicting emotional needs that are hidden away are:

- Help to feel comfort and safety with the parent.

- Support to accept nurturing. These children find it difficult to let down their guard and allow the parent to provide them with comfort and care.

- Co-regulation of emotion that is hidden. These children dissociate or cut-off from feelings. Like children with ambivalent patterns of attachment these children also struggle to regulate emotion but they deal with this in a very different way. Instead of the feelings emerging in an uncontrolled way they are inhibited. The children do not learn to handle these feelings.

- Help to trust emotion and to know that it will be acceptable to others. The children do not express the way they are feeling because they fear that this will push the parent further away. They feel safer if they contain their feelings rather than express them.

Catherine's early life was different to Zoë's. She learnt to relate to adults with an avoidant pattern. Her early experience taught her that showing emotions overwhelms other people. Catherine's need of Fiona was frightening for Fiona and so Catherine learnt not to show this need. She stopped trusting her feelings and learnt to be very vigilant of the mood and behaviour of other people.

When she moved in with Jenny and Martin, Catherine could not relax and express, or even understand, how she felt. Instead she would think about how to behave depending upon the situation. If she thought that Jenny and Martin wanted her to be happy, she would be happy. If they asked her if she would like to go shopping, she would decide whether they wanted her to go and answer accordingly. At school she figured out how to behave by watching the other children. She kept her own feelings locked tightly away. In this way others would not witness them, but neither could she understand how she was feeling.

As time has gone on Catherine is relaxing a little. At nine years of age she can enjoy feeling a part of this family, can relax and enjoy some spontaneous feelings of pleasure and happiness. The more negative emotions continue to be difficult however. If she experiences a moment of sadness, for example, and it is not tightly controlled she experiences fear. Catherine then becomes very angry with Jenny and Martin. These angry outbursts can be intense but will be quickly over as Catherine gains control again. She will also be angry if she feels especially close to them; maybe they are having a loving time together. At these times Catherine can be quite provocative, trying to put some distance back into the relationship.

In some ways looking after Catherine is less tiring than looking after Zoë. Catherine is often very compliant, and she will play, read or draw happily by herself. She is also quite self-reliant, not wanting their help and being uncomfortable with comfort when she is hurt or distressed. If Catherine falls over, for example, she will call out that she is all right almost before she even touches the ground. She is generally quiet and well behaved.

Over time however this has become quite wearing for Jenny and Martin. They feel as if they can't quite get hold of Catherine; the relationship does not feel quite real. They try and cuddle Catherine and make a fuss of her, and she will cuddle them back, but always Catherine seems to be trying to please them rather than enjoying the relationship with them. They try to help Catherine understand her feelings but worry about how impressionable she is. If they tell her she is feeling sad, Catherine readily agrees. Like a very young child Catherine can only understand her inner life through the eyes of her mum and dad. These interactions are important for her; only after this help from her parents is she able to understand how she feels herself.

Jenny often feels guilty; she spends a lot of time with Zoë and she is aware that she isn't giving enough time to Catherine. The fact that Catherine does not complain only adds to her guilt.

Jenny and Martin need to parent Catherine differently to Zoë. They need to give Catherine some space, and allow her time to be distant from them. It is hard work for Catherine to spend too much time with them; she needs to relax by herself. Jenny and Martin are careful however to also make some demands on Catherine, to spend time with them and to let them help her. They provide a gentle challenge to her not needing them. They are careful to demonstrate to Catherine that they are going to keep her safe and that they will be available to comfort her when she experiences distress. They talk to her about feelings, describing their own feelings and making guesses about how Catherine might be feeling. They try to mirror her inner feelings, thoughts and beliefs back to her, to help Catherine become more in touch with her internal mental state.

A trip to the dentist, for example, gives Jenny an opportunity to talk to Catherine about her own anxiety when taken to the dentist as a child. She talks about how her tummy would churn up whilst waiting to go in. She notices Catherine clenching her hands and wonders if maybe Catherine feels a little anxious. Although Catherine protests that she is not feeling anxious, Jenny reassures her that she will stay with her throughout.

Jenny and Martin also decide to look for opportunities to nurture Catherine. If she has a cut or bruise they pay special attention to it. Jenny spends time helping Catherine to style her hair, providing opportunities for close physical contact. Catherine is not too comfortable being cuddled but they find out that she likes having her feet massaged. Special 'mum' times for Catherine consist of a foot massage whilst they talk about their day. This is an opportunity to talk to Catherine about how she is feeling. 'I bet you were really pleased that the teacher read out your story. Were you thinking how much the teacher liked your story? Maybe you felt like smiling.' Or 'That was really mean of Ben to take your pencil without asking. Did you think that he should have found his own pencil? I wonder if you felt very cross with him.' This time always ends with Catherine's favourite activity, reading a story together.

Jenny and Martin are coping with two children who both need to experience feeling safe and secure and both need to trust in their parents' reliability and responsivity; but they are expressing this in very different ways. This is hard work and they often feel despondent. Although Zoë is hard work they at least feel needed by her. It is difficult to keep on providing Catherine with the experience of a relationship that she appears so uncomfortable with. Progress is very slow and it is particularly discouraging to see how Catherine quickly turns back to her old ways of comforting herself when she is especially stressed. They always know that something is bothering her when she sits sucking her thumb and twiddling her hair until she pulls it out. Often they wonder if they are 'right' for Catherine, whether someone else might be able to reach her more easily. It is an act of faith for Jenny and Martin to continue parenting Catherine in this way day after day, trusting that this will be helpful for her in the long run.

Parenting the child with a disorganized/controlling attachment pattern of relating

The child who brings a disorganized, controlling style of relating into the new home expresses the need to be in control very clearly. 'You will do as I want. It will be done my way. I will take control of everything.' These children can appear angry and manipulative. They can overtly control, or they may be subtler, controlling behind the parents' back. Stealing and lying are common. The children appear tough but are often very scared inside. Thus the children's expressed need is:

- to be in control.

The conflicting emotional needs that are hidden away are that they:

- need help to feel safe. Predominantly the children do not feel safe or secure, and do not know how to elicit help from others.

- need a low stress environment. These children are not able to tolerate very much stress. They quickly dysregulate, or become emotionally overwhelmed. This then leads to an increase in the controlling behaviours as they try to feel safe or secure again.

- need help to develop *emotional regulation*. The children have very little capacity to regulate their feelings. They quickly become overwhelmed and the feelings are acted out rather than understood and processed.

- need help to develop *reflective function* abilities. The children have very little ability to stop and reflect on how they or others are feeling. They react but rarely stop and think.

Marcus arrived in his placement with Rita and Frank determined to show them who is in control. He needs to be in control of everything. Marcus's early experience has taught him that to appear weak is to be hurt and so he keeps on demonstrating how strong and powerful he is. He is defiant, quarrelsome and often very insulting to Rita and Frank. He is very 'in their face' as he demands, refuses or complains.

Marcus however can also be loving and helpful. He will give Rita a cuddle or willingly help with tasks around the house. It often feels like looking after two Marcus's rather than one. He is either 'golden' or obnoxious. There is no in between.

One area that Rita and Frank find particularly difficult is Marcus's tendency to lie to them. He goes upstairs for a shower, comes back still with dirty hands and face and insists that he has taken the shower. Nothing they can say shakes his conviction that he has indeed taken this shower. They also find that if they leave small change around, it will go missing. Again Marcus swears that he hasn't had it, although the sweet wrappers in his bedroom tell another story. Even more seriously he will appear with items from school, including a mobile phone on one occasion. He concocts elaborate stories to explain how he has come by these.

Marcus's need to feel in control is so strong that Rita and Frank find it difficult to oppose it. If they try to take control themselves they find themselves in endless control battles, which Marcus always wins. They need to find a way of maintaining the important boundaries whilst allowing Marcus some measure of control within these.

Marcus's overriding need is to feel safe. It is important for Rita and Frank to provide a tight structure and routine with a high level of predictability. They also try to remain calm and quiet. They know that signs of disapproval, irritation and, of course, anger increase Marcus's level of fear, provoking even more difficult behaviour from him.

This is challenging; despite their best efforts Marcus can provoke them to anger. They have to learn to be very aware of their own rising stress levels so that they can walk away before he gets too much for them. This is more difficult because they need to provide such a high level of supervision. Marcus wants to play out with the other lads in the neighbourhood but he quickly gets into trouble. The other boys don't like the way he tries to take over the games, or his anger when things don't go his way. Rita and Frank make sure that he only goes out for short periods; and that he has opportunities to bring friends home instead, where they can keep a closer eye on him. Unfortunately Marcus resents this, feeling that he isn't being allowed what the other lads have.

Rita and Frank also learn quickly not to provide too much excitement for Marcus. In the early days they wanted to give him experiences he had previously missed out on. They would plan a treat. Marcus would eagerly look forward to this, but his behaviour became worse and worse the closer it came. Not wanting to disappoint him they would go ahead with the plan, only to have to cut it short as his behaviour became more difficult. Marcus was not able to manage his increasing excitement; he became dysregulated quickly as this emotion overwhelmed him.

An increase in anxiety has the same effect, as demonstrated by his increasingly difficult behaviour. Rita and Frank try to spot Marcus's increasing level of arousal, stepping in early and spending more time with him as they try to regulate this arousal for him. They also try and slow Marcus down, helping him to stop and think. Marcus finds it very difficult to understand the link between his behaviour and its consequence. Rita and Frank try to provide him with short, clear instructions and to help him understand consequences. 'When you do this, then...', 'If you do that then...'

Caring for Marcus is a full-time job for Rita and Frank, and they try to support each other as much as they can. If one of them is becoming angry or frustrated the other tries to step in to provide a break. They also make sure they keep talking to each other. Marcus often plays one off against the other. 'Rita said I could...', 'Frank promised me...' He also tries to persuade one of them of some injustice done to him by the other. Sharing these experiences and planning consistent responses are an important element of their parenting of Marcus.

Parenting the child who has not learnt to selectively attach

The child who has experienced severe neglect in early life has been deprived of experiencing a parent as either available or unavailable to meet emotional needs.

The parent is simply not there often enough for the child to begin to conceive of people being available to help soothe distress. Thus these children do not understand that relationships could be significant or important for them. They will use relationships opportunistically and indiscriminately.

The expressed need is:

- If I need something I will use whoever is around.
- I will not commit to relationships at more than a superficial level.

The hidden needs are:

- for an available, dependable, continuous parent, but not having experience of this, the child has no sense that this is a possibility.

Luke arrived in placement with Jackie as if he had always lived there. He shows no sign of missing his mother or his sister. He makes few demands on Jackie but talks excitedly to anyone who comes to the house. He acts as if everyone is his best friend. This can be quite endearing although his apparent trust of everyone means that he has to be carefully supervised. If Jackie turns her back in the park Luke might just as easily walk off with one of the other mothers rather than seek her out. If a respite break is arranged Luke goes off happily and then arrives back as if there has been no break.

Jackie needs to teach Luke what a parent is. Luke has missed out on so much in his young life that he needs to be shown that parents can cuddle, feed, provide for and generally be available.

Luke also has to be taught how to treat other people. A cuddle for the postman needs to be re-directed back to Jackie. If he tries to tell the man in the corner shop his life story Jackie explains that it is fine to talk to her, but not to talk in this way to people they only know casually.

These lessons are only slowly learnt. A lack of early critical experience combined with learning difficulties means that it is very difficult for Luke to learn to behave with people differently. Whilst he becomes used to, and even enjoys, the high level of nurture that Jackie provides for him he continues to experience difficulty in moving beyond superficial relationships: relationships in which he gets what he wants but cannot understand that he might reciprocate. He cannot develop a deeply satisfying mutual relationship with Jackie.

Part 2

A Model for Parenting the Child with Difficulties in Attachment Relationships: Providing a Secure Base

7

Introduction to the Model and Creating a Secure Base

In this chapter I provide an overview of the house model of parenting (see Figure 7.1).

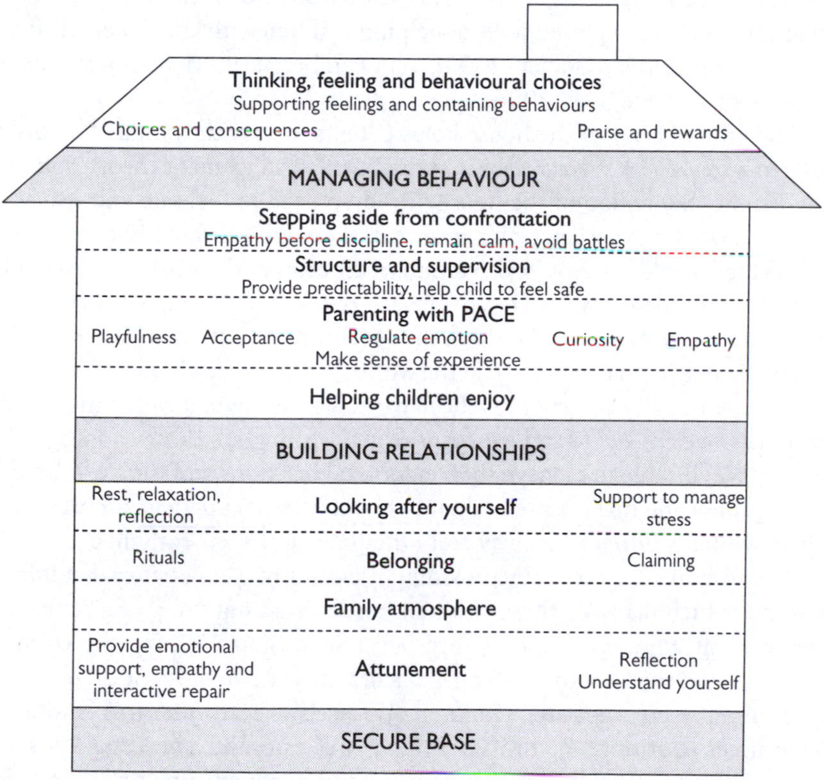

Figure 7.1 contents:

- Roof: **Thinking, feeling and behavioural choices** — Supporting feelings and containing behaviours — Choices and consequences — Praise and rewards
- **MANAGING BEHAVIOUR**
  - **Stepping aside from confrontation** — Empathy before discipline, remain calm, avoid battles
  - **Structure and supervision** — Provide predictability, help child to feel safe
  - **Parenting with PACE** — Playfulness — Acceptance — Regulate emotion — Make sense of experience — Curiosity — Empathy
  - **Helping children enjoy**
- **BUILDING RELATIONSHIPS**
  - Rest, relaxation, reflection — **Looking after yourself** — Support to manage stress
  - Rituals — **Belonging** — Claiming
  - **Family atmosphere**
  - Provide emotional support, empathy and interactive repair — **Attunement** — Reflection Understand yourself
- **SECURE BASE**

Figure 7.1 The house model of parenting (Adapted from 'The House Model of Parenting' in Golding et al. (2006). Copyright © John Wiley & Sons Ltd. Reproduced with kind permission.)

In the following chapters we will work through this model, exploring each element in depth, whilst considering the difficulties and challenges you might meet along the way.

Attachment theory can help us to understand the difficulties that children living in foster care or adoptive homes can experience. Understanding the influence of early experience on the way that children respond to later parenting can help us to make sense of challenging behaviour and emotional difficulties. Understanding the children is a starting point for helping them to have a very different experience of attachment relationships. However, if children are going to be able to develop a more *secure attachment* relationship in their new home then they will need to experience a very different type of parenting. This parenting needs to go beyond meeting the typical needs of children to also helping them to recover from their early experience.

The house model of parenting is based upon our knowledge of how children build *secure attachment* relationships in infancy, and how this can be adapted to help older children to also achieve a more *secure attachment* with foster carers or adoptive parents. This model draws on the work of a number of clinicians who have explored ways of helping children with attachment difficulties, for example Mary Dozier (2003), Vera Fahlberg (1994), but most notably the work of Dan Hughes (2006).

The ground floor of the house helps parents to provide a home that offers children a *secure base*. A *secure base* is at the heart of attachment theory and also provides the foundation of the house. Children need to feel safe and secure. If children have the experience of a *secure base* they will confidently explore and learn in their world. They will also return to the arms of their parents when they need love, care and comfort. The attachment system and the exploratory system will be in balance allowing the children to feel confident in their parents and in their own capacity to be effective in the world. Within such a home children can develop emotionally and cognitively. In particular they will develop the capacities for *emotional regulation* and *reflective function.* Through these developing abilities they will be able to manage their emotional reactions and they will be able to think about and make sense of their past and current experience. This in turn will allow the children to recover from the trauma of their early lives.

Parents build *attachments* by providing the parenting experience that infants need, but which many of these children have missed out on, in particular the experience of *attunement*, and an absorbed relationship. Helping the child to experience and enjoy emotional engagement with the parent is critical if he is to benefit from *secure attachment*. Children also need to learn that this emotional connection can at times be broken without a catastrophic consequence. They will be able to re-establish the connection and experience being loved, supported and comforted, even when the disruption to the *attunement* was caused by their own behaviour. This is called interactive or relationship repair. Children need to learn that fundamentally they are good even though at times they make some bad choices. The parents therefore need to find ways to provide these attunement/re-attunement cycles as explicitly for the older child as they would do for a toddler or young child. The child will then feel secure within the relationship.

To foster such security parents need to provide a *positive family atmosphere*. When people living closely together experience different emotional states these will adjust so that one emotion predominates. Thus remaining calm and positive will over time allow the child to also experience such feelings. To maintain such an atmosphere parents will however need to learn how to avoid being drawn into the emotional state being experienced by the child. It is not uncommon for children to react to their past experience. They use the current home as a stage on which they re-enact their early experience. Other family members unwittingly become the supporting actors for this theatre. If children experienced chaotic, negative and highly aroused family life then this is what they expect and try to generate in their new home. It can be challenging for parents to maintain a positive atmosphere when the child's experience has been so negative.

As the parents learn to control the emotional rhythm of the house, claiming, and a feeling of *belonging*, occurs. Children are helped to feel part of the family. These may be strange experiences for the children, and may at first be difficult and overwhelming. Feeling that they belong to the family can generate difficult feelings of betrayal and loyalty to the birth family, especially for children who moved at an older age. The children will need sensitively supporting with these complex feelings so that they can enjoy being part of family life whilst still retaining feelings for their original family. Where the children have ongoing contact with their birth families these conflicting feelings can be even more complex and difficult to manage.

Understandably the parenting task when looking after children with complex patterns of attachment, influenced by their early, difficult experience, can be very stressful, and emotionally exhausting. Parents also need to *look after themselves*. They need to make space for reflection and for rest and relaxation. Understanding their own reactions to the child can be important. Parents will need time apart from their children when they can attend to their own needs in order to remain emotionally able to continue the task of parenting the challenging child.

The upper floor of the house helps parents to use the secure base in order to build a deeper relationship with their child. As children develop relationships they will be able to experience a sense of *enjoyment* and fun within the family

The parents need to find ways to remain emotionally engaged and available to the child. Dan Hughes (2006) suggests a certain attitude (PACE) that the parents can hold which will help them to maintain a level of emotional engagement. If they can stay curious (C) about why the child is behaving as he is, they will be less likely to feel cross or frustrated. Curiosity leads to understanding, which helps the parent to accept (A) the child and the reasons for his behaviour. This in turn will help the parent to provide the child with *empathy* (E) and support alongside the discipline he needs. At times a playful (P) stance can also diffuse a situation and help the child to behave in a more acceptable way. In this way *parenting with PACE* provides the child with the experience of love (L) and kindness; the parent offers the child a supportive PLACE within which he can begin to experience a very different attachment relationship.

An attitude of PACE is not the same as tolerating difficult behaviour. *Security* and trust are increased by an appropriate degree of *structure and supervision* tailored to the individual needs of the child. This will provide children with boundaries so that they can learn to behave in ways that are acceptable within the family. Additionally parents will find it helpful if they can *step aside from confrontation* through calm, empathic responses to the child.

A *secure base*, a calm, positive emotional atmosphere and parenting that offers the child the experience of emotional connection, acceptance and *empathy* all provide a containing structure for the child symbolized by the house. Within this home the child will learn to enjoy belonging to the family.

The roof of the house represents the management of difficult behaviour. Good behavioural management rests on an understanding of the links between *thinking, feeling and behavioural choices*. Children are helped to make good behavioural choices because their inner experience, what they think and feel, is accepted. Parents strive to understand the thinking and feeling that led to the behaviour, providing acceptance alongside clear behavioural management. This is communicated via *empathy* before discipline techniques provide choices and logical consequences and the child is helped to manage the consequences and to enjoy praise and rewards.

The house model of parenting therefore provides children with a home within which they can develop emotionally and cognitively. As they develop a more *secure attachment* they can learn to use the support and care on offer and with this can start to make sense of their emotional life. They will develop the ability to regulate themselves emotionally and behaviourally. With this will develop the flexibility of thinking that leads to the capacity to inhibit impulses, develop problem-solving abilities and manage different situations capably. This in turn will lead to a greater capacity to make sense of their experience past and present and to recover from the trauma of early adversity.

The challenge of parenting children with difficult attachment relationship histories

Offering children a parenting experience that provides love, security and comfort can be a challenge in itself, but helping children to accept this experience presents its own set of challenges.

Children may not believe that they deserve love and care. Often the only way that they can make sense of their early experience is to develop the belief that they are bad, that they somehow deserved the abuse, neglect and loss of family. In this way children are able to preserve a belief in parents as good. It is they who were not good enough. They will now set out to prove that this is true within their new home.

> It has been a difficult day for Catherine. She has always found school a struggle. She is capable but she does not believe in her abilities. She is often reluctant to commit work to paper for fear of making a mistake. However, she is developing some trust in her teacher and has been growing in confidence. Today a supply teacher takes the class. Catherine is thrown back into her fear of not being good enough. She spends much of the day quietly avoiding the tasks set. The growing frustration of the teacher, who finds Catherine's passive resistance difficult to cope with, only increases Catherine's fears that she is going to fail. On top of this there is an odd number in the dance lesson; Catherine is the one who does not have a friend to work with!
>
> When Jenny picks Catherine up from school she finds her tired and non-communicative. Jenny is disappointed; she was hoping that Catherine would be in a good mood tonight. Her aunt is visiting and she wants the children to make a good impression. She quietly reminds Catherine of the visit and tells her that she is sure Aunty Jean will enjoy meeting such a good and kind girl. Catherine's anxiety rises as she hears this; deep inside her she just doesn't feel good enough.
>
> Catherine is rude and unco-operative for the rest of the evening as she shows Jenny and Martin how wrong they are about her.

Alternatively, the experience of parents not being able to care for them may lead the child to doubt parent availability. They are left feeling that the new parents must meet their every need and wish or else these parents are no different from their biological parents.

> To add to the disaster of Jenny and Martin's evening Zoë throws one of the biggest tantrums they have seen in a long while. Jenny has asked Martin to take over in the kitchen whilst she takes Catherine aside for a quiet word. They ask Zoë to keep Aunty Jean company. Zoë's anxiety increases as neither Jenny nor Martin are available for a while. She gets out a puzzle and starts to put it together. As she gets stuck she looks to Aunty Jean for some help. Aunty Jean hasn't got her reading glasses with her so she tells Zoë to wait for mum to come back down. Zoë, unable to wait, goes to the kitchen to find Martin. He tells her he will be there in two minutes. Zoë, still not satisfied, goes up to Catherine's room to find Jenny. Catherine angrily tells her to get out of her room; Jenny more quietly reminds her that she is not allowed in Catherine's room but reassures her that she will be down soon. Zoë cannot hold it in any more. She needs to know that Jenny and Martin are there for her, and she needs to know it now. Her anxiety and fear take over as she erupts in anger and frustration.

Being able to use the parent as a *secure base* starts with the experience of a parent who is interested and attentive. The parent keeps the child in mind, showing him that she will be there when needed, much as parents do with their infants. In addition the child needs to experience the parent as reliable and the structure to the day as predictable. Morning, bedtime and school routines follow a consistent pattern. Through these things children learn that they matter to the parent. This in turn helps them to develop a belief in their own strengths and abilities. The parent believes for them, providing opportunities for the children to gain a sense of accomplishment. The children will gradually learn to accept a view of themselves as effective in the world. They will learn to trust the parent and to trust themselves.

The parenting challenge is therefore to provide children with a consistent and emotionally enabling experience of being loved and cared for. This will provide them with security and safety whilst allowing them to develop a different way of understanding themselves and their parents. Children learn that they are worthy of love and care and that parents are capable of providing this experience.

A further challenge to this parenting is that the children are likely to have gaps in development. They will need nurturing and care that helps to fill these gaps. The lack of key experiences in early childhood will impact on both emotional and *cognitive* development. Often children will be functioning at a different age to their chronological age. In particular poor early parenting can be very disruptive to children's emotional development, leaving them emotionally immature. They might be experiencing a *secure base* for the first time. They might need parenting that is relatively young for their age. On the other hand they are also trying to fit in at school and within the community. They need help to acquire age-appropriate academic and social abilities. The parent is left feeling that they are parenting a child whose needs keep shifting across the developmental age span.

8

Empathy and Support from the Secure Base

Children who are unable to experience a family as a secure base are likely to be highly anxious, and have difficulty trusting their parents. Children can display their anxiety and lack of trust through difficult behaviour. Much of the parents' time can be spent managing this behaviour or trying to ward off the next outburst. This can feel like 'walking on eggshells'. The parent finds it difficult to relax around the child.

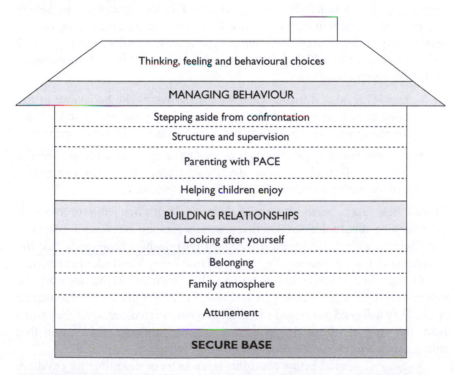

Figure 8.1 The secure base (Adapted from 'The House Model of Parenting' in Golding et al. (2006). Copyright © John Wiley & Sons Ltd. Reproduced with kind permission.)

Alternatively the child might be very compliant, almost too good to be true. She might be easy to manage but the parent is uneasy. It feels like there is something missing in the relationship. Whether anxiety is 'in your face' or 'hidden from view' children will only begin to feel secure within the family if they feel that their internal experience is accepted and supported.

Providing children with a *secure base* (see Figure 8.1), from which they can develop confidence in themselves and others, requires a large amount of empathic support. The use of *empathy* is therefore a key element within the house model of parenting. *Empathy* relies on emotional understanding and the ability to make emotional connections with another person. These ideas will be explored here but this will also be built on throughout the discussion of this model.

What is empathy?

Empathy is a quality in which one person understands the perspective of another, accepts this perspective as belonging to the other person and conveys this understanding and acceptance back to the person.

Being able to empathically listen to another person is essential if we are to build a relationship with him. To empathize with someone you need to listen deeply, paying attention to the words and also to the thoughts, feelings, beliefs and perceptions underlying the words. If we understand and accept what a person is expressing, and can help him to experience this understanding, he will feel connected with us. This deepens the relationship and provides a platform for further communication.

- *Empathy* is most difficult when we disapprove of the behaviour of the other person. We become focused on the behaviour and stop noticing the thoughts, feelings, beliefs and perceptions also being expressed.

- *Empathy* can also be forgotten in our haste to help someone solve a problem. Instead of empathically listening and conveying our understanding we jump in with offered solutions.

In both these cases a person is more likely to modify his behaviour or join with us in thinking about solutions if he first experiences being deeply understood.

Children with difficulties in attachment relationships have rarely had the experience of feeling emotionally connected to another. This lack of experience means that they struggle to understand their own emotions, to read the emotions of others or to anticipate how another might behave in response to them. They will need prolonged and clearly communicated *empathy* if they are to learn that they can be understood, that they are 'understandable', and that others can accept even their most frightening feelings.

Empathy is essential before providing boundaries or discipline for children. The children have often had little previous experience of parents behaving in a consistent and sensitive way connected to their own behaviour. Thus the children find it difficult to link what the parent is doing or saying with what they have just done. Without this experience the children find it difficult to appreciate cause and effect. They just experience the parent's behaviour as random and this fits their expectations that parents are 'mean'. They will not associate it with their own behaviour. They will become defensive, and this will prevent any true learning from the situation. If you can offer understanding and *empathy* your child will in turn get a sense of being understood. This feeling of emotional connection helps your child to attend both to her own behaviour and the behaviour of others. She will learn to appreciate the connection between her behaviour and your behaviour, and thus to respond in ways that lead to particular responses from you. This deepening emotional connection also helps to strengthen the relationship between you. As children experience a genuine, meaningful relationship they will want to behave in a way that meets with approval and pleasure. Your child is no longer just pleasing or protecting herself but is trying to please you. In this way communicating *empathy* leads to discipline becoming effective and your child learns how to behave in a socially acceptable way.

A longer period of empathic listening will also help your child to think with you about a problem and to consider different solutions. Without the *empathy* first, children can experience attempts at problem-solving as being critical of them. Again they can become defensive and stop listening. The experience of *empathy* can help children to feel understood, to feel accepted, and to feel that the problem is manageable because it can be shared. Sometimes this is all children will need; not all problems have solutions and children may just need to be understood and to have their feelings accepted in order to be able to cope. Sometimes empathic communication can pave the way for some joint problem-solving.

Supporting internal experience and managing behaviour

Children need support to trust in the family as a *secure base*, from which they can develop healthy relationships. Only within such relationships will the child feel accepted and cared for; this in turn will positively impact on her behaviour. It is the child's behaviour however that is most evident. Parenting strategies often focus on achieving behavioural change. These aim to help children develop acceptable behaviour and to reduce their use of behaviours considered unacceptable. Focusing on an insecure child's behaviour is like paying attention to the top of the iceberg. If the hidden iceberg is ignored then, whilst the day-to-day behaviour may be managed, ultimately the child will not be receiving the support she needs to really feel secure. Relationships will remain superficial and ineffectual, and behavioural change will be temporary in response to the immediate circumstances.

The hidden iceberg consists of the child's internal experience, all the feelings, thoughts and beliefs that underlie the child's outward behaviour. Often emotions are poorly understood or managed by the child; feelings drive her behaviour. Similarly beliefs are implicit, hidden at an unconscious level, leading to inflexible responding. Parenting needs to be focused on understanding the feelings and beliefs that the child is having and communicating this understanding via *empathy*. *Empathy* will help the child to understand and ultimately manage her own feelings and beliefs, and true behavioural change will follow.

In order to help children find security, therefore, the management of behaviour needs to be accompanied by support for the child's experience. It is important that the child feels that this internal experience is accepted, even when it is expressed through behaviour that is unacceptable.

Support is needed when strong feelings and beliefs are expressed through clearly challenging behaviour or through more *passive-aggressive* behaviour, acts of spite that occur behind the back, such as stealing or damaging property, as a way of expressing anger that can't be shown openly.

It is important neither to avoid situations in which strong feelings will emerge nor to minimize emotional outbursts. You need to show your child that you can cope with her feelings and that you will still be there for her. Your child will learn to trust and feel secure when you continue to be available and are not frightened or overwhelmed by the strong feelings that she is expressing.

It is equally important not to deny the beliefs your child holds. Telling a child who knows she is a 'bad kid' that this is not true is unlikely to reassure or to change her mind. She is most likely to stop sharing her beliefs with you. Empathizing with how hard it is to feel that you are a 'bad kid', and demonstrating your belief in her whilst accepting her own beliefs, is more likely to help her to develop newer, more adaptive beliefs over time.

Experiencing *empathy* alongside clear boundaries and limits on her behaviour will help your child. *Empathy* for the experience underlying the behaviour, and discipline and limits for behaviour, communicates that the internal experience is accepted even though the behaviour is not. Your child can then be helped to find alternate ways to express this experience. Whilst you will sometimes need to put some space between you because of your own feelings of hurt and anger it is important that overall your child does not feel rejected by you. You need to look for opportunities to keep her close even when the behaviour is pushing you away. You will also need to find ways to reconnect with her when you have taken some space for yourself. This communicates to your child that the relationship has survived the latest difficulty.

A *secure base* will be experienced when parents accept that, even if not openly expressed, a large part of the insecure child's behaviour is governed by feelings of anxiety, fear and the need for comfort. These feelings themselves can be very frightening for children whose early experience of having such needs was met with hostility, rejection or pain. The children may try to bury such feelings, by acting the clown, putting on a smile or caring for others. tively they may express the feelings in unhelpful ways such as through a infantile/helpless behaviour. These behaviours can lead to a temporary tion in the anxiety, fear or need for comfort, which then starts to build again. Figure 8.2 demonstrates a typical cycle as arousal in response to a trigger leads to behaviour and a temporary reduction in the arousal before it starts to build again.

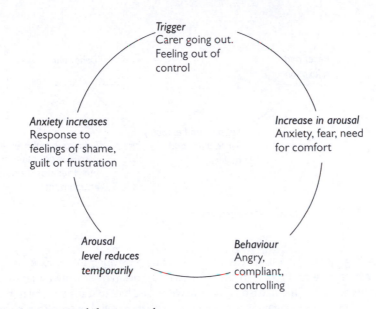

Trigger
Carer going out.
Feeling out of
control

Anxiety increases
Response to
feelings of shame,
guilt or frustration

Increase in arousal
Anxiety, fear, need
for comfort

*Arousal
level reduces
temporarily*

Behaviour
Angry,
compliant,
controlling

Figure 8.2 Anxiety–behaviour cycle

The arousal–relaxation cycle, discussed in Chapter 5, can be used to provide a predictable, consistent and reliable response to the child. This simulates the experience an infant has with a sensitive parent (see Figure 8.3). Increased arousal leads to behaviour that can be challenging. If this behaviour is contained without providing *empathy* and support for the underlying experience, the attachment relationship is not strengthened. However, if the child also experiences support for difficult feelings of shame and frustration, and *empathy* for uncomfortable beliefs about being not good enough, she will experience feelings of relief and relaxation supporting the developing attachment relationship. Ultimately she will experience reduced shame and begin to believe in herself more positively.

Jenny has just collected Zoë and Catherine from school. Both girls are feeling a bit fractious; it is nearing the end of term and they are ready for the school holidays. Catherine has a spelling test the next day and is worrying about learning

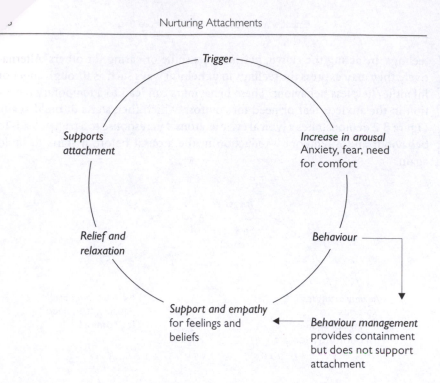

Figure 8.3 Using the arousal–relaxation cycle

the spellings. Jenny promises to sit with her and go through them. Zoë, as always, needs to re-connect with Jenny following a period of time away. Jenny is feeling tired; she too has had a busy time at work, and had to leave several things unfinished in order to get to school on time. Unfortunately, before she can see to either girl, the phone rings. She tells Zoë and Catherine that they can watch some television and goes to deal with the phone call. When she comes back she find uproar. Zoë has picked up Catherine's old teddy bear to cuddle whilst she watches television. Although Catherine hasn't bothered with this bear for quite a long time, seeing Zoë with it she now wants it. Jenny takes the bear away from both of them and makes sure they are sitting apart in different chairs. She reminds them that if they can't watch the television nicely then it will be turned off. She goes into the kitchen to make a much-needed cup of tea. Jenny has dealt with the immediate problem, and for a while the girls are quiet. However, Catherine's anxiety about her spellings remains and Zoë is still feeling in the need of some comfort and attention from Jenny. It won't be long before the girls start quarrelling again.

In this scenario Jenny stays calm and deals clearly with the immediate behaviour. What she doesn't do is provide empathy for the girls and the anxiety and need for comfort that they are experiencing. Their level of emotional arousal therefore remains high and unregulated.

Imagine instead that Jenny comes back into the room; seeing the teddy she decides to use it as a fun way of distracting the girls. She picks the teddy up and has a serious conversation with it. She solemnly tells teddy that Zoë has been a big girl at school all day and now she is in need of a cuddle. Catherine is worried about her spellings; she is learning some very difficult words at the moment. The girls watch curiously as they hear their experience expressed and understood. Jenny now sits down with them. She gives Zoë a cuddle and asks Catherine to show her the words. Zoë snuggles in to Jenny and they look together at the list of words Catherine has to learn. 'Wow, Catherine, these are hard words, no wonder you are worried that you won't be able to learn them. I tell you what, I am going to have a cup of tea and then I will sit down with you and we will go through them together. Perhaps teddy can help us.' Catherine giggles as she cuddles the teddy bear to her. Zoë, sensing that Jenny is soon going to be unavailable, starts to cry. Jenny holds her and quietly says: 'Zoë, you have been such a big girl all day, and now you are very tired. I think you need some more cuddling at the moment.' She notices Zoë visibly relax as her feelings and her need is acknowledged. She picks Zoë up and says: 'Guess who is waiting for you in the kitchen?' They go into the kitchen where Zoë is delighted to find her own teddy washed and just about dry in the drier. She wet the bed the previous night, and he had been in need of a wash. Zoë holds the teddy to her and watches Jenny making her tea. She is now happy to sit next to Jenny whilst Catherine is helped with the spellings. It will soon be time to make tea but now that both girls have experienced empathy for how they are feeling there is a chance that they will manage to play together whilst tea is made.

What can you do when the child rejects your empathy and support?

A child who continues to reject despite all your efforts can place a large strain on you and on the relationship. You are left with doubts about your own efficacy and hurt at the rejection. This may also trigger feelings relating to earlier rejections that you have experienced. These feelings then get mixed up with the feelings in the present and you can find yourself responding to your child in ways that are unusual for you. It can also take a toll on your own health, as you are left with feelings of anxiety, anger or depression. You will need intensive support to help you maintain empathic responses whilst understanding the reactions that you are experiencing.

Living with children with emotional difficulties therefore provides a complex range of challenges. Understanding the experience that drives the behaviour can be a full-time job on its own. You are also trying to convey this understanding back to your child whilst staying in control of your own emotional responses. Parenting with *empathy* is a first step towards helping a child to experience security. This helps the development of an *attachment*. The child now has a relationship within which she can experience being valued and can value others in return. The child will be able to use this relationship for support with her internal experience, and to learn appropriate behaviour. *Empathy* and support will lead to the child experiencing a *secure base* within which she can

...ence safety and nurturing and from which she can develop a deeper, more secure relationship. Behavioural change will however be slow, sometimes frustratingly so, and the continuing need to respond empathically and supportively whilst correcting unacceptable behaviour can be emotionally draining.

> Rita and Frank are struggling with Marcus. He has just gone back to school after a half-term holiday. They had a good week. Marcus, without the day-to-day stress of going to school, was in a relatively relaxed mood. In addition the good weather meant that he could get out into the garden each day and let off some steam. It felt like they were making a bit of progress.
>
> Two days back at school and this progress feels like a distant dream. The school have phoned on both days; Marcus has been fighting in the playground again. The teacher asks them to have a chat to Marcus. Their hearts sink; these chats about school behaviour never go well.
>
> Marcus arrives home, the door bangs and the school bag is thrown down. As soon as he sees Rita he starts demanding. Rita sympathizes with Marcus about his difficult day at school and calmly asks him to take his shoes off and to put his bag away. Marcus swears at her and storms upstairs. With a deep sigh Rita follows him upstairs meaning to sympathize with him about a difficult day at school. Her resolve leaves her however when she sees Marcus coming out of the bathroom. How can anyone make a mess like that in such a short time? Angrily she tells Marcus to stay in his room until tea-time. Frank arrives home a short time later. He innocently asks Rita if she has had a good day. Rita gives a good imitation of Marcus as her frustration spills over!

What can you do when you have no more empathy left?

The behaviour being expressed can be very difficult to deal with on a day-by-day basis. You are not only having to stay two steps ahead, staying aware of what your child is doing and why, but also having to deal with your own emotional reactions to her. You may experience anger when she is aggressive, defiant or non-compliant. You may experience frustration when she won't do something you know she is capable of; or you may experience hurt when her behaviour is very rejecting of you. In addition these behaviours don't reduce quickly; each day leads to the same patterns of behaviour and the same emotional reactions.

Parenting can therefore be emotionally draining. It is difficult to maintain *empathy* for a child especially when her behaviour feels personally targeted.

You will know that *empathy* is low when you find yourself responding to your child with:

- anger
- despair that you are not understanding or helping your child
- feelings that you cannot continue to provide a home for your child

- feelings that your child is selfish and ungrateful
- frustration that your child is not taking responsibility for her behaviour.

In these situations you can quickly find yourself in an escalating spiral of frustration. Without *empathy* for yourself or your child you are likely to lurch from difficulty to difficulty. It is at these times that support is most needed. You may not feel like going out to the support group or lack the energy to pick up the phone, but time to talk with others who understand, to offload some of your frustration and despair will provide you with a much-needed release. You can then start to think about your own needs. Are you getting at least some time for yourself? What opportunities do you have to re-charge your own emotional batteries? Stop, and give yourself some *empathy*. This is a difficult child, and she is giving you a hard time. Remind yourself of the progress you have made, however small. In the longer term you might also find it helpful to find some time to think about your child more deeply. Think, perhaps with a professional, with your partner or with another foster or adoptive parent, about the behaviour your child is displaying. What is the meaning of the behaviour? How does this relate to his past experience? How does this relate to possible difficulties in forming relationships?

As you re-establish some *empathy* and acceptance of your child and her difficulties you may feel ready again to think about the way you are parenting and to try some different approaches.

As you participate in such reflections you may become aware of patterns in your reactions. Perhaps there is some aspect of the child that always seems to get to you. You may be able to cope with any amount of verbal abuse, but the lying gets to you every time. Maybe you can cope with the untidy bedroom and the lack of showers but bad table manners put you totally on edge. Of course your child sussed you long ago. If she wants to 'push your button' she knows exactly what to do. Understanding your own idiosyncrasies can increase your tolerance for the behaviour of your child. Often being driven crazy by a particular behaviour relates to experience in your own past.

Jackie has been finding Luke especially difficult. His bed-wetting has been getting more frequent and the endless washing of bedding has sent the washing machine into a final decline. Now Luke has taken to stealing even more compulsively. He seems to be hoarding a whole range of things, not just food. Jackie found all the CDs in his room, removed from their cases, together with a collection of paper clips, rubbers and, bizarrely, all the handles from her dresser. Jackie had not realized that he could unscrew them.

Empathy is at an all-time low as Jackie experiences frustration at the slow progress they are making. She is finding it harder to maintain a loving attitude towards Luke and she even finds herself disliking him at times. She begins to view Luke as ungrateful after all she has done for him. She feels especially angry when she watches him talk so sweetly to their elderly neighbour.

Jackie confides in her social worker, Alan, about how she is feeling, and suggests to him that she may not be able to continue much longer. Alan listens to her sympathetically. He does not try to tell Jackie what a great job she is doing, but allows her to fully offload about how hard it is right now. Alan suggests that maybe they could arrange a consultation with the psychologist to explore why progress appears to be so slow.

Jackie finds this consultation really useful. She feels deeply listened to and experiences empathy and understanding for her frustration and despair. Jackie and Alan re-explore Luke's past history as the psychologist asks detailed questions. She then helps them to connect some of this past history with his current behaviour. Jackie begins to understand more clearly how the chronic neglect has been deeply damaging to Luke and how his capacity to enter into a fully reciprocal relationship may have been permanently compromised. Jackie feels sadness returning for the little boy who not only has to cope with a learning disability but an emotional disability as well. As they think together about the support Luke needs they get encouragement from the small signs of progress he is making. When he fell from the swing the other day he very clearly looked to Jackie to help him. Jackie finds some strength and empathy returning. She also realizes that it is not only Luke who will need long-term support. She arranges another meeting in a couple of months' time. She does not want to feel quite so low again.

Understanding the impact of past experience on parenting

We have all encountered a range of relationships in the past. Some have been rewarding and some more difficult. All these relationships will influence us in some way. They can increase our confidence, or reduce it. It is not unusual for our children to remind us of some of the more difficult experiences from our past. When this happens it becomes harder to maintain *empathy*.

Rita was married to Tony before meeting Frank. They had a turbulent marriage. Tony was a domineering man who had a traditional view of marriage. Physical violence was not uncommon and Rita often had to explain away a black eye when she went into work. Rita became more and more anxious, culminating in quite frequent panic attacks whenever she felt intimidated by people. Fortunately she had supportive parents and they helped her to leave him. She lived in fear of him turning up on her doorstep for quite some time.

The impact of this relationship has stayed with her, but Frank is very different and for the most part she has been able to put it behind her. Gradually the anxiety and panic attacks reduced.

Since they began caring for Marcus however she has begun to experience occasional panic attacks again. She visits her GP and he refers her to a counsellor. In talking it over with her Rita comes to realize that her increased anxiety is associated with Marcus. In particular Rita starts to notice that when Marcus is demanding and verbally aggressive she becomes more anxious. This surprises Rita because although Marcus is difficult she never actually feels threatened by him. It appears that his behaviour is triggering for her the memory of her relationship with Tony. Instead of responding to Marcus, she is instead reacting to a relationship now well in the past.

Perhaps the most influential of past relationships are those we experienced with our own parents. These can have the longest lasting influence on the way we relate to others, and also determine how we respond to later relationships. Our own experience of being parented is particularly relevant when it comes to our own parenting behaviour.

We have all had experience of being parented, although this experience can be very variable. This experience has an influence on the way we approach parenting the children we care for. If this is done non-reflectively then we will adopt both positive and less desirable parenting styles, as we experienced them. We become our parents. Even when we consciously want to avoid a certain parenting style that we were subjected to it is surprising how often we find ourselves slipping into the same practice. It is not sufficient to remember what happened to us; we need to make sense of this experience in order to move beyond our past and to become the parents we would like to become.

When parenting children with difficulties in attachment this becomes even more important. Studies have shown that children are more likely to form a *secure attachment* with a parent who has a resolved attachment 'state of mind' as an adult (Dozier *et al.* 2001). This does not mean that parents have to experience an ideal childhood, but they do need to be able to reflect upon their experience and to have resolved for themselves any difficult experience that they have encountered. They can make sense of what has happened and the impact it has had on them, and have reached an acceptance of this.

We might notice that we respond to a particular behaviour of a child in a rigid, inflexible way. Whilst we can deal with a range of difficult behaviours one particular behaviour always 'pushes our button', and we respond despite ourselves. Often some reflection about our own early experience makes sense of this for us. As we understand and recognize this we find we are better able to manage the behaviour that previously was so difficult for us.

As a child Martin had a difficult relationship with his mother. Although she could be fun loving, and he remembers good times with her, there was another side to their relationship that was more difficult. She had very high expectations of him; her disapproval was never far from the surface. She never actually said very much to him, but he would know by the frostiness of her manner. She would turn away from him and suddenly he would be outside of their relationship

looking in. As he grew older and began to live his own life, this side of their relationship eased a bit. Living at a distance he was less exposed to either her expectations or her disapproval. She herself had also mellowed as she had grown
older and was more relaxed. Martin had therefore not thought much about this
side of his mother for many years.

A pattern is developing with Catherine however that leads him to re-visit
old memories. Jenny notices that Martin is quick to get angry with Catherine.
She is surprised at this as he is generally a calm man and he has endless patience
for the more difficult tantrums that Zoë displays. He also manages Catherine's
more violent outbursts better than she does; she often hands over to him at
these times. Catherine can however blank him and he flares up. Typically Martin
would be trying to help Catherine with something. She might be trying to tie her
shoelaces or opening a difficult biscuit packet. As Martin intervenes Catherine
turns away, a determined look on her face. Catherine does not like needing
help.

Talking to him one day Jenny asks Martin what he finds so difficult. 'I don't
know really. It feels like I've let her down somehow, like my help isn't good
enough. When she is so determined not to be helped I feel like I don't really
have a connection with her. We are trying so hard to build a relationship with
her, but she won't let us in.' As he is talking, a memory of his own mother suddenly comes to mind. She had asked him to fetch a towel out of the airing cup-
board, but it was a little out of reach. As he stretched up to get it the pile of
towels came tumbling out. His mother didn't speak to him, but brushed past
and determinedly began picking them up. Martin watched helplessly. Martin
suddenly realizes that Catherine is reminding him of his mother. As with her he
is left feeling not quite good enough, as if he has failed to meet some level of expectation. Instead of supporting Catherine with her fear of needing him he is
left reacting to her with the anger he felt at his mother for expecting too much.

Exercise 8.1 can help you to think about your own attachment experience a little
more deeply. The questions are designed to help you reflect on your early
experience and the impact it has had on your parenting. It can be helpful to
write some answers down so that you can reflect upon these again in the future.
Answering these questions can be surprisingly emotional, and this exercise can
be difficult to do. It may re-awaken some sad or painful memories or it may
highlight experiences that you didn't have as a child. It can be helpful to do this
exercise with someone you trust, who can support you with the feelings that
it arouses.

Exercise 8.1: Understanding your own attachment history

1. When you think about your parents what words to describe them come to mind?

   Do these words give you a clue about the parenting you experienced?

2. How would you describe the relationship that you had with your parents as a child?

   How have these relationships changed over time?

   Are there ways that you try to be like or not like your parents?

   Do you think that these relationships have impacted on you as a parent?

3. Were there other people in your life that you felt especially close to as a child?

   Did these relationships have a big impact upon you?

   Do you feel like these relationships have influenced you as a parent?

4. When you were upset as a child what would you do?

   How did your parents respond to you when you were upset?

   Is this similar or dissimilar to how you and your children are?

5. When you were happy or excited as a child what would you do?

   How did your parents respond to you when you were excited?

   Is this similar or dissimilar to how you and your children are?

6. What ways did your parents use to discipline you as a child?

   How did this feel to you as a child?

   Are these methods that you use with your own children?

7. Can you remember early separations from your parents and how you felt?

   Did they help you to leave and return to them confidently?

   How comfortable are you now with your children going and returning?

8. Did you ever feel rejected or hurt by your parents, either physically or emotionally, or have any other traumatic experiences as a child?

   How do you feel about these experiences now? Have they stayed with you?

   Have these experiences impacted upon you as a parent?

9. Did you lose anyone close to you as a child?

   Were you helped and supported with this loss?

   Do you feel that you have accepted this loss or does it still cause you pain?

   Do you feel that this experience has affected you as a parent?

10. Overall how would you describe your relationship with your parents?

    How much do you feel that this relationship has influenced your parenting?

    What would you like to change about the way you have developed as a parent?

    What has been positive about your development as a parent?

Adapted from Siegel and Hartzell (2003, pp.133–134)

9

Attunement and Empathy

The experience of *attunement* with a responsive, sensitive parent is a prerequisite for a *secure attachment* (see Figure 9.1). This experience of emotional connection provides the infant with the necessary experience to develop trust in and experience security with the parent. When this experience is absent or only inconsistently available this will to some extent compromise the development of trust and the capacity to feel safe and secure within relationships. Older children,

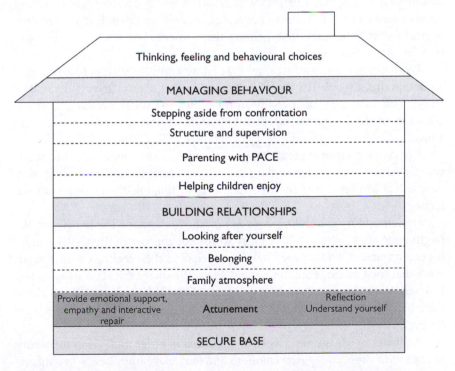

Figure 9.1 Attunement (Adapted from 'The House Model of Parenting' in Golding et al. (2006). Copyright © John Wiley & Sons Ltd. Reproduced with kind permission.)

who have difficulties in experiencing a *secure attachment*, need to experience a parenting relationship within which they can experience their emotions being understood. They can learn to share the experience of joy and fun and to be supported with feelings of anger, worry and sadness. They can equally learn that when they need comfort the parent will notice and meet this need. Alongside these *attunement* experiences the child also needs to learn that disruptions to *attunement* can be repaired. Discipline, disapproval or frustration from the parent does not signal the end of the relationship. *Attunement* can be re-established.

What is meant by attunement?

Relationships that are highly empathic provide emotional *attunement* for children and are more likely to lead to the development of secure attachments. Children have the experience of connection with another that is consistent and provides contingent responses to their communications and their needs. An attuned response helps children to feel understood and connected to the adult. As well as attending to verbal communication the adult mirrors the vitality and affect experienced by the children. In fact the ability to understand the non-verbal communication of children is important for connecting emotionally. Often it is the non-verbal communication that really communicates how children are feeling. Children, as well as adults, are generally poor at putting feelings into words. From an attuned state the adults can then lead the children to a different experience thus helping them to regulate stress, emotion and impulse. *Attunement* therefore relies on *empathy*.

By showing *empathy* we are showing that we know how the person feels and we accept this. *Empathy* is a way of helping the other person to feel fully understood. This brings us emotionally in tune with the other person. *Attunement* allows us to share emotion together. Enjoyable experiences are amplified and stressful experiences are reduced and contained.

Eye contact, facial expressions, gestures, movement, voice tone, and touch can all convey our understanding to another person. Understanding why people feel as they are is an important start to helping them cope with the feelings.

Understanding the feeling does not mean we condone the behaviour. We might understand why a child is angry whilst not approve of the way the anger is demonstrated. Children need help to understand their feelings. *Empathy* tells them that their feelings are understandable and manageable. It is okay to feel this way. With this understanding children will be able to start to think about their behaviour and will accept support to change the way they show their feelings.

An infant needs the experience of *attunement* in order to develop the ability to cope with stress, to regulate emotions and to manage impulses. When infants are first born they have little or no ability to regulate even at the physiological level. The parent externally regulates body temperature, for example, by controlling the clothing the infant wears and the temperature of the room. With maturity the infant develops temperature regulation mechanisms such as shivering, flushing and sweating.

Similarly with *emotional regulation*, in infancy the adult controls the emotional environment providing stimulation or calmness in response to the infant's moment-by-moment needs. Under-stimulation leads to boredom and, if extreme, to failure-to-thrive whilst over-stimulation leads to the baby 'switching off', and if extreme the infant learns to dissociate to stress. *Dissociation* is a mechanism that prevents a person becoming overwhelmed; however, it is also maladaptive in that whilst in a dissociated state the person is unable to learn or develop abilities to manage stress more easily. Thus, whilst protective, dissociation can be harmful if it becomes excessive.

The attuned parent provides the right amount of stimulation to arouse the baby from boredom or to calm the baby who is becoming overwhelmed. As the parent consistently regulates external stimulation for the infant and soothes internal distress he gets an experience of *emotional regulation*. In time the child will use this experience to develop the ability to regulate emotion. Children learn to manage anger and frustration, to cope with boredom and to deal with stress. Without this early experience older children will quickly become overwhelmed with how they are feeling. They will not be able to tolerate frustration, excitement, stress or anger; and will demonstrate this poor capacity through challenging behaviours.

Thus the ability to regulate emotion is dependent on *attunement*; the parents' ability to match the feeling state of the infant by matching the intensity and vitality of the infant's behavioural and verbal expressions. The parent connects with the infant at a preverbal level. The infant can feel a sense of continuous connection that will help him develop the ability to regulate and integrate the feelings he is experiencing and later to develop an integrated sense of self.

The attachment relationship that develops out of these attuned communications provides the child with the experience necessary to develop a coherent sense of self and to manage and learn from emotional experiences.

Older children who have not experienced these attuned connections early in their life will move into foster or adoptive homes with weak abilities to regulate either at the emotional or behavioural level. This can be expressed through dysregulated behaviour within which they are *impulsive*, quick to feel frustrated or angry. Alternatively children might cut-off from how they feel, unaware of all but a very limited amount of what is felt internally. In fact some children are so uncomfortable with noticing their feelings that they will use their behaviour to avoid this experience. They might provoke their parent to anger, for example, as a distraction from the experience of sadness.

These children need help to experience and feel comfortable with attuned connections to their parents. If the parents can provide them with daily experience of *empathy* and *attunement*, connecting to hidden as well as expressed feelings, the children will gradually be able to experience, acknowledge and feel comfortable with their inner life. Alongside this the experience of connection with another will lead to a strengthening of the relationship and a more secure feeling of attachment.

Managing difficult behaviour within attuned relationships

The attachment relationship is the relationship within which the child learns what is acceptable or not acceptable behaviour. This is the process of socialization, and is essential if a child is going to fit comfortably into the family, community and school. Allan Schore (1994) describes the importance of the emotion of *shame* for these developing social abilities. When the parent expresses disapproval or provides discipline for the child this will create a state of mis-attunement and the child experiences *shame* and an increase in negative arousal. A young child cannot regulate this increasing arousal and is reliant on the parent to provide support or co-regulation. Following this the parent ensures that a state of re-attunement occurs so that the child once again experiences feeling loved and cared for. These sequences of *attunement*, rupture and re-attunement provide the child with the experience needed to learn to control impulses and to behave in socially appropriate ways.

Unfortunately older children moving into foster or adoptive homes without this early experience find it very difficult to learn socially appropriate behaviour or to enter into a relationship that provides attunement/re-attunement experiences. As children encounter *shame*-filled experiences they will display the behaviour that can be so damaging to them and the family. They are not able to regulate their own experience of *shame* or to use relationships to help them with this. *Shame* increases and the children, unable to manage this, become defensive by blaming themselves: 'I am bad, I will always be bad' or blaming others: 'It is not me. It is always someone else'.

Acceptance and *empathy* for your child will help you to manage his behaviour in ways that makes *shame* manageable rather than unmanageable for him.

- An angry response to your child's behaviour will increase his sense of *shame* and leave you both in a relationship that lacks *attunement*.

- An empathic but firm response will, over time, allow your child to take responsibility for his behaviour whilst experiencing an attuned relationship.

Thus your child is helped when you respond to his behaviour and underlying feelings with *empathy* and matter-of-fact consequences. It is helpful if you avoid displaying a tense and annoyed attitude. Such an attitude communicates that the relationship will be used to punish misbehaviour. Calm consequences and *empathy* for the emotional state of your child will instead communicate that the relationship can be helpful to him.

Empathy can also be displayed for your child's response to consequences. Support and accept your child's need to pout or remain annoyed. This communicates that the relationship is alive and well. You accept his need to reject it at this time but leave the door open for when he wishes to re-establish positive contact again.

It is important that attention is paid to *interactive repair* following episodes of difficult behaviour or distancing from your child. This re-establishes the positive atmosphere and reduces feelings of *shame*. Your child needs to know that this has not damaged the relationship, that he is still cared for and valued. Time spent letting him know that the relationship is all right will allow you both to once more experience *attunement* together.

This is not a time to continue to chastise, to discuss consequences or to try to teach what is acceptable or unacceptable. Thinking about the behaviour and its consequences can come later. For now it is important that you just spend time enjoying being together again, and for helping your child feel supported and comforted.

At the age of eight Zoë has made progress with Jenny and Martin, although she can still be very emotionally demanding. She has now developed some capacity to emotionally regulate her increased arousal and is not quite so dependent upon being with Jenny all the time. She is also making some progress at school and has managed to maintain one or two friendships.

Zoë can however still display some very difficult tantrums when her new-found abilities to manage her emotional arousal desert her. These are particularly apparent when Zoë cannot have something she wants. For Zoë, being told 'no' is especially difficult. She does not listen to the reason, or stop to consider the fairness of the adult response; instead this triggers for her a deep sense of not being good enough. It is as if not being able to have something provides evidence of her lack of worth. 'I am not loveable, I will not be loved.'

One day Zoë and Jenny are out shopping. They have had a good day, and Zoë is enjoying having Jenny to herself. The good feelings however come to a sudden halt when they go to buy Zoë some new pyjamas. She has been growing quickly lately and is in desperate need of these. Zoë finds the ones she wants, but unfortunately they do not have her size. Jenny tries to explain but Zoë isn't listening. She has heard that she can't have them. Jenny tries to keep her calm but Zoë is getting more and more agitated. As the noise level increases Jenny starts to feel cross; other shoppers are beginning to notice. She talks sharply to Zoë. This just increases her anxiety and sense of shame further and she starts to run out of the shop. Jenny is concerned now. She doesn't want Zoë running out into the road. She runs after her and grabs hold of her. Zoë is now in a panic. She kicks and screams. Jenny holds her tight; she forgets everyone around as her attention focuses on this screaming, panicking dynamo in her arms.

How could she get so distressed so quickly? Jenny feels enormous sadness for a little girl who can't even buy a pair of pyjamas without feeling that it is the end of the world. She holds on tight, sensing the strength of Zoë's fear and anger. She talks with increased vitality and affect: 'Wow, Zoë, you are very mad that we can't get the pyjamas. I think you are really cross with me. You think I am so mean for saying you can't have them.' Now she talks more quietly to her. She tells her how sad it is that the pyjamas were the wrong size. She can see how upset Zoë is and wonders if it feels like she can never have what she wants. How scary that feels; it feels like she isn't good enough to be given what she wants. Zoë is quietening now; feeling understood she clutches tightly to Jenny. She feels the reassurance in Jenny's arms and Jenny's voice. Jenny reminds Zoë that she loves her and will always be there for her. Even when she says no to things she will still love her. Zoë is beginning to feel calmer now. They remain there for some time and then Jenny asks her: 'What shall we do about the pyjamas, Zoë? You still need some.' Immediately, Zoë's head goes down and she starts to tense up. Zoë is experiencing the shame of having made such a fuss. Jenny, calm herself now, notices this and provides more reassurance. She has to regulate the increasing shame so that Zoë can start to think about what she wants. 'It's okay, Zoë, you were very upset. Now you have remembered how much I love you we can think about the pyjamas.' Zoë looks up and Jenny offers her a choice. 'We could go back to the shop and order the ones you like so that they can get your size or we could have a look in a different shop for some others.' Zoë chooses to look in another shop and hand in hand they walk on. Jenny breathes a sigh of relief. If only she could always stay this calm with Zoë and help her through the episodes, but it is so difficult. Zoë's tantrums seem so unreasonable until she remembers the depth of fear underneath.

Interactive repair is also important following times when you have been emotionally unavailable to your child. Perhaps you have found it hard to like him because of behaviour he is displaying. You may have withdrawn because you feel angry and are concerned that you might 'lose your cool' or maybe you have experienced stress elsewhere in your life. Your child needs to know that the withdrawal is temporary whilst you look after yourself.

Children's previous experience can leave them hyper-sensitive. For example, when the parent is distant, or preoccupied, they may be quick to assume that it is because of their own 'badness' or the 'meanness' of the parent. This may seem like proof that they will again be abused or neglected or that the placement will end and they will be rejected. Time spent talking to your child about your emotional withdrawal, apologizing for any displays of anger or temper and offering him reassurance about your continuing availability will help to counter these beliefs, allowing the building of trust and dependency over time.

How to help children experience attunement through relationship-based play

The use of *empathy* can help you to find ways of giving your child experiences of an attuned relationship. *Attunement* is not only helpful for managing the more difficult behaviour displayed. *Attunement* is also the basis for more fun-filled aspects of relationships. Through fun and time spent together you can help your child to experience the relationship as joyful.

Introducing fun and playfulness with children who have lacked this experience early in their life can present its own challenges. The children will be puzzled and even frightened by the strangeness of this experience. Alternatively they may be reluctant to engage with the activity for fear that they will enjoy it but then lose it again.

The children have typically missed out on relationship-based play experience when young. This play, which absorbs the child and parent together, is an important precursor to enjoying joint attention to tasks or activities.

Interactions that are playful, interactive and empathic can help the child to feel special and connected to the parent. In this type of play the main task is enjoying being together. This is different to more task-focused play when for example the parent helps the child to complete a puzzle or to learn colours. Relationship-based play makes minimal use of toys but lots of use of the relationship between the child and parent. This play dramatizes for children that they are special and loveable, that others can be responsive. This increased focus on each other during play can be helpful for older children who experience difficulties with relationship.

Jernberg and Booth (2001) suggest the following dimensions to this play.

Structure the play

Children may be helped if the adults set limits, define boundaries, keep the children safe and help them to complete sequences of activities. Children can let go of the responsibility for maintaining and controlling interactions and can enjoy the experience.

Parents may also need to initiate interactions – if they wait for children to choose to play with them it may never happen.

Parents can be directive in play, for example, 'We are going to…', rather than 'Shall we…?', but still direct the play in response to the child's reactions. *Attunement* will be important in order to be able to guide the play in response to the child. For example, the parents might notice the child getting too excited and stimulated. They can direct the play to soothing and comforting activities. They might notice the child being restless and bored. They can direct the play to challenging and exciting activities.

Engage the child

This helps to establish and maintain a connection with the child, to focus on him in an intense way and to surprise and entice him into enjoying new experiences. The parents aim to be exciting, surprising and stimulating. This draws the child into becoming engaged in the activities.

Nurture the child

Parents help the child to experience warmth and tenderness. They can soothe, calm and comfort him when appropriate. This reinforces the message that he is worthy of care and that adults will provide care without him having to ask. For some children the experience of nurturing can be quite frightening. These children will need sensitive and gentle challenges to their resistance to nurture. This allows them to gradually become comfortable with nurturing activities.

Challenge the child

Parents encourage the child to move ahead, to strive a bit and to experience a sense of mastery. By encouraging him to accomplish an activity, with adult help, he feels more competent and confident.

It is quite likely that your child will initially resist playing in this way. He may fear getting close to you. He thus resists intimacy, often trying to stay in charge to keep you at a distance. You will need to stay with it. Find ways to surprise him into being engaged with you. Help him learn to trust. You may need to build in brief playful interactions until he can manage longer times. Thus your child is helped to find pleasure in the interaction.

Jackie feels that Luke needs a lot of relationship-based play with her. This type of play is ideal for teaching him about parents and the availability of parents to meet his needs and to regulate his behaviour and emotion. She tries to introduce this type of play throughout the day; this might be as brief as a quick blow on his cheek or a tickle as she passes, but can be extended to singing nursery rhymes whilst she gets him dressed in the morning or some exciting water play at bath time. Additionally she introduces a daily play session when she plays with him in a more structured, reflective way. She plans these sessions depending upon what she wants Luke to learn about. For example, when she wants Luke to learn that mums can take care of hurts she gets out the lotion and cotton wool. She plays a game of 'finding the bruises', carefully tending to each bruise as they come across it. Similarly when she wants Luke to know that she can help him to regulate his behaviour she introduces some fast-paced, challenging play that leads to feelings of excitement. She intersperses this with quieter, calmer play. Luke experiences Jackie being in charge helping him to cope with growing excitement and helping him to calm down from this as well.

As Luke responds to these playful interactions Jackie also finds her own feelings for Luke change. She is becoming better able to judge what he needs from her and Luke is benefiting from this highly responsive parenting. She is starting to feel like she has a relationship with him. Moments of quiet nurturing feel more real and connected. Luke in turn is becoming more needy of her and quite clingy at times. Jackie has been warned that Luke might become more attention-needing of her as he begins to understand relationships. She therefore does not see this increased neediness as a problem but as a sign of progress. Luke is beginning to understand that Jackie is there for him.

Helping children develop understanding through attuned relationships

The experience of an attuned and dependable relationship helps children to develop emotionally and cognitively. They can learn to understand and manage the emotion that they are experiencing and the emotion they see in others. To help children, parents need first to make sense of the behaviour and underlying thinking and feeling. They can then help children to make sense of themselves and those around them.

Parents can help by talking about feelings. Reflective dialogues involve talking about what is happening internally and externally. For example, 'John is breaking the toys because he is feeling very angry. His mum didn't turn up to contact today'; 'Daddy is not having dinner because he is feeling upset right now. He is upset that his watch got broken.' Parents can raise questions and be open and curious. The child is angry that the toys have to be put away. The parent comments: 'I wonder if you think I don't like you because I want you to tidy up?' The child is helped to become aware of underlying thoughts. This in turn helps to reduce the emotional response.

These types of dialogues help the child to understand mental states and feelings in self and others. The child learns *reflective function*, to understand what is going on in his own mind and in the mind of others. He is then better able to *mentalize*, to make predictions about what might happen, and what others think and feel. This then allows improved planning and problem-solving.

This in turn helps the child to identify his thoughts and feelings, to experience these as valid and to use support to help express them. With this understanding the child learns to regulate feelings and impulses. Instead of feelings emerging unpredictably and intensely, as he acts without thinking. He will learn to stop and think and to control the expression of his feelings.

Learning to reflect and think in the present can also help children to process what has happened in the past. They can begin to develop a *coherent narrative* about their experiences. The development of such a narrative allows children to move on from their experience and to respond more flexibly in the present.

Luke has continued to thrive with Jackie but despite all the progress that he is making in learning about Jackie, and how she can take care of him, he still finds it especially difficult to reflect. He is so reactive to the way he feels there is very little time left to think. He is also highly active, with very little pause; he doesn't notice what he or others are thinking or feeling, and if he did he wouldn't have a language to talk about this. Jackie has worked hard to develop more emotional understanding with Luke over the years. She comments often about the way she is feeling or what she thinks Luke may be feeling. She has bought some games about feelings to play with him and she sometimes watches television with him, commenting on the characters in the programmes. At ten years Luke can now describe what he thinks someone might be feeling in pictures, and he is sometimes able to guess what Jackie is feeling; he continues to struggle with describing how he is feeling.

Jackie has new neighbours. Carol and Graham have recently moved in with their two children, four-year-old Jamie and his two-year-old sister Becky. Jackie is surprised to see Luke strike up a friendship with Jamie, and even more surprised at how well they get on. When Luke plays with the other children on the estate he always seems to get into trouble, fighting with the other children, stealing from the shop on the corner or, on one occasion, breaking the windows of the greenhouse of their elderly neighbour Mr Perks. Jackie has grown accustomed to the many complaints about Luke. With Jamie however he appears a different child. They play co-operatively together and he is even gentle with little Becky. Surprisingly he never seems to think that the games Jamie wants to play are 'babyish'.

This leads Jackie to think about her parenting of Luke. She wonders if emotionally he is younger than she thought. Is she expecting too much of him? She thinks about all the differences in parenting a ten-year-old compared to a four-year-old. Jackie starts to adjust her parenting of Luke a little, not expecting quite as much from him, explaining a bit more to him and stepping in a little earlier when he is struggling.

Without realizing it Jackie is also helping Luke to improve his ability to emotionally regulate. As Jackie steps in and provides co-regulatory experience, Luke is beginning to learn about his feelings and how to manage them. This in turn improves his capacity to think. As he remains a bit more emotionally regulated Luke is able to listen to Jackie and to learn about how his behaviour links to his feelings. With time Luke will develop some capacity to mentalize, to understand how others are thinking and feeling and to start to link this to his own behaviour and how he thinks and feels. This continues to be a slow process. Luke still has the appearance and the attitude of a ten-year-old, and often Jackie expects more of him than he can actually manage. In addition Luke remains very susceptible to increases in stress. If his teacher is away from school, for example, Luke's anxiety increases and his fragile ability to self-regulate reduces. Luke becomes more dysregulated and angry. Jackie tries to find ways to keep stress low for Luke whilst also helping him to cope with the typical stress-filled day of a ten-year-old.

10

Protecting the Family Atmosphere and the Development of Emotional Regulation

At the heart of the house model of parenting is the family atmosphere (see Figure 10.1). Learning to stay calm, to stay in control of your own reactions and behaviour, and therefore to be in control of the atmosphere in the home is key to providing an environment within which children can heal and develop. You are not in control of how your child behaves but you can control your own reactions and behaviour. This can also lead to changes within your child.

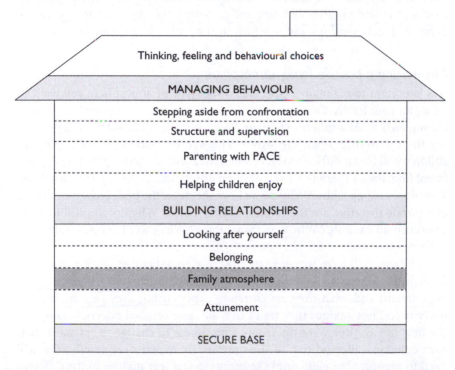

Figure 10.1 Family atmosphere (Adapted from 'The House Model of Parenting' in Golding et al. (2006). Copyright © John Wiley & Sons Ltd. Reproduced with kind permission.)

What is a family atmosphere?

Children need to live within a safe and nurturing home. Within this home children experience mutual enjoyment, respect, opportunities for learning and for fun. As children experience consistent boundaries and limits on their behaviour, feelings of safety increase. A family atmosphere of *empathy*, sharing, security, love and fun provides children with a positive experience within which they can learn to trust and feel secure.

Unfortunately many of the children who live in foster and adoptive homes have had previous experience of a very different family atmosphere, an atmosphere that might be characterized by tension, hostility, rage, fear and isolation.

Signs of anger, tension or discouragement in the substitute home can trigger for children memories of this original atmosphere. The children may feel at home with this; they have previously learnt how to live in such a home and it can confirm what they know about themselves and others. In fact some children work hard to make the home like this; it can feel quite scary to experience something very different, even if we feel it is a lot healthier for them. Other children quickly experience an increase in feelings of danger and insecurity. Their behaviour becomes a defence against these feelings and worries.

Children need to experience a home environment that is markedly different from their original environment. An ongoing atmosphere of relaxed *empathy*, sharing, fun and predictable safety and security helps the child to experience dependable relationships within which healthy attachments can develop.

learn to trust & feel secure

Maintaining a positive family atmosphere

It is important to maintain a clear idea of the type of atmosphere you want to create for your family. Often parents have had considerable experience of maintaining such an atmosphere before the child moves in. The hard work is protecting the atmosphere when she arrives. This can be extremely challenging, as children will find it difficult to feel comfortable with something that is very different from their experience. Even physical differences can be a puzzle for them. Why do we eat on tables? Why do we have sheets on the bed? How much more of a puzzle therefore are the emotional differences? Why do you still love me when I am so naughty? Why won't you hit me? Why can't I get you really mad with me?

Children will have strong expectations of how families work and what a family atmosphere is like. When they experience incongruity between their expectations and what they are currently experiencing they feel anxious. In order to feel less anxious they try to recreate their original experiences within the new home. They want the family atmosphere to change to resemble their own emotional life and that of their previously experienced family. You will need to support your child until she begins to feel less anxious in the different family atmosphere.

To maintain the family atmosphere:

- Stay calm. You will find it easier to stay calm if you can feel *empathy* and acceptance for your child, and the anxiety experienced in trying to adjust to the new family.

- Be firm and consistent. You need to create an expectation that your child will fit in to the new home, that she will, with help, be able to adjust to the family rules. You will help her to adjust with a relaxed, matter-of-fact and instructive attitude that engages her. If you become harsh, critical, complaining or negative your child may feel closer to her original experience and is less likely to change or adjust.

- Discipline must be clear and predictable, but also must reflect the atmosphere of mutual enjoyment and respect. Firmness doesn't need to be intense, very serious or provided with annoyance. Instead you need to adopt an attitude of being empathic and supportive whilst remaining firm in your expectations.

- Help your child to feel liked and wanted even when she is misbehaving. Provide her with an expectation that she will, with support, be able to respond to the limits and boundaries in place because she is a good person. Provide consequences with *empathy*, avoid being pulled into angry confrontations about this and quietly empathize with her distress whilst remaining firm about the consequence.

- Bad behaviour is therefore met with clear consequences alongside respect for the choices that led to the behaviour and *empathy* for feelings about the consequences.

- Provide nurturance to your child even when she is being hostile and defiant or when she is 'giving nothing back'. Respond to hostility and rejection with *empathy*. Avoid taking her behaviour personally but remain calm, interested, patient and persistent. Help her to trust and ask for help.

Remember that it is okay to have a bad day, to mishandle a situation. All parents need to allow themselves to make mistakes. This also models to the child that it is okay to make mistakes. It is helpful to spend some time repairing any disruption to the relationship when feeling all right again. In the meantime give yourself some time and space to recover your equilibrium.

Over time it is hoped that your child will adjust to the family environment and will start to feel settled, comfortable and secure with this approach. This will be reflected in her behaviour as she spends less time trying to stay in control of you, and of the atmosphere, and more time enjoying being part of the family.

These behavioural changes whilst important are the outward signs of something much more fundamental. With this approach children are not just learning how to conform to your expectations, how to fit in with you and the family, but are learning about themselves. One of the core difficulties children who move into foster and adoptive homes often have is difficulties with *emotional regulation*; whether they express this through dysregulated, emotionally driven behaviour or through *dissociative*, withdrawn behaviour, the child is not able to understand or manage emotion in a healthy way. Living in a calm, accepting atmosphere with a high level of *empathy* and support will gradually help the child to learn about the emotions she experiences, and to manage these in a self-regulating way. She not only fits in with the family but also can be a fully participating member able to respond emotionally, behaviourally and socially to other family members. Sibling fights, difficult 'stressy' days, and bad moods won't disappear but will feel less extreme and more normal. The child will also be able to find a way back from these more easily. Instead of these difficult days confirming to her how bad she is or how horrible parents are, they are just seen for what they are. That was a bad day, now it is over. Time to move on.

As Marcus enters early adolescence he continues to make progress with Rita and Frank, although he continues to be a challenging boy. He is responding to them and beginning to enjoy the calmer family environment that they are trying to create. It still surprises them however how quickly Marcus can disrupt this atmosphere when he is more stressed and then their home becomes much more chaotic. Frank has felt particularly provoked at these times, and has been afraid that Marcus could push him to the point of hitting him; a clear echo of Marcus's experience with Richie. By working together however Rita and Frank are learning to manage these periods and Marcus is finding it harder to re-create his early home environment.

Rita and Frank strive to maintain calm responses to even the most provoking behaviour displayed by Marcus. By supporting each other and tactically withdrawing at times they are managing this a reasonable amount of the time. They have also learnt not to be too hard on themselves when they don't manage it. They remember how difficult Marcus is to care for, supporting each other, as they feel low. By avoiding feeling guilty or frustrated they are more able to get back to the calm responding they are aiming for.

Regular respite is also helpful, providing them with well-earned rest time as well as an opportunity to check out with each other that they are maintaining consistency. They can also plan how to handle particularly difficult behaviour that Marcus is displaying. Marcus hasn't given up his attempt to control them and family life but there are times when he is able to relax with them.

Developing emotional regulation

Over time this parenting approach can help children develop the capacity to regulate emotions.

Children who have experienced poor parenting early in life may have failed to develop good *emotional regulation* skills. This means that all emotion is difficult to manage – positive emotion such as feeling excited or pleased as well as negative emotion such as anger, fear or sadness.

These children will have a low threshold for managing emotion. When they reach this threshold they become overwhelmed by the emotion and they either dysregulate or dissociate. This can be thought of as an emotional thermometer (see Figure 10.2). If children have a low threshold for managing emotion it will only take a small increase in arousal before they are overwhelmed.

Dysregulated behaviour is expressed as explosive behaviour. The child is unable to cognitively process information (to think about what is happening) but is being driven by emotion. In the brain the thinking parts of the brain are inactive whilst the emotional parts of the brain are overactive. Whilst children are in this state they will not respond to reason. The parent needs to keep them safe until the behaviour subsides and they start to think again.

Normal threshold for emotional dysregulation or dissociation

Low threshold for emotional dysregulation or dissociation

Figure 10.2 The emotional thermometer

Dissociation is a cutting off from the emotion. It is as if a switch has been turned off within the child. She withdraws, freezes or becomes very compliant, with an absence of emotion.

Dysregulation and dissociation are normal processes. We can all respond in these ways if our emotion gets strong enough to overwhelm us. The difference is that children who have not developed good *emotional regulation* skills get to this point much quicker. They need help to learn about their feelings and to manage these so that their threshold for reacting in these ways gets higher.

As an infant these skills are developed through close contact with the parent. Imagine a baby distressed because she is hungry. The parent must first calm the baby before she is able to feed. Rocking, cuddling and soothing allows the emotion to reduce and the baby will then suckle.

This experience teaches children how to manage their own emotion so eventually, as they grow older, they can regulate emotion without help. Children who have not had sensitive parenting early in life will find this diffi-cult. The parent needs to replicate the process, co-regulating with the children when they are getting over-aroused. Cuddling and soothing touch can be helpful along with activities such as warm baths, massages, and listening to relaxing music.

Additional Theory: The process of attachment and the developing brain

The aims of the house model of parenting are to help children manage their feelings, develop positive beliefs about self and others and to display less chal-lenging behaviour. This helps the child to develop a more secure attachment to her parents. In order to understand how this parenting approach can help the child, some thought needs to be given to the developing brain.

Development of the brain is *experience-dependent*. This means that brain development is stimulated through interactions with others. At birth the brain is undifferentiated. The brain has a lot of potential but the way it develops will depend on the experience the baby has. Differentiation – different parts of the brain taking on different functions – occurs within a social context. Thus the brain is a self-organizing system. It organizes itself and the way it works in the context of relationships. There are also sensitive periods for development. Thus attention, perception, memory, motor control, modulation of emotion, capacity to form relationships and language all develop at certain times within a child's development. These sensitive periods are times when the brain is ready to develop a certain function, and just needs the right experience to make this happen. If this experience doesn't happen then the brain will not function as well. As we have seen, the development of *emotional regulation* is very dependent on the child experiencing a regulating relationship with an adult. This requires some experience with an empathic, sensitive adult. When this doesn't happen

the brain will be much less good at self-regulating emotion. Whilst these abities might still develop given the right experience, it will take a longer time and
the resultant abilities will be more fragile than if the child had received the right
experience at the time when the brain was most ready. Some abilities, like the
ability to see, may never happen if experience doesn't occur during the sensitive
period.

Figure 10.3 demonstrates some important development within the brain. It
can be helpful in envisaging this to imagine the brain as actually three brains.
Margot Sunderland (2006) describes this very clearly. The first brain, the reptilian brain, is at the bottom. This brain needs no external experience to develop.
The infant is born able to function physiologically. For example, breathing,
digestion and circulation are all controlled from this part of the brain. Surrounding this brain is the second brain, the mammalian brain. This is our emotional
brain where we feel things, and we react to these feelings. Finally surrounding
this is the third brain, the rational or thinking brain. Here we think, assess situations and solve problems.

There are some aspects of the emotional brain that are already functioning
at birth. For example, the amygdala is the brain's alarm system. It tells us when
we should be afraid and it mobilizes us to take action. This is mature at birth; the
baby needs no experience to feel fear or to go into the fight/flight mode
governed by the reptilian brain.

Other aspects of the emotional brain and especially its integration with the
thinking brain are much more dependent upon experience, and especially social

Cerebral cortex		Amygdala
Integrated brain functioning		Alarm system
Thinking Planning Impulse control		Fight Flight Freeze
	Orbito-frontal cortex	
Immature in early childhood	Maturation dependent upon nature of attachment relationship	Mature at birth
Development dependent upon empathic and sensitive interactions	Leads to ability to regulate emotion	Threat, stress hormones such as cortisol released, activates amygdala

Figure 10.3 The developing brain

experience. Thus the orbito-frontal cortex, a part of the brain that is situated just behind the eyes, has an important role in being able to regulate emotion. This part of the brain develops within an attachment relationship. Similarly the development of the cerebral cortex, which is dependent on the brain functioning in an integrated way, also occurs through the experience of relationships. Thus the child will always be able to react, to experience feelings, and to act on this without thought, but the ability to manage feelings, to think things through, and to plan are very dependent upon the experience of relationship she has had. Children will be active, *impulsive* and quick to react; with sensitive and empathic care they will also be able to regulate their emotion, inhibit impulses, and think things through.

The process of infant attachment on the developing brain

To fully understand how the brain develops it is helpful to understand the process of infant attachment. Understanding this can help to make sense of the behaviour of children who have not had good early experience. *Attachment* occurs through a range of experiences. These influence development and the absence of these experiences can increase the risk of later difficulties for the child.

ABSORPTION

Absorption represents the experience of the infant and parent early in the child's life. Both partners in this dyad are very preoccupied with the other; this preoccupation provides the necessary experience for the infant and parent to accept or claim each other. This is the beginning of the development of a relationship between them, and of the infant developing a sense of self within this relationship. The parent demonstrates that he will reliably meet the child's needs whilst the infant learns that she has some ability to control the relationship to get needs met. Trevarthen (2001) calls this *primary intersubjectivity*. The infant and parent discover each other in a reciprocal relationship and in the process discover more about themselves.

Peter Fonagy and his colleagues (Fonagy *et al.* 2002) describe an important part of this early relationship, termed *affect mirroring*. The parent interprets the child's emotion for her by reflecting this emotion using exaggerated tone of voice, and facial expressions. This is done in a way that children know that this is not the parent's feelings but is a reflection of what they themselves are feeling. In this way children come to understand their own feelings.

If the infant gets very poor experience of *primary intersubjectivity*, an absorbed relationship with a parent, as a child she may have difficulty in trusting others and/or relying on herself to get her needs met. This can be expressed in two different ways:

- The children might remain preoccupied with their dependency needs. They don't learn to trust others to be available and responsive and so demand attention in order to ensure that their needs are met. Their behaviour is therefore very attention-needing, and controlling of others.

- Alternatively the children can be quite dissociated from their dependency needs. They manage the belief that others will not be available and responsive by ignoring or suppressing their needs. They learn to rely on themselves instead of others, demonstrating an inappropriate self-reliance.

The absence of *affect mirroring* can have quite complex effects on children. In essence children are unable to find their psychological self in the mind of their parents. The parents are not helping their children understand what they are feeling but are instead preoccupied with their own feelings about their children. This means that the only information the children have about how to experience themselves is the parent's own thoughts and feelings towards them. This 'alien', non-mirrored view of self then becomes internalized as a core part of the self, but not related to the child's emotional or *cognitive* state. The child will fail to build up a coherent, co-ordinated sense of a psychological self.

David Howe (2005) explains how abusive parents reject what is going on in the child's mind, or are hostile and contemptuous towards it, so that the child internalizes a hostile, persecutory sense of self. Neglectful parents on the other hand fail to recognize or acknowledge what is going on in the child's mind. The child internalizes an abandoned self. Children find these internalizations difficult to live with and therefore project them on to others. You can find yourself cast into the role of hostile or abandoning parent even though you have not parented your child in this way.

ATTUNEMENT

Attunement is another important element of intersubjectivity or the sharing of a relationship. The parent provides the infant with an experience of emotional connection with another that is consistent and provides contingent responses to her communications and needs. An attuned response is an empathic response that helps the child to feel understood and connected to the adult. The child learns to trust in the availability and responsiveness of the adult.

The lack of experience in an attuned relationship leads to children having difficulties with trust in others. This can be expressed in a range of ways. Children might learn not to trust others at all or alternatively they may be over-trusting, displaying an over-reliance on the other person. Some children will persistently trust the 'wrong people'. They become attracted to and involved with groups of older children or young adults who exploit them or direct them into delinquent activities. The attraction of this group is that it offers a source of apparent safety when they can't feel safe with the caring adults.

Overall, therefore, children have difficulty forming and maintaining appropriate relationships. Having not experienced reliable *empathy* from others children have difficulty in feeling *empathy* for others. This makes it difficult for children to enter into reciprocal, mutual relationships.

REGULATION

The intersubjective experience of absorption and *attunement* with another also provides the experience of regulation for children. Allan Schore (1994) describes how parents provide their children with an experience of *attunement* by recognizing and connecting with the arousal state being displayed. At this stage the parents follow the children's lead, accepting the arousal state that they are signalling. Thus the infant–parent emotional state becomes synchronized in a way that provides a sharing of positive emotion and a containing of negative emotion. The parents are then able to lead the children into a different, regulated emotional state, for example soothing a distressed child, calming an overexcited child, stimulating a bored child. The child learns that distress can be managed and transformed and that pleasure and excitement can be shared and modulated.

Through a process in which adults initially regulate for children, and then co-regulate with children, the children learn to regulate stress, emotion, impulses, *shame* and rage. If this process does not occur, or is experienced patchily and inconsistently, a child will fail to develop the capacity for regulation. She reacts to the lack of regulation abilities by:

* dissociation – avoidance, withdrawal, disconnection, 'spaced-out'
* hyper-arousal – panic, rage, volatility.

These are unconscious, defensive processes; the children are not able to regulate and self-soothe.

Difficulty in regulating impulses leads to children lacking the capacity to assess risk, or to stop and think. The children can be destructive, a danger to self and others, constantly in trouble, socially unacceptable, and easily led.

If children are not helped to regulate *shame* they will experience disintegrative *shame*, overwhelming their sense of self. Children are unable to experience guilt for behaviour, but are instead overwhelmed with a sense of badness. Thus the children do not take responsibility for behaviour, learn from mistakes, nor make choices. As a defence against this the children blame others or become very perfectionistic.

When children lack regulation capacity for rage, they are unable to manage anger. This can lead to aggression and destructiveness. These children elicit fear and anger in others and are terrified of their own sense of being dangerous. They have difficulty making or keeping friends.

THINKING AND AWARENESS

Through a process which Trevarthen (2001) called *secondary intersubjectivity*, the child learns about the world of people, events and objects. The child and parent together focus their attention outwards. This shared attention helps them both to explore the world and learn about the impact of this world on each other. The child learns about the world through the meaning the parent gives it. As the adult helps her to make sense of the world she develops the capacity to think. In this way children learn that the world, themselves and other people make sense. This in turn allows children to reflect upon, process and learn from experience.

Learning about the world also involves learning about the mental states (thoughts, feelings, beliefs and desires) of self and others – in other words having reflective function or a *theory of mind*. This helps children to understand the thoughts, feelings, beliefs and desires they hold and that others might have different thoughts, feelings, beliefs and desires. *Theory of mind* typically develops in children between the age of three and four years, providing they are interacting with parents who are helping them to become aware of mental states in both themselves and in others. Understanding mental states helps children to make sense of behaviour and therefore to understand the social world within which they live. A researcher called Elizabeth Meins has highlighted the importance of the parent being *mind-minded* in order to help the child understand mental states (Meins *et al.* 2002). Parents who are *mind-minded* are able to translate psychological experience of the child into a coherent dialogue. ('Look how upset you are. I guess you really wanted to play with the car. Are you thinking that Joe is really mean not to let you have it?') The parent is not just responding to the child's behaviour but is also interpreting what the behaviour means. This in turn develops the child's mentalizing skills, and facilitates emotional understanding and regulation.

When children lack a relationship within which they are enabled to make sense of the world, they are left with poor mentalizing abilities. They struggle to make sense of the world, and especially the mental states of self and others. This means that they find it difficult to explain their own behaviour or to predict the behaviour of others.

When children lack a relationship to help them to make sense of the world they are at increased risk for a range of *cognitive* deficits. Cairns and Stanway (2004) highlight some of the difficulties children may have when early experience has not supported the development of information processing, the ability to make sense of experience. Children can lack the ability to see the world from different perspectives – 'you are sad because…'; 'that person wants to…' – and therefore *empathy* development is compromised. Learning is made especially difficult because of difficulties in generalizing learning from one situation to another, and because of a lack of cause-and-effect thinking. It is also typical to find that children can't distinguish fact from fantasy, or mine from yours, and therefore lying and stealing are common.

This description of developing attachment illustrates how important the relationship is to the developing child. The child who has not had good relationship experience will find it very difficult in a number of ways. The use of family atmosphere, *empathy*, and sensitive parenting can begin the process of providing children with this necessary experience. The challenge is to provide this experience for a child who has already developed within different relationships. Being absorbed and attuned with an older child, developing regulation and thinking ability, can all be enormously challenging. Change will take a long time as the child has to learn a different way of being with others, and this has to translate into changes at the level of brain as well as behaviour.

There is an old adage that you can't teach an old dog new tricks. The dog has to unlearn old behaviour before it can learn the new behaviour, and this can be a challenging, although not impossible task; much easier when the dog has learnt the behaviour for the first time as a puppy. This is also what adoptive and foster families are helping the child to do. The child needs to learn new ways of behaving and managing her emotional experience. These new ways won't replace what she learnt when she was younger but will provide her with more flexibility, more options and choices and a greater capacity to cope with a range of situations.

11

Creating a Feeling of Belonging for the Child

We discussed in the last chapter the importance of family atmosphere to help children adjust to the family and to start to feel comfortable. This, over the longer term, can help children to adjust both at the behavioural and emotional level. In this chapter we consider how to supplement this use of family atmosphere with activities that give the children a sense of belonging in the family. Much as a baby feels claimed within the early relationship, the older child also

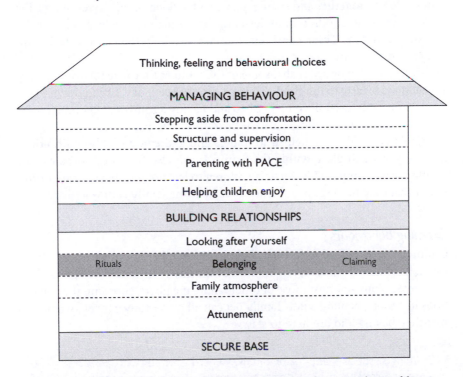

Figure 11.1 Belonging (Adapted from 'The House Model of Parenting' in Golding et al. (2006). Copyright © John Wiley & Sons Ltd. Reproduced with kind permission.)

needs to actively develop a sense of belonging if he is to fully adjust to being a full member of the family (see Figure 11.1).

The use of family rituals and claiming behaviours to help children feel that they belong

Children need to feel a sense of belonging and to feel part of the family in order to feel secure. This helps children to cope better at times when they are away from the family. Paying attention to rituals and routines and explicit ways of 'claiming' the child can help him to develop a feeling of belonging.

Rituals and routines

Families have many rituals and ways of doing things that can be quite perplexing for children coming into the family. Not knowing these rituals can make the children feel like outsiders, that they don't belong. Time spent helping your child to understand 'how we do things here' can help him adapt and fit into your family.

Many rituals develop out of our awareness. We are not aware that we do things in a certain order, or follow a certain routine. Others may be more explicit. We sit together and share a pizza and a video on Friday evenings, for example. Helping children to understand these rituals can help them to feel a part of the routine. These consistent routines also help the child to feel more secure, and life to be more predictable.

Carers need to be aware that some of the routines they take for granted may appear quite bizarre to the child. Taking a shower every day, sitting down to eat meals at the table, even sleeping in a bed and having a consistent bedtime can be very perplexing for a child who hasn't had this experience.

Children need to be helped to understand and enjoy rituals and routines that are already in place within the family. It can also feel good to be part of creating new routines. This can help children to feel not just that they are fitting in but that they have some influence over how the family is developing.

Claiming behaviours

Children can be helped to feel they belong in a number of different ways. Photographs around the house, celebrations of the day they joined the family, their own possessions amongst those of other family members, choosing the decorations in a room, naming a new family pet can all powerfully convey to children that they belong and are here to stay.

> Claiming is especially important for Luke; when he arrived with Jackie he had no sense of being special or belonging to someone. Jackie is careful to find ways of

demonstrating that Luke is her child, using visual reminders such as photographs, and a door sign that says 'Jackie and Luke live here'. She makes sure that his moving-in day is treated as a special anniversary and she involves Luke in making decisions that affect both of them. For example, Luke helps her to choose the colour for their new carpet. When friends come around Jackie uses the opportunity to show Luke how people come and go but he remains as he belongs with her. It is particularly helpful when Jackie cares for her two nieces whilst their mum goes into hospital for a minor operation. Jackie shows Luke that he is different to them, and also helps Luke to understand how much they miss their mum and look forward to going home.

Probably the behaviour that is most likely to interfere with the process of claiming a child within a family, and can make it hardest to maintain the positive family atmosphere, is anger. Children can display anger in a range of ways, but each of these can be very destructive to family relationships.

Helping children who are angry

Children with difficulties in forming and enjoying attachment relationships often use anger to cope with feelings of low self-worth and fear of rejection. The anger can be:

- a defence against the feelings about self. The child instead blames others and expresses anger towards them.

- a way of coping with the fear of rejection. The child pushes the parent away, rejecting before being rejected.

- a way of testing commitment. 'This is how bad I am. Will you still love me?'

- an expression of frustration at events or feelings that feel out of control to the child.

- a way of managing feelings that the child feels are intolerable. For example, if the child finds feeling sad intolerable he may use anger as a way of blocking the feelings of sadness.

By the time Zoë is ten years old Jenny and Martin have made substantial progress. Zoë is now much more mature and more able to talk about how she is feeling rather than demonstrating this through her behaviour. She sometimes leaves little notes around the house to tell Jenny and Martin that she is sad or cross. She will also talk with them without being so quick to 'lose it'. Her emotional outbursts still occur, but are not so frequent and more quickly over.

Catherine on the other hand appears to be more difficult as she moves into her teenage years. Jenny and Martin often notice her winding Zoë up, trying to provoke her into an angry outburst. Catherine has always put a lid on her own emotion; Jenny and Martin now wonder how much Zoë's temper tantrums have helped her with this. Could Catherine somehow experience these outbursts vicariously, reducing her own need to display her feelings?

They have also noticed that Catherine's previously infrequent outbursts, although still short lived, are becoming more frequent. Jenny is particularly concerned about this as she feels in other ways her relationship with Catherine is improving. This improvement in their relationship is leading to some conflict for Catherine. She has a deep-seated fear of not being good enough. She fears that Jenny will see how bad she is and will not want her any more. When she feels particularly close to Jenny this creates anxiety for Catherine; she becomes angry both as a way of managing the increase in anxiety and to demonstrate to Jenny how bad a young person she really is.

Catherine has also had many questions recently about Fiona who she barely remembers. Becoming a teenager has led to a need to find out more about herself. Catherine's growing independence is accompanied by a need to strengthen her own sense of identity. This in turn provokes sadness in Catherine – sadness for a mother who she barely remembers – and because of the fear that her mother, Jenny, could not love her because of who she is. Catherine cannot handle feeling sad; she has always managed to cut off from the feelings she experiences, dissociating from any connection with them. This is becoming harder to do. Provoking Zoë or becoming angry herself is a way of inhibiting the intolerable sad feelings.

Displays of anger for Catherine are therefore complex as, in adolescence, she comes to terms with who she is all over again. Anxiety and sadness, a fear of not being good enough and of rejection, together with a changing relationship with her sister, all contribute to the increase in provocative, angry behaviour alternating with compliant and loving behaviour when she is feeling calmer.

A colleague of mine, Betsy Brua, helps parents understand children's angry outbursts by using the image of a volcano; she provided me with the visual image in Figure 11.2 (Brua, personal communication).

Calmness → Trigger → Build-up → Explosion → Wind-down → Remorse → Calmness

Figure 11.2 The volcano

Things can go along fine until a *trigger* is experienced. The child's behaviour begins to *build up* until an *explosion* occurs. After the explosion, there is a *winding-down* stage that is then followed by a return to *calmness*. There may be a period of *remorse* before the child returns to normal. Sometimes the triggers are unclear and the outbursts appear suddenly and unpredictably. In addition the wind-down stage may be characterized by numerous further eruptions before calmness is finally restored.

You can think about how you can help the child at all these different stages, each being dealt with differently.

Calmness

Maintaining a positive emotional atmosphere will help to develop periods of calmness in the home. This means avoiding being pulled into confrontation with your child but staying calm, clear and empathic. If your child is being oppositional or non-compliant calmly state the consequence and walk away ('When you...then...' Or 'If you...then...'). Maintain clear boundaries and expectations without getting angry. It is helpful to acknowledge the effort your child is making, however small, and to provide *empathy* for how hard this is.

Children with experience of chaotic, unpredictable and unresponsive parenting will benefit from extra predictability and consistency. This can be difficult if you like being a bit *impulsive*, doing things on the spur of the moment. You need to assess whether your child can cope with such spontaneity. If not you may need a bit more predictability; gradually help him to become more secure with unpredictability.

The trigger

Outbursts tend to occur for reasons. This may be, in common with all children, when the child is not getting something that he wants, being stopped from doing something or feeling bored, tired or unwell. Children who struggle to manage their feelings are likely to be triggered much more quickly and easily. They reach the threshold for tolerating stress sooner and thus explosions appear to occur more suddenly and more extremely than in other children. Even nice events can be stressful and therefore can lead to similar reactions. If your child doesn't tolerate stress well then treats and family outings need to be carefully planned and monitored. It may be better to plan a few small, low-key outings than a major event. Going to the park to feed the ducks, a family picnic, or a shared video may be easier for your child to manage than a trip to the safari park. These also have the added advantage that they can be ended earlier if you notice him beginning to struggle. Your child ends the experience positively and is none the wiser that it is earlier than it might have been.

For children with experience of abuse or neglect, additional triggers can be reminders of past experience, feeling fear, feeling not good enough, experiencing *shame*, and perceiving rejection from others. Children who are hyper-sensitive to being rejected can perceive even neutral expressions or statements from the parent as rejecting, leading to explosive behaviour. These triggers can be very unexpected and difficult to spot. You might notice patterns in how your child is behaving; puzzling about this with him may throw further light on it. ('I notice you get very angry when I say no more television. Do you think I don't like you and that is why I am saying this?') Often however the children themselves do not understand these links. You may have to try different reassurances, see what makes a difference to your child. ('I love you very much, but now it is time to turn the TV off. Shall we spend some time doing that puzzle?')

The build-up

The build-up can happen relatively slowly or can occur very quickly. As the explosion starts to build up there may be opportunities to intervene. With careful observation you may notice signs of stress building up that you hadn't noticed before. Sometimes however this is not possible and your child just 'explodes' with no warning.

When you are aware that stress is building you could try distracting your child, diverting him to an activity which is stress reducing, spending a bit more time with him so that he can use you to help manage the stress or producing something novel which helps him to focus away from the stressful trigger. For young children special toys can be kept to use at difficult times. Sometimes active ignoring might be useful in diffusing the situation, especially when your child is trying to goad you into a reaction. In these instances however it is also useful to think about why he wants to goad you; he may need support for some other feeling. For instance, a child might try to engineer an outburst when feeling anxious.

For some children humour or playfulness can stop the build-up; behaving unexpectedly can stop children in their tracks. Soon they are joining in and giggling with you.

Children who have experienced frightening parenting in the past, either because their parents have hurt them or because they have not been available and responsive to them, will be feeling afraid during the build-up. As they experience an increase in stress they will be anticipating lack of help, or worse, physical punishment for their behaviour. This can accelerate the process, building the stress more quickly and thus leading to earlier explosions. Some of these children will respond to being held and cuddled at this time. This can help them to feel safe and contained, allowing them to calm down. You need to be mindful of your child's previous experience. If hugging triggers memories of past abuse this may create further anxiety. You will need to find a different way to hold him which doesn't trigger this anxiety or you can stay close, without touching, and talk in a calm, safe way allowing your voice to 'hold'.

The explosion

Children vary in the length and severity of their outbursts and there is no easy answer as to how to handle the explosion. You need to try to stay calm and remember that it will not go on forever. At this time you will not be able to reason with or talk your child out of it. Concentrate on keeping him safe. Any talking should be calm and reassuring, helping him to feel supported. You need to let him know that he is safe and that you will be able to help.

Although you probably feel upset and angry, showing these feelings will only prolong the outburst. Find ways to stay calm; try to say positive things to yourself, take deep breaths, count to ten. If you are feeling very wound up it is best to walk away, if this can be done safely. This will be easier if there is another adult who can take over.

The wind-down

During the winding-down stage, some of the diversion and distraction strategies that are used during the build-up phase can be tried again.

Cuddling at this stage can be a powerful way of letting young children know that they are all right and that you still love them. Older children might welcome a cuddle too, or at least a reassuring pat on the shoulder. For children uncomfortable with touch, use words to give the same messages.

The message should always be that whilst the behaviour is unacceptable, you would like to help him to find a different way of showing how he is feeling. This is not the same as rewarding the explosive behaviour. This only happens when you give in to children as a result of their behaviour.

As your child is calming down, it is better not to discuss the outburst. This is likely to trigger further outbursts whilst emotions are still not fully back in control. Your child is not in a receptive frame of mind and will not be able or willing to see why his behaviour was unreasonable. If you feel that you need to discuss the outburst choose a quiet time when everyone has fully calmed down. *Empathy* and *attunement* at these times will help him to listen.

If your child has done any damage or made any mess during the outburst this will also need leaving for now. When calmness is restored, and he is feeling supported, then you can discuss quietly how he will tidy up or make amends. Supporting children at this stage is a powerful way of demonstrating that they are still loved, thus reducing their feelings of *shame* and sense of badness.

Remorse

When children have wound down, they will sometimes experience a period of remorse. They may say that they are sorry, that they will never do it again. This is an important stage and builds on the *interactive repair* during the wind-down period. You can provide *empathy* for how hard it is for your child to cope with the strong feelings and give the message that you will help him with this. Don't worry however if he is not expressing remorse. Trying to get a child to apologize is rarely effective. At most he says sorry to keep you quiet but it will not feel genuine. Children generally do feel bad after an outburst, but for some children the feelings of *shame* are too overwhelming. They defend against these feelings by not acknowledging their sense of badness about the behaviour or sometimes by blaming others. As you help your child to cope with the *shame* and as you reassure him that you will continue to love him then he will gradually be able to acknowledge sadness for what has occurred.

12

Looking After Yourself

Making time for yourself is something parents find very hard to do. Looking after children, managing a household and fulfilling work commitments can mean that looking after you is very low down the priority list. Yet it should be the number one priority. Without time for yourself there will be no opportunity for re-charging batteries, thinking or planning. Rest, relaxation and reflection

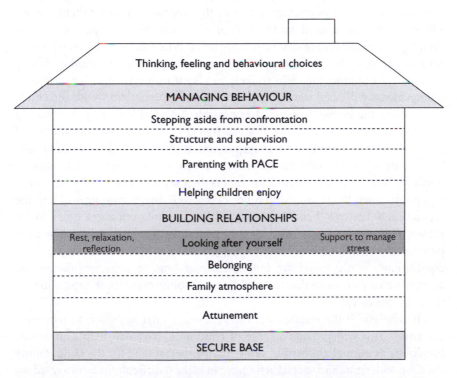

Figure 12.1 Looking after yourself (Adapted from 'The House Model of Parenting' in Golding et al. (2006). Copyright © John Wiley & Sons Ltd. Reproduced with kind permission.)

are all essential elements of parenting, especially when parenting children with emotional and relationship difficulties (see Figure 12.1).

Making time for reflection and relaxation

When caring for and working with children with difficulties in attachment it is very important that you have opportunities to spend time away from them. If your child is struggling to go to school this can be even more important. Respite breaks and holidays, as well as times for yourself, are very important both to re-charge batteries and to think about the best way of caring for her.

Children may struggle with these necessary breaks from parents, especially when they fear abandonment and loss. This inevitably presents a dilemma; the parent needs a break but taking a break can appear to be contributing to the child's difficulties. It is not uncommon for a period of 'pay-back' upon your return, leaving you to wonder whether the break was worth it. It can also be difficult to find alternative carers for your child, especially when behaviour is very challenging. Baby sitters can be difficult to find and extended family are not always available or keen to provide this kind of practical support. Despite all these difficulties it remains an essential part of the parenting approach. Therapeutic parenting as described in this model is very emotionally demanding and intensive. Breaks are as essential a part of this approach as any other element. Allowing time for yourself whilst your child is at school can be part of this, but evenings out or short breaks are also important. When these breaks can be built naturally into a child's routine, with a grown-up child or another family member for example, the child is likely to take it in her stride. More complex arrangements will need some thought and careful preparation with the child.

Making the breaks as planned as possible with stable arrangements using the same substitute carer is ideal. The children get used to the change as a part of their routine, and do not see it as a response to anything they have done or said. When parents do not take breaks and the pressure builds up, a break may be needed as a response to a crisis. The child is then separating from the parent at a low point, when the relationship is not doing well. Inevitably she will link the separation to her own behaviour, and will fear a more permanent break in the future. This can lead to a large amount of testing the relationship when the parents return, making it difficult for the parent to get the relationship back to equilibrium. Whilst crises are inevitable from time to time, regular respite arrangements can mean that the child doesn't only experience separations at times of difficulty.

It is helpful if the respite carer can follow a similar approach to parenting the child. This will provide a sense of continuity. It is also helpful if respite breaks are as normal as possible, rather than a special time for the child. Filling the time with treats and special activities can make it difficult for her to re-adjust to normal life when her own parent returns.

Children can be helped to feel that they are still in the parents' mind during a break. Time spent planning the break with your child and letting her know what you will be doing whilst you are apart can help the experience to feel less threatening. She could be asked to look after something for you; a message that you will be returning. Telephone calls or sending a card can also help her to stay connected with you whilst you are away. This experience of continuing connection with the parent can be very helpful, especially for the child with a large degree of separation anxiety. Even spending time away from the parent when at school can lead to a large amount of anxiety for some children. Knowing that the parent is continuing to think about them can be very helpful to children in coping with separation.

Although Zoë is now ten and Catherine thirteen, Jenny and Martin have not yet left them overnight. This is presenting them with a dilemma. They want to travel abroad to a golden wedding anniversary of a family member, but they do not think that the girls will cope with this event. If they do not take them it will mean leaving them for a few days.

Jenny and Martin have some good friends who have also adopted two children, and they rather courageously offer to have the girls. After some deliberation Jenny and Martin decide to take up this offer. About a month before they are due to go Jenny and Martin tell the girls. Predictably Zoë is very upset; she clings to Jenny begging her not to leave her. Catherine on the other hand appears indifferent, taking the news in her stride, although Jenny and Martin feel that she isn't as untroubled as she appears. They decide to plan the weekend, involving the girls as much as possible, and with an emphasis on when they will be coming back. They make calendars of the month to put up in their bedroom illustrating the few days away amongst a sea of days either side when they will be with them. They also get out the family albums showing Catherine and Zoë the couple celebrating the anniversary and who else will be there. Catherine helps Zoë to make cards for the couple, and while they are at it for the friends they are going to stay with! Martin draws maps for the girls, marking on the route they will take to get to the hotel and more importantly the route back home. Finally they buy Zoë a teddy bear with a little recorder inside for personal messages. For Catherine they buy a new make-up mirror; it has a mirror on one side and space for photographs and messages from Jenny and Martin on the other. Jenny and Martin leave a message for each girl reminding them how much they love them and when they will be home.

The day before they are due to go they visit the friends' house. Jenny goes through the girls' usual routine, and leaves them with a supply of peanut butter! She also leaves notes to be given to the girls whilst they are away. These say how proud they are of them and that they are missing them. On the morning itself Jenny hands each girl one of her scarves, telling them she wants them to look after these for her, and she will collect them back when she returns.

> The stay goes smoothly. Zoë is a bit tearful and clingy, especially at bed-time. She insists on marking each hour on her calendar so that she can see when Jenny and Martin will be back. Catherine appears fine, although she is a bit quiet and she becomes quite frustrated when she can't find her homework for school the next day. Overall however they appear to cope. They are both pleased to see Jenny and Martin when they return and for a few weeks Zoë is clingier than usual but overall Jenny and Martin are glad they had gone.

Finding ways to spend free time is not as difficult as making the time in the first place! Relaxation, support and reflection all need time away from the children and together they help you to feel strong and emotionally able to continue.

Relax
It may feel impossible at times but it is important to make time for hobbies and interests, for meeting friends and spending time with your partner. If you don't feel like socializing or being busy, allow yourself evenings in when you can take a bath, read a book, or watch television without being interrupted by your child. Learning a relaxation exercise does not take very long and, if practised regularly, can be very helpful at times of increased stress.

Use support
You will need a good support network including some people who will have similar experiences to you. Friends and family are obviously an important source of support, but difficulties in sharing confidential information, or a lack of understanding on their part about why you are fostering or have adopted, might mean extending your support network more widely. Support groups or individual support from foster and adoptive parents can be helpful. Support can also come from other professionals who know your child, or are willing to listen to you talk about her. Some people will be able to offer practical support; others may provide emotional support. Knowing there is someone to phone when things are tough can make a huge difference to whether you will cope or not.

Make time for reflection
All parents need time for reflection. This can allow you to think about your child's behaviour, to understand it and to reflect upon your response to it. This can help you to acknowledge your own feelings of anger, sadness and despair. It can also help in maintaining a sense of humour.

Take opportunities to think about your child, and your reactions to her. Learning from how things have gone, thinking through the reasons for behaviour or exploring the links between your child's current behaviour and her past experience are all very difficult to do during the heat of day-to-day care. Maintaining a journal, or talking with someone who has some understanding of your child, can help you to think things through, make plans and review and revise plans in the light of experience.

You may need time to think about realistic day-to-day goals, and to revisit these at times of increased stress.

If you are caring with another person you will benefit if you have time and space to talk to your partner. This can help you to provide a consistent response to your child and to explore issues you are facing. Caring for a child who has difficulties in making and maintaining relationships can place a huge strain on marriage or partnerships. If this isn't talked about, it will simply build until the relationship reaches breaking point.

Partners need especially to think about a child who is responding to one parent very differently from the other. If this is not thought through, resentment and frustration can quickly build up. Time for reflection avoids *splitting*. This is when a child tries to respond to one parent as the good parent and the other as the bad parent. In the absence of good communication it is very easy to fall into these roles.

Understanding and managing feelings evoked by the child

If you find yourself experiencing anger, tension or discouragement this will be communicated back to your child. This leads to increased insecurity and often an increase in the difficult behaviour being displayed. Thus a vicious circle can quickly set in.

Children will experience certain feelings in response to the feelings of the parents:

- fear or rage in response to anger

- anxious and guarded in response to tension and pessimism

- hopeless in response to discouragement.

When you habitually find yourself reacting to particular behaviours of your child, it can help to reflect on this.

You might be experiencing *projection*. These are feelings projected into you by your child. If you experience an emotional reaction that seems to be extreme you could consider whether you may be experiencing the emotion that your child is experiencing. Time spent with someone suffering from depression can leave us feeling depressed. We may pick up on the anger that someone is feeling and find ourselves experiencing this anger as if it is our own. Understanding these reactions means that you can support your child, providing her with some sense of containment and *empathy*.

One day Jenny is telling Martin about her friend's daughter. She has been getting into drugs and the friend is 'out of her mind' with worry. 'I don't know,' says Jenny. 'You make so many sacrifices for them but can't your children let you down? Mind you, Kate has always had a stubborn streak. She can be a manipulative little madam.'

Unbeknown to Jenny and Martin, Catherine hears the last part of the conversation and mistakenly thinks that they are talking about her. The next few days are quite strange. On the surface Catherine appears much as usual but Jenny finds herself feeling angry with her. She can't put her finger on it but she experiences a distance from Catherine, a feeling of estrangement that hasn't been there before. Catherine is polite and compliant but Jenny feels that she wants to shake her.

Fortunately for Jenny and Catherine's relationship Catherine confides in a favourite teacher. She tells her that she hates her mum; after some probing Catherine lets on that her mum doesn't like her because she is stubborn and manipulative. The teacher is concerned enough to let Jenny and Martin know and after some reflection it all becomes clear. Jenny and Martin sit down and have a quiet talk with Catherine, at the end of which they make her promise that if she does any more listening at doors she will make sure she knows who they are talking about!

Alternatively it might be that your child is acting as a trigger to an unresolved issue from your own past. As discussed in Chapter 8 it might be helpful to reflect upon your own experience of being parented, or on previous relationships that you have had, and to think about how this might impact on your role as a parent. When strong emotions are triggered in us it becomes difficult to continue to respond flexibly. We are caught up in our own emotions and we no longer think clearly. It is easy then to over-react to your child. You may need time apart to reflect on your responses to her. Does any person or event from your past experience come to mind? Often exploration of our attachment history can give us clues as to why we are responding to a child in a particular way. Does your previous experience help to make sense of the emotional reaction? Being able to understand such a reaction will ensure that you are more in control next time it happens. You will be able to return to more flexible responding.

Stress and coping

Everyone experiences stress in their lives and at low levels this can be positive. Stress can help us to be motivated and enthusiastic, helping us to cope, and to achieve goals we have set for ourselves. Too much stress however can be problematic leading us to feel unwell and unhappy. Increased stress interferes with coping.

Coping can be thought of in terms of resources and demands:

- *Resources*: These are the things that are drawn on for support. They can internal, for example health, fitness and confidence. They can be external, for example support, pay and holidays.

- *Demands*: These are the things that have to be done or managed, for example, getting children to school, attending meetings, employment, managing difficult behaviours.

The balance between resources and demands determines your ability to cope. When you have more resources than demands you will be able to cope. If demands exceed resources however you are likely to find yourself not coping very well.

Coping = more resources than demands.

Not coping = more demands than resources.

Exercise 12.1 gives you an opportunity to think about your own resources and demands, and thus to think about how you can improve your ability to cope.

Exercise 12.1: Making changes
What are the demands upon you? Do you have sufficient resources to cope? Try to think of one achievable thing you could do to reduce the demands on you and/or to increase the resources available to you. See Figure 12.2.

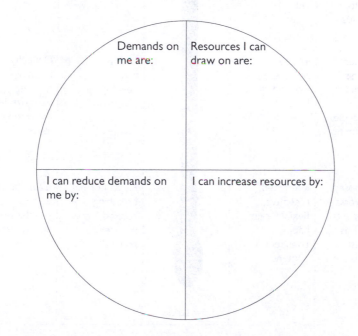

Figure 12.2 Making changes

Stress thermometer

You can notice when you are becoming stressed because of the impact this has on your body, your behaviour, your thinking and your feelings. Carolyn Webster-Stratton (2001) uses the idea of a stress thermometer to help you monitor changes in these as your stress builds up (see Figure 12.3 below).

What am I thinking?	What am I feeling?	High stress	What is happening in my body?	How am I behaving?
I'm bad, I'm hopeless, I'm a bad parent. This is too stressful.	Angry. Furious.		Heart racing, neck muscles tight, chest tight, clenched fists, teeth clenched, headache.	Yelling, hitting.
No matter what I do nothing changes. It's useless. It never helps.	Defensive, guilty, withdrawn, frustrated, sad.		Shallow rapid breathing, sweating, tense muscles.	Threatening, withdrawing.
I'm not sure I can do this. Maybe this is too much for me to handle. Maybe I'm no good.	Irritated, anxious, worried.		Pacing, headache developing.	Difficulty listening, thinking narrows, less open to new ideas.
It's supposed to get worse before it gets better. This won't last forever. I can make a difference. I can help...	Interested, receptive, flexible, calm, happy, confident, content.	Low stress	Heart normal, breathing relaxed, muscles relaxed.	Calm, pleasant, able to problem-solve, able to listen.

Figure 12.3 The stress thermometer (Adapted from Webster-Stratton (2001). Copyright © The Incredible Years. Reproduced with kind permission.)

Everyone will deal with stress in different ways, and have their preferred means of reducing this stress. As long as these are working this is fine. If the stress is continuing to increase it might be time to revisit the strategies. It may be time to find ways to increase resources and reduce demands.

Exercise 12.2: Stress thermometer

You can think about the way you react to increasing stress using this sheet (see Figure 12.4). Think about what you think and feel and how these change as you become more stressed. What do you notice happening in your body as you become more stressed, and how is this noticeable in your behaviour?

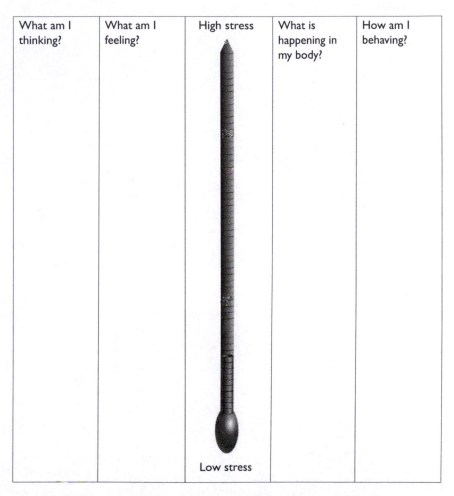

What am I thinking?	What am I feeling?	High stress	What is happening in my body?	How am I behaving?
		Low stress		

Figure 12.4 Stress thermometer exercise

Part 3

A Model for Parenting the Child with Difficulties in Attachment Relationships: Building Relationships and Managing Behaviour

13

Helping the Child to Enjoy Being Part of the Family

In Part 2 we focused on how parents can increase security and support for their children. The foundation to the relationship between the child and parent is a *secure base*. The parent provides the security the child needs in order to be able to trust and rely on adults and to feel confident about moving away and exploring the world. This trust develops out of the experience of attuned relationships.

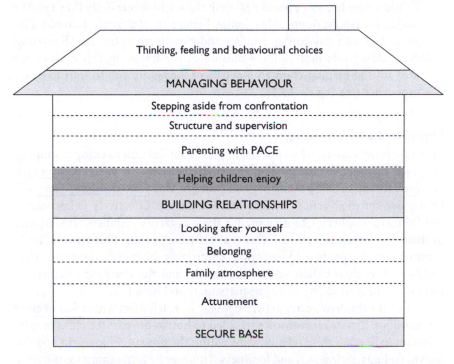

Figure 13.1 Helping children enjoy being part of the family (Adapted from 'The House Model of Parenting' in Golding et al. (2006). Copyright © John Wiley & Sons Ltd. Reproduced with kind permission.)

Children need opportunities to experience *attunement* and to learn that this relationship isn't lost at times of rupture, but can be recovered through the process of *interactive repair*. This parenting is provided within a positive, calm and harmonious family atmosphere. Children's responses to this very different experience can make it hard to maintain this atmosphere. The parents will need to help the children to feel they belong in the family and to experience family enjoyment. Parents will only accomplish all this if they look after themselves as well. Time for rest, relaxation and reflection are essential prerequisites when children have difficulties with attachment.

Helping children feel secure and supported is the starting point for developing a relationship with them. In this part we consider relationship-building more explicitly. In the absence of a healthy, secure relationship, behaviour can be contained or managed but this will have less impact on the emotional progress that the child will make. Once a reasonable relationship is formed then behavioural management can be used not only to contain difficult behaviour, but also to help children learn to behave in socially appropriate ways. Children will begin to make emotional progress, developing increased confidence in their ability to manage their own feelings, to understand the thoughts and feelings of others and to make sense of their own experience.

If children are to grow up and deal with the world successfully they need to start within the family. Being able to enjoy being part of a family, to build relationships, deal with day-to-day conflict and participate in fun are all starting points for doing this more widely outside of the home. In this chapter we consider ways of helping children feel part of the family and to start to enjoy this experience (see Figure 13.1).

Enjoyment and belonging

There are many reasons why children might find it difficult to enjoy belonging in a foster or adoptive family. Their early experience may have left them with a pervasive feeling of being bad, not good enough. This *internal working model* will be a guide for their actions within the new family. Effectively it becomes a self-fulfilling prophecy. Children predict the way family members will respond to them. They then behave as if this is already happening. This pushes family members into the predicted interactions confirming the initial prediction. Thus children enact their beliefs within the family, and the resulting interactions interfere with their ability to enjoy, participate and have fun.

Often the children's early experience may have left them with a fear of close relationships. If close relationships have led to hurt in the past the child may be reluctant to develop close relationships within the present. Enjoyment and fun lead to feelings of closeness and fondness. This may be frightening for the child who then resists participating in family activities or relationships. If children do let their guard down and find themselves enjoying a day it is not uncommon for the next day to be particularly difficult. The children act in a way that spoils the close feelings that were developing and therefore gets things back to a state within which they feel less anxious.

Children may fear enjoyment because they anticipate that it will end. They fear the loss of something they are starting to like and the anticipation of such loss builds up anxiety and distress. To end this anxiety children ruin the enjoyment. They feel calmer spoiling the enjoyment than waiting for it to end.

Children may experience a conflict of loyalty between their new and previous families. Having fun, taking part and enjoyment may all feel like a betrayal of their family of origin. They therefore remain disengaged as an expression of their loyalty.

Additionally contact with their family can, in some circumstances, contribute to children's difficulties in engaging with a foster family. Sometimes families use contact to give messages such as: 'You will be coming back to us; you must be naughty in order to get sent back home' or 'Don't trust these people'.

There are therefore many reasons why you might need to help your child enjoy and participate in family life. It is easy to think that by providing positive, fun experiences he will naturally enjoy and take part in them. When this doesn't happen you may feel demoralized and rejected by him. Seeing a Christmas present destroyed the day after Christmas or having to hastily leave a theme park with a child in mid-tantrum can feel very frustrating. You may wonder why you are bothering.

It may be helpful to think instead that your child needs to learn to manage these treats. It may be important to take things slowly. Not to plan big treats or days out but allow him to get used to more typical activities – a visit to the local park, playing a board game before bed. These activities can be gradually increased, allowing him to become accustomed to doing things within the family. Regular family time with familiar activities can help your child become used to doing things as a family in a way that feels safe and comfortable, because it is predictable.

Understanding why your child needs to sabotage an activity can help you to deal with this empathically and supportively. Whilst he may need to experience a consequence for the behaviour this can be provided within a context of 'I know how hard this is for you'.

In addition talking with an older child about feelings of conflict and of feeling not good enough can help his behaviour become understandable, leading to more flexibility in behaviour. Often the reasons for behaving as they do are poorly understood by children, and are unconscious responses to feelings of anxiety, conflict or failure.

You may need to find activities that your child can engage in and that provide a sense of accomplishment in order to help him discover that he is good at some things. Provide low-key, descriptive praise: 'You have really given a sense of movement to the horse you have drawn' rather than: 'That's a great picture of a horse.' Children may find this easier to listen to and therefore be less likely to reject it as too different from how they feel about themselves. As children increase their *self-esteem* and sense of *self-efficacy* they will also feel closer to the family and more able to feel like they belong.

> Marcus really struggles with treats and praise. His own sense of badness conflicts seriously with being told he has done something well. His teachers have learnt this to their cost. Work that is praised is torn up and thrown down; if he is rewarded for getting on with the other children, mysteriously he will be at the centre of a fight during the very next break. It is as if he cannot tolerate being told anything good about himself. Before long the teachers will discover how bad he really is. He fears losing what he is starting to like.
>
> With Rita and Frank, Marcus is beginning to relax a bit. He has now lived with them for six years, and has tested their commitment to him in every way that he can think of. Whilst the placement has teetered often and has been at breaking point a few times somehow they have always found the will power to continue. The support they have received and sufficient opportunities for respite have allowed them to carry on. They have also learnt from experience not to expect too much. In the early days Marcus would spoil anticipated trips before they happened or would behave so badly they had to end them early. They learnt not to plan too much in advance and to keep outings very simple.
>
> Marcus discovers he enjoys going for walks, and flying a kite. He also demonstrates a particular aptitude for boxing. This especially pleases Frank; as a keen boxer himself he enjoys working with Marcus and helping him to develop his technique. Although able, Marcus still cannot compete however. Losing is just too difficult for him. Frank has tried to get him involved in a local club for young people but the friction between Marcus and the other boxers has led to too much trouble. Frank continues to take Marcus with him and hopes that in time Marcus will learn to cope with boxing with other young people.
>
> Rita is trying to get Marcus more interested in his identity. She is hoping that by increasing his understanding of his roots he will develop a stronger sense of self and start to believe in himself a bit more. She helps him to find out about his father's favourite reggae music, and enlists his help in making some Caribbean food. She wonders if they could invite a school friend round to sample it. She hopes that this will help him to develop a sense of pride in his heritage rather than always expecting to be ridiculed by the other children. She is also hoping to take him to the carnival next month. They will watch this year, but she wonders next year whether she might get him participating in the parade without this being too overwhelming for him.

When children are really struggling to live in a family it may be that they have missed out on important socialization experience when they were younger. Understanding the socialization process and especially the role of *shame* may lead to increased understanding about children's difficulties and provide ideas for intervention.

Marcus's lying has been a major source of concern for Rita and Frank. He will lie rather than admit to something or just to maintain a sense of control over Rita and Frank. His tall stories can be extravagant, often of the strength and power of his birth dad Richie or to recount a tale of some activity he had with him. Rita and Frank might believe the first but they very much doubt that Marcus ever went on these outings with his dad. The most infuriating behaviour however is Marcus's tendency to blame everyone else rather than admit to anything wrong. Whatever has gone wrong it was always someone else. If the teacher calls Rita about his behaviour Marcus always has a story about why it was not him. Rita and Frank fear that if Marcus won't take responsibility for his behaviour then he will not really make progress.

All of these behaviours are linked to the shame that Marcus experiences on a daily basis. All the small, or not so small, things that go wrong during the day, a cross word from Frank when he bumps into the table, a school mate not including him in a game, another young person calling him racist names or commenting on his hair, add to the sense of shame that Marcus experiences. Only by blaming others and spinning tall stories is Marcus able to feel good about himself, allowing him to hide away from the shame that threatens to overwhelm him. Rita and Frank struggle with this. They are very keen that Marcus start to feel more responsible, but all their attempts seem to drive him further and further into his blaming of others and his lying. They have had to learn not to confront him with his behaviour but instead to provide empathy for the reasons that lead to the lying; helping Marcus to feel more in touch with his day-to-day experience.

Shame prevents children from feeling a sense of belonging within the family and interferes with their capacity to take part in and enjoy family activities. Parenting that supports children in their experience of *shame* and provides them with experience of *attunement* and *interactive repair* will begin to help them to cope with the *shame* they are experiencing. Empathic discipline that provides *empathy* for the reasons the child got into the situation, and support for managing the consequences of this, will gradually help him to use discipline to learn how to behave appropriately. He can then feel a sense of belonging in the family. The child will be able to enjoy the family activities that everyone is taking part in.

Additional theory: Socialization and shame

Figure 13.2 illustrates the socialization process that occurs as children move from infancy to toddlerhood. As children mature the *attunement* experiences they engaged in with their parent now help them to learn socially appropriate behaviour. They learn what is acceptable and unacceptable as they experience the *shame* that is associated with breaks in this *attunement* caused by the need for limit-setting and discipline. The *interactive repair* following these breaks communicates to children that everything is okay. They are still loved and valued and

1. Attunement	Emotional connection. Child and parent share and enjoy positive emotional state, manage and contain negative emotional state.
2. Limit-setting, discipline	State of attunement is abruptly broken. Child experiences shame, an unpleasant emotional state.
3. Interactive repair	Carer helps child manage feelings of shame and conveys continuing love and acceptance of child.
	Child develops capacity for emotional and behavioural regulation and learns to express appropriate and inhibit inappropriate behaviours.

Figure 13.2 Socialization process

the relationship is intact. It has survived the need for discipline. The children learn from this experience because they have got back into an attuned state with their parents.

When this sequence does not occur, as in Figure 13.3, children will not have the experience of a *secure attachment*. The lack of a relationship within which children can experience themselves as loveable, alongside ineffective *attunement*, poor discipline and little relationship repair, all leave the child with an excessive experience of *shame* that is not contained by an adult. They will not be able to manage the *shame* that results from this. Thus the child is overwhelmed and learning does not take place.

1. Little experience of attunement	Child does not experience states shared or contained.
2. Discipline occurs with rejection, humiliation or anger	Shame is excessive.
3. No or delayed interactive repair	Experience of shame is not integrated. Child unable to develop capacity for regulation. Child develops sense of self as bad.

Figure 13.3 Impaired socialization process

What is shame?

Shame is an affect, a complex emotion that develops later than the development of more straightforward feelings or emotions such as anger, joy or sadness. *Shame* is uncomfortable for children and therefore children will learn to limit shame-inducing behaviours. In this sense it is protective, because it helps children to behave in a way that is safe and helps them to develop relationships.

> For example, a father and child are walking along a road. They have been reciting nursery rhymes and are enjoying each other's company. The child suddenly runs into the road; in a panic the father pulls him back. He is cross and shaken. The child experiences a sudden break in attunement and is filled with shame. He cries and the father comforts. The attunement between them is re-established. The child prefers this feeling to experiencing the shame. He is less likely to run into the road again in the future.

Toddlers constantly test boundaries. They learn through experiences of *shame* and re-*attunement* to regulate their impulses and thus to behave in socially acceptable and safe ways. The experience of *shame* has been integrative. Dan Hughes (2006) suggests that the experience of integrative *shame* allows children to experience guilt. Instead of feeling shameful, impacting on their sense of self as bad, the children experience guilt about the behaviour. This in turn provides them with a motivation to alter their behaviour in order to reduce such feelings of guilt in future.

For children with insecure attachment relationships the experience of *shame* is more likely to be disintegrative. They do not experience the attunement–shame–re-attunement cycle but instead they experience unregulated *shame* that overwhelms them.

Many experiences of disintegrative *shame* lead to *shame* becoming part of the core-identity: I am a shameful person. This person becomes chronically angry and controlling of others. When children have not had the experience of appropriately graded doses of *shame*, and the support and reassurance needed to help them to manage this, the *shame* engulfs them. They feel alienated and defeated, never quite good enough to belong. Children are trapped in *shame*. They feel abandoned and the *shame* becomes toxic. This leads to a state of development within which children experience difficulty both regulating emotion and thinking rationally. Children are left unable to respond flexibly or to control impulses.

The experience of *shame* is uncomfortable, but within the context of a *secure attachment* relationship it is manageable. The children will seek re-attunement and comfort. However, experiences of disintegrative *shame* lead children to seek to hide from others or deal with it in other dysfunctional ways. For example, they may:

- constantly lie, often pointlessly, to hide themselves from others
- defend against the pain by becoming controlling and domineering, or rigidly perfectionistic
- try to attack the source of the pain by blaming or punishing others.

14

Learning to Parent with PACE and Building Relationships with Stories

In this chapter a parenting 'attitude' is introduced that has been found to be very helpful to adoptive and foster parents parenting children with difficulties in attachment (see Figure 14.1). This is followed by some thoughts about communicating with children and young people through stories.

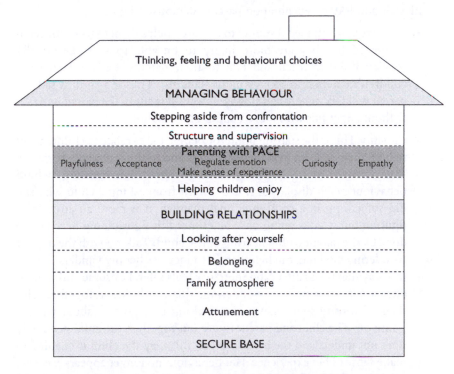

Figure 14.1 Parenting with PACE (Adapted from 'The House Model of Parenting' in Golding et al. (2006). Copyright © John Wiley & Sons Ltd. Reproduced with kind permission.)

What is meant by PACE?

PACE (playfulness, acceptance, curiosity and *empathy*) is suggested by Dan Hughes (2006) as a way of helping the adult remain emotionally engaged and available to the child. It is recommended that parents develop this attitude as a habitual way of relating to their children. Through an attitude of acceptance and *empathy* the parent is available to co-regulate the child's emotional state. This leads to an improved ability in the child for emotional regulation; she is able to manage her feelings. Through an attitude of curiosity and wondering, the parent is available to co-construct meaning with the child. This helps the child to develop the capacity for *reflective function*; she is better able to make sense of her experience.

Devised as part of a therapy for children with attachment difficulties, it provides an important guide to parents, helping them to demonstrate to their children that they are available and sensitive to their needs. The parent becomes attuned to the child through a stance of acceptance and curiosity, *empathy* and/or playfulness. This combined with feelings of love for their child (PLACE) means that the parent is meeting the emotional needs to be loved, nurtured, protected and understood.

PLACE and PACE depend upon parents demonstrating:

- *Attunement*: An attuned response to children helps them to feel connected to the adult. They are more likely to be able to stay emotionally regulated and to listen and talk to their parents. Parents match the children's emotion to convey understanding. Thus if a child is sad the parent will talk quietly and slowly. If a child is angry the parent will talk without anger but with more vitality and emotion.

- *Curiosity*: This is the starting point for being able to relate to children and to help them to learn to manage feelings and to think about experience. This includes wondering with a child about the meaning behind behaviour being displayed. It is different from asking a child why she did something in a confrontational manner. It is more an attitude of figuring out what is going on. Sometimes this figuring out needs to be done by the parent within hearing of the child. Talking with the dog, or wondering out loud, can help a child to increase her own understanding in a way that is less direct and therefore feels safer. For some children, or after a period of indirect wondering, this can be done together with them. Curiosity sometimes means making best guesses about what is going on. The child and parent figure out together; the child genuinely does not understand the behaviour. In this way the child is enabled to make sense of her experience. Her behaviour no longer appears random, or evidence of her 'inner badness'; instead it arises out of her experience, and the child now has more choices about how to react to her experience.

Having an attitude of curiosity can lead to feelings of *empathy* for children. A parent's sadness when his child misbehaves can support the child in a way that anger cannot. The child will then be more willing and able to think about her behaviour and the consequences that ensued.

- *Acceptance*: Following curiosity comes acceptance. Acceptance means understanding why children behave in a certain way. The adult accepts both the behavioural choices the child is making and the feelings that underlie these choices.

  Acceptance conveys understanding rather than a condoning of the behaviour. As children feel understood they will be more willing to think with the adult about the consequences to the behaviour that they now face.

- *Empathy*: Acceptance is conveyed to children through *empathy*. To empathize the parents need to enter imaginatively into the experience of the children. Acceptance of this inner experience is communicated to children helping them to feel that their inner life is important and valued.

- *Playfulness*: At times a playful attitude can be a key factor in helping children feel connected within the relationship. A light-hearted, relaxed and playful attitude can help the child, sometimes unexpectedly, to experience fun and love. If the resistant child does not see it coming and if it is over quickly she will find it harder to avoid and disengage.

- *Love*: Children need to feel loved and special. They need to know that parents love them, whatever they do, value them for the special people they are, and will always be there for them.

The use of PACE therefore is an active interaction that responds to and reflects upon children's experience. Children are helped to feel that their inner life is noticed and valued. What the child thinks and feels is both important and understandable. This helps the child to develop improved emotional regulation skills and increased capacity to reflect upon and make sense of her experience.

Zoë has come home from school in a bad mood. An earlier phone call from the teacher has already tipped Jenny off and she is ready for her. As she comes in Jenny asks Zoë how her day has been, much as she does every day. In answer Zoë throws down her bag and kicks her shoes off.

'That bad, eh?' Jenny empathizes. 'Come and have a drink and we can talk about it.'

'I don't want a drink.' Zoë glares at Jenny and switches the TV on. Calmly Jenny puts a drink and biscuit on the side and turns the TV off.

This is what Zoë has been waiting for; the TV gives her an excuse to let out all the pent-up emotion of the day. She screams at Jenny: 'You don't love me. I always have to do what you want. I never get to choose. I hate you.'

'Wow, Zoë, you are really telling me how bad you feel.' Jenny talks to Zoë with intensity and a forcefulness that matches Zoë's mood. 'It feels like I am so mean to you not letting you have the TV on. I wonder if it feels like the whole world is mean to you today.'

'You don't understand. You can't know how bad I feel,' shouts Zoë.

Still intense, Jenny responds: 'You're very cross with me for not understanding. You really are feeling bad, and you think I can't possibly know how bad that feels. It's very hard when you feel so bad and you have a mum who doesn't understand.' A slight nod and relaxation from Zoë gives Jenny the cue to soften a bit. She reiterates more quietly: 'It's so hard when Mum doesn't understand. You have had a hard day at school and now you are all hot and bothered, and you just want to be cross with me.' Zoë nods mutely. As Jenny attunes to Zoë's mood Zoë is able to calm down and they can both share the sense of sadness that underlies the angry outburst. Jenny is now able to cuddle Zoë to her and ask what went wrong today.

'Tom is so mean to me. He never likes me. I hate him,' she tells Jenny.

'Is that why you hit him, because he is mean to you? I can see how you would feel cross if Tom is mean to you.'

'Yes, that's why I hit him.' Zoë pauses and looks at Jenny. 'How did you know?'

'Mrs Robinson phoned me earlier. She told me you had a difficult day today.'

'Yeah, and I expect she told you it was all my fault too!' Zoë replied indignantly.

'Is that what you think, Zoë? Do you think it was your fault?' Jenny is careful not to give any hint of criticism or disapproval as she talks with Zoë.

'No, it wasn't my fault. Tom wouldn't share his paints. I needed blue to finish the sky, but he wouldn't let me have it.'

'So that that is why you hit him, when he wouldn't give you the blue paint?' Jenny asks, still keeping to a conversational tone.

'Yes, I felt so mad at him. He never likes me!'

Zoë is able to start to express her feelings and her beliefs at this point. Jenny explores this further with her. 'It sounds like you were really cross with Tom for not sharing with you, and just thinking about it is making you feel angry all over again.'

'Yes,' says Zoë. 'I feel really mad with Tom. He shared with Chloe so why wouldn't he share with me? I guess he hates me.' Zoë is beginning to reflect on the incident now. The attunement with Jenny has helped her to regulate the strong emotion she was feeling. This support has enabled her to think about Tom and to share some of her fears about why he wouldn't share with her. Jenny can now be curious and empathic about the way that Zoë has made sense of Tom's behaviour.

'It sounds to me like you were angry because you thought Tom didn't like you. Do you think that not sharing is his way of showing he doesn't like you?' Zoë nods quietly.

'That must be so hard for you, thinking that Tom doesn't like you. Maybe you were thinking about all the other times Tom doesn't share with you. It must make you sad to think he dislikes you so much that he won't share with you. Now I understand why you got so angry. You thought Tom doesn't like you. It's hard to think your friends don't like you. I guess I would be angry if I thought I wasn't liked.'

Here Jenny is giving Zoë empathy for her feelings, and helping her to think about the meaning of what happened at school that day. She is letting Zoë know that her thinking and feelings are understandable. She is providing empathy for this without challenging Zoë's view of the events. In this way Zoë is helped to feel understood and supported. Now Jenny can start to gently challenge Zoë's view of the event and Zoë will be able to listen and to think about it. This will also help Zoë to think about the consequences of her own behaviour.

'I wonder if Tom is always mean to you. Can you think when he has been nice to you?'

'No, Tom is always mean,' Zoë replies. 'He doesn't know how to share. The teacher is always telling him off.'

'Do you think Tom maybe didn't share with you because he is not good at sharing? I wonder why he shared with Chloe?'

Zoë thinks about this. 'The teacher told him to share with Chloe. Maybe that's why he shared the paint with her. The teacher didn't tell him to share with me. He still doesn't like me though.'

Zoë is beginning to think about the events in a different way. She is not completely ready to change her view but is prepared to think more flexibly about it. Jenny can now help Zoë to think about her own behaviour.

'I wonder how Tom felt when you hit him. Do you think he was upset?'

'Yeh, he cried. I think I hurt him. I was so cross I couldn't have the blue paint and I hit him. Yeh, I think it must have hurt.'

Zoë is thinking deeply now and starting to connect the different behaviours of herself and of Tom. Often Zoë is so focused on how mean everyone is for not liking her that she does not understand how her behaviour can lead to different consequences. In this conversation with Jenny she is able to think about cause and effect. This in turn leads to her being able to think about how she might behave differently. She decides that she will say sorry to Tom when she goes into school the next day. She runs up to her bedroom to get one of her special pencils to give him as a peace offering.

In this example Zoë has responded well to the attitude of PACE that Jenny demonstrated. Of course it does not always go as well as this. Jenny had time to think about it because of the telephone call from school. She was able to reach a state of attunement with Zoë quickly; sometimes Zoë is so angry and desperate it is hard for Jenny to match and pace her mood. Equally Zoë was receptive to the empathy she was hearing; when she did experience shame this did not overwhelm her and Jenny's continuing empathy was able to help Zoë to regulate and to think. Most importantly Jenny felt up to the challenge of Zoë today. Some days when she is tired, trying to share her time with Zoë and Catherine or preoccupied, it is hard to stay so sensitive and empathic. Each time Zoë and Jenny have these PACE-led interactions however Zoë is feeling a little more secure. This in turn builds Zoë's receptiveness to Jenny and their relationship is strengthened. Zoë feels loved; she feels she has a PLACE in Jenny's heart.

The use of PACE with discipline

The use of PACE is not aimed at directly changing children's behaviour. Rather it is used to help children feel connected. This in turn builds trust and security. It is likely that in time this will also lead to change in the child's behaviour.

It can be hard maintaining a focus on the feeling and thinking underlying behaviour. You may be deeply concerned about the behaviour being displayed, and in particular about the responses your child is likely to meet if she displays this behaviour out in 'the real world'. Discipline that aims to link the behaviour with consequences can be used to help children to learn what is and isn't acceptable behaviour. In order to maintain the feeling of trust that is being developed however it is important that discipline is not angry or too shaming for a child. PACE followed by discipline can help you to remain calm and supportive and the discipline to be measured.

Whilst this sounds quite straightforward it can be very difficult to implement an attitude of PACE within your day-to-day parenting of your child. We are not used to stopping and thinking about why a child is behaving as she is; and we unknowingly have lots of beliefs about how children should behave, usually based on our age-related expectations. It therefore takes practice to put these expectations aside and to start to be curious about the individual child in front of us. It is important not to get too frustrated when this doesn't come easily and not to be too hard on yourself as you slip back into a more typical parenting stance. Like the child, take one day at a time and use reflection times to think about what has worked well and less well.

Reflection times can help to maintain an attitude of curiosity, even when it is hard to keep this going in the heat of parenting. This curiosity will lead to improved understanding of your child. This will help you to increase your acceptance of her and to therefore be more curious on a day-to-day basis. Without this acceptance it is easy for discipline to become angry and confrontational. To help your child improve emotionally and not just behaviourally it is important that discipline starts with *empathy* and warmth.

This can give parents some concerns; acceptance can feel like putting up with behaviour. Parents may be especially concerned for the child outside of the home as they meet with teachers and other adults who will not be so accepting. Acceptance is however not the same as tolerance. It does not mean that you should just 'put up' with difficult behaviour. Acceptance does mean starting where the child is, understanding her inner life and how this is being communicated. By expressing *empathy* for the inner thoughts and feelings of your child, she will experience containment and support for this inner experience. This helps her to feel safe. You can then provide the guidance, feedback and limit setting that will eventually help her to express thoughts and feelings in a less challenging way. Finally by spending time with your child, helping her to become re-attuned, you are reminding her that she is still special. You both stay emotionally engaged with each other, despite the difficult behaviour being expressed. Your child learns that bad behaviour is not the same as being bad and this will increase her confidence that she can behave in different ways and that she will be supported when not able to manage this all the time.

Sometimes, and especially for some children, talking directly with them about their behaviour or about their experience is too difficult. They continue to experience this as an indication of their own badness and they become stuck with overwhelming *shame*. At these times more indirect ways of helping children to reflect on themselves and their experience is needed. Play and drawing can be one way of doing this. Joining with children as they play and draw and commenting on these can help them make sense of experience. For example, talk to a child about the animals she is playing with: 'That baby calf looks very frightened because he can't find his mummy. Do you think he needs some help to get back to her?' Or comment on a drawing in a way that might link to the child's own experience. 'The girl in your picture looks very angry. Look how strong she is fighting the men; do you think she is very frightened? I bet she could use some help even though she is so strong.' Notice that this type of talking does not focus directly on a child's own experience. Children do not need these links to be made, and such direct talking can be quite scary. They will learn about their own experience by thinking about the characters in their play and drawing. Story making can be a powerful but non-directive way to help children think about their own experience. Sharing stories helps children to explore whilst also helping the relationship to develop.

Building relationships with stories

Stories have always been used as a means of communication, to teach, to build relationships and for understanding. We all make sense of our own experience through the creation of stories. This is sometimes referred to as a '*coherent narrative*'. This narrative is what we use to understand and integrate our life experiences. The narrative is a dynamic story, changing as we experience, as we learn more about ourselves, and as we develop our understanding of our pasts. Stories can be autobiographical. 'When I was six my grandmother died…' Or they can be metaphorical. 'Once upon a time there was a young owl. This owl was feeling very sad because…'

Stories are a powerful tool for building relationships with children. Sharing a story is a unique bonding experience, a platform for experiencing *attunement* and developing an attachment relationship. They can also be used to convey *empathy* and acceptance, and to help children reach a deeper understanding about their experience. Stories can facilitate healing and can foster growth and development.

Stories can be:

- written for the child
- written together
- drawn from children's literature including fairy stories, stories written for children who have particular experiences (e.g. children who are bereaved), or stories that particularly appeal to the child
- read together
- you can be the reader or the audience
- told through play, drama and artwork.

Lacher and colleagues suggest creating the following stories for children with attachment difficulties (Lacher, Nichols and May 2005):

- Claiming narratives. The story is used to let children know that they should always have been loved and cherished, that they will now be loved and cherished, and to help children feel that they belong in the family.

- Developmental narratives. Stories can help children to experience imaginatively developmental experiences that were missed early in life. They can help children develop skills, grow emotionally and learn about relationships.

- Trauma narratives. These stories help children to process past experience. They help children make sense of events and the thoughts and feelings that they are left with. In this way the feelings become manageable and the experience becomes integrated into the children's life narrative.

- Successful narratives. Children can use stories to learn about who they are, what has happened to them, and who they might be. They can provide guidance for new behaviours, help children think about choices, and understand cause and effect. Stories can help children understand values, and can provide support and encouragement.

Nancy Davis (1996) provides useful advice to guide the creation of stories for children. Stories provide a message direct to the unconscious of the listener. There is therefore no need to interpret the story for the children or ask them questions about it to check that they have 'got it'. If children want to talk about the story they could be asked what they felt about the story. More typically a child will want to get on with another story, hear the story again or go on to another activity.

In the beginning of the story the child's situation will be mirrored in some way. Metaphors can be used to help the child hear the story rather than becoming overwhelmed by her own experience. Plants, animals or objects can be used to help create the metaphor. For example, if the child especially likes trains then the main character could be a train; if the child's interest is in a princess this will guide the choice of character.

When writing a story it can be helpful to identify the main character as the same sex as the child and to make the family constellation the same, e.g. if the child has a younger brother and an older sister the story character (whether inanimate or animate) can have the same siblings.

Metaphors or symbols can also be used to represent the process of change – this could be through the use of dreams, heroes that the child is keen on, fairy story characters, or familiar people, all of whom have the wisdom to help the main character.

Themes are best if they are positive rather than negative, and the main characters can be given the power within themselves to solve the problems, albeit with a little help from wise friends.

Messages can be conveyed through the narrative of the possibility of change and growth, and the helpfulness of looking to others for assistance.

In the next section there are some examples of stories written for children living in foster care.

Stories written for children

A 14-year-old girl, Claire, wrote this first story for her younger foster sister. I worked with Claire to help her to understand why this little girl found living with them difficult at times. This story came out of our work together.

A new beginning: the story of how Joey came to live with Kanga and Roo

Once upon a time there was a family of kangaroos who had a daughter named Joey. Joey was three years old. She was light brown in colour, but she was different from the other kangaroos because she had a large brown spot on her left leg. She was also different in her family as she was very sporty. Her mum and dad were lazy compared to most kangaroos. Joey sometimes felt upset by this, as she wanted someone like her to play with. Her parents disapproved of all her sportiness. They would like her to be a calmer kangaroo. One day her parents confronted her with this and Joey felt upset and annoyed. Because Joey wouldn't be calm they put her in her room.

That night Joey began to feel hungry. As Joey went to go downstairs her door would not open. She pushed and pulled the door, but it was stuck – she was locked in! Joey felt scared and confused. She didn't know if they would ever let her out. The next day her parents let her out and at the breakfast table they had another row about her being calmer. Joey did not like this and felt angry. Joey was frightened that they might lock her in again and so she ran away.

She ran and ran in one direction without looking behind her. She eventually stopped after what felt to her like a day's worth of running. She looked around herself and felt lost. She didn't recognize anything. She was further from home than she had ever been before. She looked around and felt very scared. She didn't know what to do and she didn't know where to go. She felt that she had been very naughty running away, and that her parents would never forgive her. She decided to look around for something to eat because she hadn't eaten for a long time. She couldn't find anything, so feeling tired and hungry she sat down and she was so exhausted she fell asleep. The next day she woke up with a growling tummy and a stiff back. She still didn't know what to do. Joey started just walking, hoping to find some food. As she came to the clearing she saw a bunch of kangaroos and ran up to them.

She found herself amongst a cluster of kangaroos. They asked her loads of questions and eventually she was given some food. Then the chief kangaroo from this herd took her back to his own house whilst they decided what to do next. The Chief asked her why she had run away from home. Joey felt ashamed and she was a bit worried about telling him.

The Chief was kind and patient. Eventually Joey told him about the row with her parents. Joey was told that it was okay to be sporty and that she shouldn't have been locked in her room without food. The Chief then told Joey that she would have to go to a new family and this family would look after her better. Joey felt very frightened that she had got her family into trouble. She felt that it was all her fault and that she should have kept quiet.

The next day the Chief came home later than usual and told her that he had found a new family for her that would be loving and caring. However, they had never fostered before and they were feeling very nervous about meeting Joey. They didn't know what to expect. They were also excited and couldn't wait to meet Joey. The Chief wanted Joey to meet them to see if she liked them.

The Chief tells Joey all about the new family. There is a mum called Kanga and a little girl called Roo. Roo is four years old and enjoys sport very much. Her favourite sport is volleyball. Joey feels excited by this as she has never had a sister and more importantly she has never lived with someone who has the same interests as her. However, she feels upset that she won't be returning to her family and will be going against their wishes. She worries how they are feeling. She wishes she could see them. The Chief tells her that this is not possible at the moment and that she needs to settle into her new family.

Two weeks later Joey moves to her new family in Hundred Acre Wood. She feels very shy and misses her family very much. Joey finds it all strange because the lifestyle is very different to what she is used to.

Kanga and Roo make her feel as comfortable as possible. Roo even gives up her pouch with Kanga for her. Gradually Joey starts to settle in. Roo and Joey even start to squabble like normal siblings. However, Joey feels that it is her fault that they are fighting. She is not used to having a sister. Kanga reassures her and tells her that it's normal for siblings to play happily and to squabble together. Joey starts to feel fond of them but she worries that she doesn't have enough love in her heart for everyone.

Two months go by and the Chief finally comes to visit Joey and to see how she has settled in, also to give her some news about her family. The news was that the Chief had been looking for her mum and dad and after a long hunt he had found them. They were very upset and had spent some time looking for her. When Joey found out she was excited and wanted to see them. However, the Chief tells her that she is not allowed to see them until they have checked that it will be safe, but she reassures Joey that she will do this as quickly as possible. Joey went to bed that night excited with the thought that she might see her parents soon, but suddenly she gets a rush of guilt flowing through her body as she thinks that Kanga and Roo would be upset. She thinks that they will think that she doesn't like them because she wants to see her mum and dad. She wonders who she will live with, and if she goes home will she still see Kanga and Roo. She falls asleep feeling very worried.

A few days go by and the Chief returns to see Joey. He tells her that Joey won't be able to go and live with her parents. He explains that he has had a long talk with them and he doesn't think that they are able to look after children properly. Joey is upset and asks if she will ever be able to see them again. The Chief reassures her that she will be able to see them regularly and Joey feels glad that at least she will still be able to see them. The Chief also tells her that she will be staying with Kanga and Roo until she is grown up.

A month later Joey starts pestering Kanga about when she can see her mum and dad. Roo doesn't understand why she wants to see her mum and dad, as they have been horrible to her. Kanga tells Roo that although they have done wrong they were trying to do their best to bring up Joey, and they didn't know any different because that was the way they were treated when they were children. Joey still loves them and it is important that she is allowed to stay in touch with them. Roo went to bed still feeling puzzled but had a little idea about it.

Over time Joey began to settle in more and more and accepted the fact that she would never be allowed to live with her mum and dad. Sometimes Joey would get angry and upset but most of the time she was happy having Kanga and Roo as her family and still visiting her mum and dad.

I wrote this next story for a teenager who liked the science fiction television series *Stargate*. This story addresses the issue of expressing emotion. Like the android this teenager did not want to have feelings. The story aimed to help her think about the possibility that strength could come out of painful emotions.

In the eye of the storm

Sam and Jack stepped through the Stargate onto a world that they had not seen before. They looked around curiously but found nothing remarkable. The sun shone brightly in the sky and the landscape was green and lush. They had been sent out on a reconnaissance mission to assess the possibility of sharing technology with the inhabitants. It was also a time for the two of them to spend some time together. Time to come to terms with feelings for each other that they couldn't share or talk about.

They walked forward tentatively but had not got more than 200 metres when a woman appeared as if from nowhere. She walked towards them rapidly. From a distance she didn't look any different from the human women they had left behind on the other side of the Stargate, but as she got closer they did have an uneasy feeling that there was something different about her. Her eyes had little expression, it was hard to see what she was thinking, and her face was almost mask-like. Sam and Jack felt uneasy. They didn't really know what to expect. However, the introductions passed smoothly. The stranger, whose name was Trance, accepted their presence on the planet without fuss and they were soon following her to a nearby city. Here they were greeted like minor celebrities and they found little time to talk to each other as they were shown around the city.

In many ways the level of technology was not dissimilar to Earth except for one interesting aspect. The planet had a hostile climate for six months of the year. During this winter the inhabitants all lived underground. A team of mechanics worked all year round maintaining an environment that could sustain the population through the worst of the season. Trance was one of the mechanics. Jack paid particular interest to this. Here was a possibility for sharing technology that might be to Earth's advantage. He followed Trance around as she went about her duties. Jack admired her calm efficiency and ability to cope with minor crises without getting ruffled. She worked closely with a man called Brix and the two appeared a competent and efficient team. Jack spent the next two weeks in the company of these two. He enjoyed their company. He enjoyed his time with Sam, but it was always a strain. He had to work hard to keep his feelings hidden. The ironic thing was that he knew she was doing the same. They had agreed long ago that working in the same team meant that they shouldn't have a relationship, but it was difficult to maintain this feeling when working in such life and death situations. Jack envied Trance and Brix's easy relationship. They could clearly depend on each other but there was no underlying tension.

At the end of the two weeks Sam and Jack went back through the Stargate to report their findings. They felt sad to be leaving the planet, as their stay here had been a welcome change from the usual danger and high drama. They eagerly looked forward to returning. They didn't have long to wait. General Hammond was excited by the possibility of technology exchange and soon had a negotiation team ready.

As soon as Sam and Jack stepped through the Stargate they knew things had changed. The climate was very different. Storms were clearly brewing and there was a feeling of static in the air. The winter had arrived earlier than expected. Fearing a worsening in the climate at any moment the team hurried to the nearby city. When they arrived the sense of panic was palpable. Sam and Jack didn't wait to be asked. They fell in with the teams, helping out where they could. As they took orders from the men co-ordinating the teams they gathered that the early arrival of the storm had caught everyone off guard. The first field generator, which was meant to control the impact of the storm, had overloaded. As it failed, the other generators had to cope with the force of the storm. Now each was failing in turn under the excessive load. If this increasing failure was not arrested then the storm would arrive in the city and they would all perish.

Sam and Jack worked alongside Trance and Brix for 18 hours. It looked as if they were winning. Parts of the town were now made safe and they were thinking about taking a break. Jack glanced over at Sam. Her hair was matted, and her face was covered in grime. Fleetingly Jack felt an ache of sadness that she would never be more than a friend. It was an ache that was suppressed with a speed that only comes from practice. He stepped back and fell in line with Trance. Brix and Sam followed closely behind. They had not gone far when there was a huge explosion behind them. They sprinted for the door but it was touch and go as the blast from the explosion hurtled towards them. With relief Jack threw himself through the door, Trance just behind him. Many hands reached out and grabbed them. In the confusion Jack could see no sign of Brix or Sam. A team of fire fighters worked furiously to contain the fires but it was another 20 minutes before all was under control. During that time and despite his protestations Jack found himself in the infirmary.

Jack suffered the medical examination with an impatience born of worry and dread. Finally he was allowed to go. He looked around the infirmary for Sam but could find no sign of her. He rushed back to the maintenance area. Scanning the mass of people he finally spotted Trance calmly working at a control panel. Jack called to her asking her where Sam and Brix were. Trance looked at him coolly and informed him that they had been trapped in the control room when the explosion occurred. It was unlikely that they had survived. Jack looked at her in horror but Trance had returned to her task unmoved by the news she had just imparted. Anger welled up in Jack. He grabbed Trance and wheeled her around.

'What are you doing,' he shouted. 'We need to go and look for them.'

Trance stared at him with her calm, impassive gaze. 'We would be of no use; there are people working to make the room safe and then they will go in. It is imperative that we get this system going.'

'Don't you care? How the hell can you be so calm?' Jack shouted. 'Brix is in there.'

'It is highly likely that Brix will not survive,' replied Trance. 'I can do nothing about this.'

Jack's anger dissipated as his bewilderment increased. 'How can you be so unfeeling? You have just lost your colleague and friend?'

'A new colleague will be assigned to me.'

'Don't you feel anything?' asked Jack.

'No, I am not programmed to feel. It is not necessary in my job.'

Realization hit him like cold ice down his spine. She was an android. Now her difference from them made sense. 'Are you all androids?' queried Jack.

'No, only half of the population. There was such loss during the storms 50 years ago androids were necessary to ensure the survivors could rebuild.'

Jack turned away. 'I'm not so ready to give up on Sam. I'm going down there.'

Twenty minutes later Jack was sitting wearily outside of the door. Despite his best efforts he had not been allowed through the door to look for Sam. He sat disconsolately looking at the floor when Trance came up with a cup of tea in her hand.

'I think you may require sustenance,' she said as she handed the tea to Jack. Jack cradled the cup in his hand as Trance sat down beside him. Jack looked at her.

'I can't imagine what it is like not to feel anything in a situation like this.'

'I think maybe I am in a good position,' replied Trance. 'Looking at you, feelings are very painful. Maybe I am better without them. If I don't feel then I won't hurt.'

At that moment the doors were finally opened and the rescue team entered the room where the explosion had occurred. Jack rushed past them scanning for Sam even before he entered the room. It was difficult to see anything through the smoke and dust. Many dead bodies were carried out past him as he continued his hunt. There did not appear to be any survivors. Hope was dying within Jack but he refused to give up. They had been in tight spots before and had always managed to get out of them. He looked across to the side of the room and noticed an alcove blocked by falling masonry. He walked over to it and peered through. He spotted her lying at the side, her arm flung over Brix. He could not see if she was breathing. He felt Trance come up behind him as he began moving the concrete out of the way. Trance pointed to the ceiling where a slab of concrete could fall at any moment. Urgently they manhandled the last beam away and Jack pushed his way through. They had no time to assess their condition. Jack pulled Sam clear as Trance lifted Brix out of the rubble.

They were back in the infirmary again, but this time Jack felt no resentment. He smiled over at Sam as the nurse adjusted the bandage she had wound around her head.

'Not a pretty sight,' Sam said weakly.

'It looks good from where I am sitting,' laughed Jack.

Brix and Trance stood nearby. 'Thank you, Sam. It was your quick thinking that saved us,' said Brix. 'If we had carried on heading for the door we would have been caught in the main blast. Pulling us into the alcove protected us from the worst of it.'

A week later and all was under control again. The storms had abated at least for now and some time for repairs had been welcomed. With relief Sam and Jack headed towards the Stargate. Trance accompanied them. As they prepared to leave, Jack looked across and saw emotion clearly registering in Trance's face.

'I am feeling sad that you are going,' she explained to Jack.

'Hey, I thought you were the girl who didn't feel anything.'

'I asked to be programmed to feel emotion. Observing you I think I may function better with feelings. I could see the pain you were feeling but also the strength that it gave you. Without those feelings I don't know that you would have been strong enough to rescue Sam.'

'He always finds a way,' smiled Sam.

As they neared the Stargate Sam and Jack touched hands very briefly and stepped through.

15

Providing Structure and Supervision

The home and the family atmosphere provide a structure for children. This structure influences how children use the support available within the family and how they manage when they leave the family either to go to school or to play. Alongside structure comes supervision (see Figure 15.1). Providing the appropriate amount of supervision for children living in foster and adoptive homes can present a challenge. It is not uncommon for children to need a greater

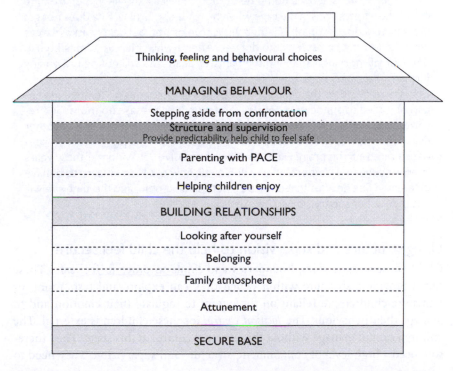

Figure 15.1 Structure and supervision (Adapted from 'The House Model of Parenting' in Golding et al. (2006). Copyright © John Wiley & Sons Ltd. Reproduced with kind permission.)

degree of supervision than might be expected. This is because they don't have emotional maturity to match their chronological age. Whilst the children might benefit from increased supervision this can also be resisted. School children, in particular, are observing the children around them, and feeling unfairly treated if they do not have the same privileges of freedom. For teens the conflict between growing up and learning to be independent, and the need for continuing supervision and support, can be an even greater challenge.

> Rita and Frank wonder if Marcus might benefit from a pet. They hope that this will be another way that they can help him to develop empathy, furthering his understanding of feelings, and ability to consider the needs of others. Marcus is very excited about this and goes with them to choose a hamster. For a few weeks all goes well. Marcus enjoys playing with the hamster and is careful to make sure it has enough food and water each day. Rita and Frank begin to relax and spend less time supervising him.
>
> One morning as he is about to go to school Rita asks if he has checked the hamster. Marcus looks at her a bit strangely but says he has. Later that morning, remembering the look he had given her she goes to check herself. She finds the cage empty, and after some searching finds the hamster, dead and hidden at the back of a drawer.
>
> When Marcus arrives home he at first denies all knowledge of this. He claims the hamster was in the cage when he left that morning. Rita does not get drawn into a discussion of whether this is true or not, but calmly asks Marcus when he put the hamster in the drawer. After a while Marcus admits he had done it that morning. He found the hamster dead, and will not be drawn any further.
>
> Rita remembers the difficulty Marcus had in a previous placement. He apparently tried to suffocate a pet dog. She wonders but says no more. She resolves to talk to her social worker about this. Can his experience of his brother dying when he was so little still be leaving its mark? How deeply is his early experience wired into his brain? Has this led to compulsive behaviours all these years later? And the most important question of all: how can Marcus learn to behave differently? She decides that it will be a pet fish next time, and this time she will not reduce her supervision so quickly.

Using structure and supervision to help the child feel secure

Children need clear rules, boundaries and limits in order to feel safe. These limits provide a structure within which they can explore and test. Young or immature children are reliant on the parent to regulate their emotion and to manage their behaviour. The *locus of control* for these children is external. The children cannot manage without this external control at this stage. They therefore need a high level of containment, structure and supervision. They need to

know what to expect in a given situation. They need to understand the rul[
they need practice to follow these.

The younger or more emotionally immature children need these limits very explicitly stated and managed. As they mature, the controls become internalized. Children are then better able to manage their emotion and their behaviour. They are less dependent on the parent for providing them with a structure within which they can behave. The *locus of control* is now internal. At this stage children need less supervision and structure. At times of increased stress however they may again need the additional support that supervision and structure can provide.

When you need to provide external control it is important that you do this with a high level of *empathy*. The additional supervision and structure is not a punishment because of bad behaviour. Rather it is a support because the child is not yet ready to manage successfully without the structure and supervision you are providing. It is important to convey this to the child and to accept and empathize with the feelings this generates.

Hughes

What is an appropriate level of supervision for the child?

When children are having trouble following rules this is a sign that they need closer supervision and limitations put on their activities. If children are having trouble behaving appropriately and if the consequences are piling up it is likely that they are not getting sufficient structure and supervision. They need closer supervision and clearer limits.

This may mean providing your child with a higher level of structure through your physical presence. You structure his day so that you can keep a close eye on him. If you are cooking tea, he can sit at the table nearby playing, reading or engaging in an activity of choice; if you need to do a job around the house he might help you. The extra time gained by having two of you working on the task can then be used to do something enjoyable together. This high level of supervision will help your child to feel safe. As he begins to feel a greater sense of safety with you he will begin to trust that you can take care of him. Often this can result in a reduced need to be hyper-vigilant; your child does not have to be concerned with whether he is safe or not, as you are there to take care of him. This in turn fosters confidence in exploration and play. Much as a young child does he will become absorbed in his own thing, whilst checking back with you from time to time.

This degree of structure and supervision is therefore proactive, ensuring that your child's emotional needs for security are being met, rather than being a reactive response to naughty or difficult behaviour. Your child will experience your supervision as loving, and thus that he is loveable, rather than as an indicator that he is naughty and intrinsically bad. In time, and with developing maturity, this high level of supervision can gradually be reduced. Be careful however not to give too much freedom and too many choices too soon. It is better to gradually ease up on the supervision. If your child struggles with a small increase in freedom you will be able to tighten up again relatively easily.

The level of supervision that children are provided with therefore needs to match their emotional maturity. It is no good providing children with the degree of supervision that is acceptable for their age if they cannot manage at this level. Hoping your child will live up to these expectations will lead to difficulties. Instead you need to provide a level of supervision within which your child can cope and then gradually support him to manage with less supervision. For example, if your child is constantly in trouble when playing out in the neighbourhood this indicates that he is not coping with this level of freedom. Opportunities to play with friends whilst you keep a discreet but watchful eye on things can assist him to problem-solve or deal with confrontation as needed. Alternatively your child may need shorter spells out with regular checking back with you.

It can be difficult to impose this level of structure and supervision when a child is either used to more freedom or is expecting to be allowed to do what same-age peers are doing. For older children behavioural contracts can provide them with clarity about what is expected from them and help them to see how they can earn more freedom in the future. It can also be helpful for these rules to be provided jointly by parents or together with the social worker to avoid a child feeling that one parent is 'just mean'. It is not unusual to see a child quickly relax under this level of supervision, provided alongside a high degree of *empathy* and warmth. The child experiences the safety of a caring relationship, perhaps for the first time.

Supervision needs to be flexible, in line with how the child is coping at the time. Thus at times of relaxation and low stress the child will manage better and will respond to being allowed to do a little more. When experiencing increased stress however it is likely that the child will need an increase in supervision and support in order to cope. Supervision and support can therefore be regulated in accordance to the child's needs at the time, within the context of their overall developmental maturity, rather than their chronological age.

Zoë, Catherine, Marcus and Luke all have differing needs for structure and supervision.

Catherine has a tendency to appear more mature than she actually is. She wants to be self-reliant and likes to do things for herself. She is uncomfortable with intimate family relationships and has used her self-reliance as a way to keep Jenny and Martin at a distance. Catherine needs structure and supervision to keep her safe. She thinks that she will be able to cope, and tends to get into situations that she isn't yet able to manage. Thus she will miss the school bus and go into town with her friends instead. Unfortunately the day they all left her there she didn't know how to get home. She ended up getting a lift with a stranger with no idea of how vulnerable she was. For Catherine the structure and supervision is also a means to help her receive help and care from parents. Uncomfortable with nurture, she can experience a relationship within which she can start to be more believing that parents will not hurt her if she lets them care.

Both Zoë and Marcus have an external locus of control through much of their childhood. They tend to believe that things happen for reasons outside of themselves and it is for this reason that they are so poor at taking responsibility for their behaviour. Zoë and Marcus need a lot of structure and supervision. Zoë thrives with the structure that Jenny and Martin provide for her. This reduces her level of stress and she is able to start to develop a relationship with them, from which she could learn about her behaviour and its consequences. Throughout her childhood Zoë is gradually learning to understand and manage her feelings. Her behaviour is improving alongside this developing capacity for emotional regulation and increased ability to think about herself and her effect on others. Zoë has been able to cope with less supervision and structure as she approaches her teenage years.

Marcus's early experience was even more damaging to him than Zoë's was for her. He too has benefited from a very predictable and structured environment, but hasn't been able to make as good progress as Zoë. As a teenager he still needs a lot of structure and supervision. This is hard for him, as he sees his peers being allowed to do more than he can do. He gets very angry, and continues to show defiance and non-compliance at times. However, he too has benefited from the clear, consistent and empathic parenting that Rita and Frank have provided. His need to control them has reduced and he is now able to engage in a reciprocal relationship within which they can engage in activities that they all enjoy.

As Luke has matured he has continued to experience difficulty in maintaining meaningful relationships. He will use a relationship as a means to an end, but does not see the usefulness of relationships beyond this. For example, he can be very compliant and loving towards Jackie when he wants something from her, but once achieved this is not sustained. Relationships provide a social structure for children. Children learn what is socially appropriate from others. They want to fit in with the social rules in order to strengthen the relationship. With only superficial relationships, Luke struggles to learn or follow socially acceptable behaviour. With poorly developed perspective-taking skills he has also struggled to develop empathy for others. Again his difficulty learning within relationships means that he struggles to understand how others think or feel. Luke does not cope well in a range of situations. He finds it difficult initiating interactions and responds poorly to any overtures by others; interpersonal conflict is therefore high and Luke is quick to anger.

His poor concentration, high levels of activity and a degree of learning difficulties increase Luke's difficulty in learning from experience. This means that he experiences high levels of stress even in typical environments such as school. For these reasons Luke continues to need a highly structured environment with routine, familiarity and high levels of supervision. He copes poorly with sudden changes of plan and even finds normal transitions such as moving between home and school or the change from term time to holiday time difficult.

In trying to get the right level of supervision in place for your child you need to take into account both his chronological age, and therefore what you expect him to be able to do, and his emotional age and what he can actually manage. It can be helpful to think of this as moving from A to B (see Figure 15.2). A is where the child is right now. B is where the parent expects the child to be either because of his age or because of what he has done previously. If A and B are different it is no good treating the child as if he is at B. This will lead to failure. The parent needs to meet the child at A and gradually help him move towards B. In this way the parent is providing *emotional scaffolding*, supporting the child to increase his abilities at his own pace.

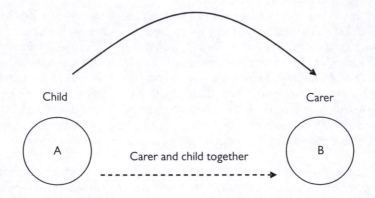

Figure 15.2 Parenting matched to the needs of the child

16

Managing Confrontation and Coercive Interactions

Nothing is more likely to interfere with the family atmosphere and to make it more difficult to maintain *empathy* than when the child is behaving in a confrontational manner (see Figure 16.1). The child seems determined to get you into an argument or to provoke you to anger. Maintaining your calm at this time can be a super-human effort.

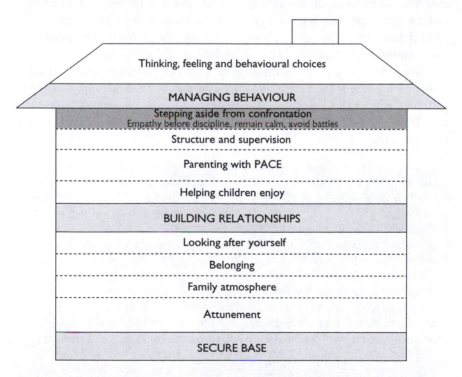

Figure 16.1 Managing confrontation (Adapted from 'The House Model of Parenting' in Golding et al. (2006). Copyright © John Wiley & Sons Ltd. Reproduced with kind permission.)

...w to step aside from confrontation

A child will be confrontational for a number of reasons.

- It helps the frightened child to feel in control, thus increasing her feelings of safety and security.

- The confrontation is an effective way of controlling the degree of attention received from the parent. The child might want to keep the parent involved and attending to her. Alternatively she might want to get some distance into the relationship.

- It helps the child displace blame and thus she avoids feeling overwhelmed with *shame* about not being good enough.

Confrontation represents a *coercive* pattern of relating to others. The child coerces the adult into maintaining attention on to her or becoming distant from her.

When children are being confrontational they will feel emotionally aroused. Their behaviour is likely to be escalating into an increasingly angry, demanding style of relating to the adults.

Whilst it may not feel like it, you do have a choice in the face of this behaviour. You can either match the pattern of behaviour, also becoming aroused and increasingly angry. This is likely to increase the confrontational behaviour your child is displaying. Alternatively you can remain calm, avoid being pulled into the confrontation, and allow her to gradually calm down in turn.

When two people are relating, their emotional patterns will gradually match each other. If the parent becomes angry then an escalating, reciprocal pattern of angry behaviour occurs. If however the parent maintains a calm emotional tone the child will calm down as well; angry behaviour de-escalates rather than escalates.

Jenny is confused by Catherine's behaviour. She can be very helpful and kind, but this alternates with days when she is much more moody and difficult. She slams doors, ignores any requests made of her and is generally difficult and unco-operative. The most difficult aspect of Catherine's behaviour at these times is when she is provocative towards Jenny. She appears to want to get into an argument with her. She will deliberately ignore a call for tea, or she will leave her bedroom in a mess. She might goad Zoë until she gets upset. All of these behaviours are ones that Jenny finds particularly difficult to tolerate. She finds herself pulled into arguments as she tries to get Catherine to comply with her expectations. The angrier Jenny gets, the more defiant and insolent Catherine is. Her 'so what' attitude just notches up the tension between them even more, and Jenny, in a final attempt to maintain some control, will punish Catherine by 'grounding' her. Catherine will angrily protest, but also appears calmer and less provocative following these grounding episodes. Jenny is concerned though because Catherine is spending little time going out with friends and a lot of time in her bedroom. She also doesn't like how easily Catherine makes her feel angry.

Jenny talks it over with Martin. Together they think through how Jenny might respond differently. She decides that she will remain calm, walking away if she starts to feel angry, rather than becoming involved in an increasingly angry dialogue. She will also provide clear and simple consequences for the behaviour. She hopes that by remaining calm and clear Catherine's provocations will reduce. Finally she will no longer use 'grounding' as a consequence. It is important that Catherine goes out and mixes with her school friends.

For two weeks following this resolve all is calm. Catherine has been difficult once or twice but nothing that Jenny can't manage. When Catherine didn't come down to dinner Jenny calmly told her that dinner would be available for ten more minutes; after that she can make herself a cheese sandwich if she is hungry. When Catherine left wet towels lying around the bathroom Jenny sympathized with her because she wouldn't be able to watch the TV programme she was interested in, as the bathroom needed tidying. Generally Catherine coped with these consequences, albeit moodily and with a few slammed doors that Jenny ignored. However, the following week Catherine tests out this new calm approach almost to the limit.

The week begins well. Catherine is going to a school disco on the Friday. Jenny feels it will be good for her to have something new to wear so she picks her up from school and they go shopping. Catherine enjoys trying on a few different outfits and is pleased with the new clothes she chooses.

By the middle of the week however Catherine is becoming provocative again. She picks fights with Zoë, refuses to do as asked and is deliberately late for school, throwing the morning routine into chaos. Jenny remains calm and clear with Catherine, but her behaviour escalates. She chooses behaviour that she knows will make Jenny angry. She leaves taps running in the bathroom, causing a small flood. Jenny finds used sanitary towels lying around her bedroom. She is managing to remain calm but is beginning to run out of ideas for consequences.

On Friday Catherine comes home from school in a difficult mood. She is rude and unco-operative; Jenny finds it very hard to stay calm. In an attempt to maintain her own equilibrium she says to Catherine, 'I can see you have had a difficult day today, Catherine. I'm sorry you are feeling so uptight but I am starting to feel cross. I want you to go to your bedroom until it is time to get ready to go out.' Catherine glares at her and heads upstairs, shouting that she doesn't care if Jenny does stop her going out. This puzzles Jenny, as she said nothing about not going out. She leaves Catherine for a while whilst she makes Zoë some tea. About half an hour before her friends are due to call she goes up to find Catherine lying on her bed still wearing her school uniform.

'Why haven't you changed, Catherine? It will soon be time to go.'

'I'm not going,' Catherine says. 'I've been horrid to you.'

'Yes you have,' Jenny agrees, 'and I will think with you about this tomorrow. Tonight I want you to go and enjoy yourself.'

Catherine looks at her, dumbfounded. 'Why aren't you going to ground me?' she asks Jenny.

Jenny sits on Catherine's bed. 'I thought you were looking forward to the disco?'

'Yes, I suppose.' Catherine doesn't sound very certain.

'Is something worrying you?'

'No, it's just, well I don't think I will go after all.'

Jenny now realizes why Catherine has been so difficult. 'I guess you are feeling anxious about the disco. I didn't realize how you were feeling.'

Catherine acknowledges this and shares her concerns that she will just be left sitting at the edge whilst everyone else has a good time. Jenny wonders how often Catherine's provocative behaviour covers up her fears and anxieties. Getting angry had prevented Jenny getting anywhere near to understanding this complex young girl who is not able to acknowledge how she feels straightforwardly. She talks with her some more, empathizing with her fears. Catherine decides that she will go but only if Martin promises to come and get her after half an hour. Martin duly turns up to collect her but it is a further half an hour before he can extricate her from her friends. She comes home smiling and enjoys telling Jenny and Martin about it as they drink a cup of drinking chocolate together.

Coercive patterns

Children may use confrontation coercively to keep parents engaged with them. These behaviours feel highly manipulative as the children display tantrums, cry, whine, yell or command the parents, often maintaining this behaviour until they get what they want. This coercive pattern of interaction is typical in toddlerhood. At this age children find it difficult to wait; they want what they want when they want it. If their desires are thwarted they quickly become frustrated and will often hit out. Children have not yet developed good language skills and therefore they communicate non-verbally. Their behaviour demonstrates how they are feeling.

As children mature they are more capable of verbally expressing how they feel and negotiating with parents to get their needs met. Older children have developed a range of social skills that help them to express their wishes. Thus coercive interactions typically reduce as children get older.

When children experience parenting that is unpredictable and inconsistent they do not develop or learn to trust their verbal skills as a means of getting their needs met. Neither do they trust their parents to be there when they need them. They fear that if they do not maintain the attention of their parents they will be ignored when they need them most. These children continue to get quickly frustrated when things don't go their way. They don't learn to tolerate delays in getting what they want. As we explored in Part 1 these children therefore retain the earlier coercive patterns of interaction as part of *ambivalent-resistant* patterns of relating to their attachment figures. These children are highly anxious. ' experience high levels of frustration and anger, but they also feel strong n___ for comfort which they are not able to communicate directly.

Frustration and anger are communicated via displays of threatening or aggressive behaviour, whilst fear, anxiety and the need for comfort are communicated via displays of compliance and appeasement. Thus expressions of anger and vulnerability are alternated in order to manipulate the parents' behaviour. This is a good strategy for a child to use with a parent who is inconsistent and unpredictable because it coerces him into more predictable responses and importantly ensures that he continues to attend to the child. When these children move into foster or adoptive homes they expect the same response from these parents as they experienced with their birth parents and therefore they maintain these ways of interacting with them.

This behaviour presents the parents with a problem. As long as they try to placate or meet the child's demands, the child will remain angry. ('I want this', 'I don't want it', 'I want that'). If the parents become angry the child changes from being demanding to being compliant and vulnerable. As the parents again change, to adapt to the child, anger is displayed once more. This alternating behaviour from the child maintains the adults' attention and forces them to behave in a predictable way. Effectively the parents are caught in a trap.

If the parents ignore the children's constant tantruming or whining, the children have to do more to attract attention. Typically the children will then become more provocative. They might do exactly what their parents have told them not to do or the very thing that they know the parents will be cross about. As the parents react they are drawn back into the coercive interaction. As the parents try to ignore this behaviour the children will again escalate their behaviour, this time into risk-taking behaviour. The children 'play' with danger to make certain that their parents are attending to them.

How can coercive interactions be avoided?

The development of this behaviour has arisen because the children have found that 'parents' are inconsistent, unpredictable or rejecting. They are not certain when the parents will meet their needs and so they become demanding and controlling. They want what they want now and they cannot tolerate the frustration of not getting it. The children need help to adapt to a more predictable experience of parenting so that they can learn to tolerate frustration and to wait to have their needs met. The parents need to adopt a consistent and calm way of managing the children's behaviour, which steps aside from the coercive interactions, without ignoring the children's need for attention. They need to hold firm to this through an initial escalation of difficult behaviour. Additionally the parents need to provide the children with an experience of nurturing care within which they can learn to let the parents help them to manage the strong negative emotions that they experience.

There is a range of parenting strategies that you can try in order to avoid being drawn into confrontational behaviour. The key to all of these is maintaining a calm, empathic stance:

- Provide consistent and predictable parenting with clear routines and structure. As your child learns to trust in the predictability she will gradually learn to trust in your availability and her need to coerce you into attending will reduce.

- You control the emotional rhythm of the house and not your child. This means that you need to stay calm and not join your child in an escalating pattern of angry behaviour. If you stay calm she is more likely to calm down as well. If you become angry or irritated this is likely to escalate the feelings of anger in both of you.

- One way of avoiding being drawn into angry confrontations is by using consequences. Calmly tell your child what consequences will occur and then walk away. Parents find that 'If–Then' and 'When–Then' statements can be very helpful, for example:

'*If* you jump on the settee *then* the television will be turned off.'

'*When* you pick up the toys *then* we will go out to the park.'

If your child does not comply you do not need to enter the battle. Just make sure that you follow through with the consequence. Your child will gradually learn that what you say does happen.

- Be positive when giving your child commands or instructions. It helps to avoid words like 'no' or 'don't'. These often trigger angry behaviour. For example, instead of saying 'Don't jump on the settee' try saying 'Let me see both feet on the carpet.'

- The use of rewards and praise can help children to learn improved behaviour. Younger children enjoy star charts and other visual ways of showing the reward that has been earned. Older children can enjoy working for points that can be traded for treats and privileges. Rewards and praise work best when they are descriptive and specific. Explain to your child exactly what you want her to do in order to earn a reward. It is important to be clear about the behaviour that is being praised. Younger children need immediate rewards and praise. Older children may be comfortable waiting for rewards.

- Children who engage in coercive interactions often have a negative *self-esteem*. They are so used to being 'naughty' that they start to believe that they are bad children. The strategies described above will be helpful as they focus attention on helping children to change their behaviour and provide them with help to behave in ways that will be approved of. Rewards and praise can especially help children to feel that they are valued. In addition finding activities that help your child experience success and making sure that she has positive time with you each day will build on these feelings.

- A child who has a strong motivation to feel in control needs help to learn to trust and rely on you. You can respect your child's need to feel in control. Provide boundaries, limits and protection but within these let your child exercise some control. In this way she can learn to rely both on self and on others.

- Another way to help your child feel that she is loved and valued is to spend time with her following difficult episodes. This is difficult because you will probably be feeling cross and worn out by then; but time spent comforting and reassuring your child, even before dealing with the aftermath of the behaviour, can provide her with positive messages that you do care and want to support her.

- These children often lack an experience of a fun or a nurturing relationship with previous parents. You may need to provide this; often a child will be helped if parented as if they were younger. Caroline Archer and Christine Gordon (2006) recommend times for family cradling when children are held and cuddled. This can be an important way of helping them to feel nurtured. Often children will also enjoy play and games that revolve around the relationship.

Children, like us all, are creatures of habit. Patterns of behaviour do not change easily, and children will work very hard to push parents into behaving in line with their expectations. This means that you may find the initial response from your child is a worsening of behaviour. You are not responding as she expected or anticipated and so she tries harder to push you back into the coercive patterns. You will need to hold firm through this escalation of behaviour until your child begins to dare to try out a different way of being with you. It is also important not to be discouraged if your child, when making good progress, appears to return to a former way of behaving. Often this occurs when a child is feeling an extra degree of stress; if you can reduce the stress you will see the more mature behaviour re-emerging.

As your child begins to respond to the increased consistency and predictability and as she is learning to calm down within the relaxed relationship you are providing you will gradually be able to decrease the amount of supervision you need to provide. Be careful not to move too fast at this stage; it is easier to ease off a bit more than to have to tighten up again. Your child might also be helped to learn some new skills at this time that can further increase their ability to manage with less supervision and external control.

Marcus is 14 years old and Rita and Frank are going through a difficult patch; they begin to disagree on how to parent Marcus. Rita is discouraged with the progress Marcus is making and wonders again whether she is the right person to be parenting him. Frank on the other hand is feeling that his relationship with Marcus has never been better. Marcus, sensing this discord, is becoming anxious. As usual in such a situation he takes control, playing on Rita's insecurity by becoming more defiant and unco-operative with her. Alongside this he becomes more charming with Frank as if to accentuate the difference between them. This type of behaviour, sometimes called 'splitting', helps Marcus to feel a sense of power. This helps to reduce his feelings of anxiety and powerlessness.

The difficulties for Rita come to a head one day whilst Marcus is excluded from school. Marcus wants to watch TV all day; Rita on the other hand is determined that he will do some schoolwork during school hours. Marcus ignores all her attempts to engage him and in open defiance continues to sit in front of the TV. Rita is becoming more and more exasperated. Concerned that her feelings will show, she leaves Marcus to it and retreats into the kitchen. She tries to phone the social worker for some advice. He is not there and so she leaves him a message. Feeling a bit stronger she again goes in to tackle Marcus. This time Marcus storms out of the room; he becomes very angry, threatening Rita. Unable to take any more Rita shouts back; she tells Marcus what a selfish, ungrateful boy he is and she doesn't know why she bothers with him. Marcus is taken aback by this unusual display of anger from Rita. He quietly goes into the other room and turns the television off. Rita is now feeling guilty for shouting at Marcus; she doesn't mention the schoolwork again and instead goes upstairs to tidy up.

Marcus is now confused and uncertain. Feeling anxious his level of arousal builds up. He follows Rita upstairs and starts to goad her. As Rita feels herself getting angry again she feels like she is a string puppet with Marcus pulling all the strings. Fortunately for her, at that moment, Frank gets home. With Frank around, Marcus settles down and Rita is able to calm herself. She talks over the day's events with Frank who is concerned at how upset she is. They both agree that they need more time to talk together, and Frank resolves to be more supportive to her when Marcus is being difficult. Rita wants to avoid being pulled into these confrontational interactions with Marcus in the future, and she needs Frank's help to do this. Marcus, sensing their renewed partnership, comes in to the kitchen and offers to make them a cup of tea. Rita and Frank look at each other and laugh.

When children begin to reduce the coercive interactions that they are engaged in they also become better able to think. Developing abilities to think, plan and problem-solve further reduces their reliance on the emotionally driven *coercive behaviours*.

Helping children develop problem-solving abilities

The ability to problem-solve is a *cognitive* skill that develops throughout childhood. It involves an ability:

- to decide on a goal
- to plan how to reach this goal
- to evaluate the consequences of different plans.

Problem-solving therefore depends on many abilities that develop during childhood. The child or young person needs to be able to think flexibly, to understand cause and effect, to be able to think from different perspectives, and to be able to inhibit *impulsive* action.

Children who have impoverished experience of early relationships often struggle to develop such abilities. Poorly developed thinking abilities are therefore not uncommon, often more typical of a younger child. Children need help to develop problem-solving skills. They need help to think about a problem, to generate solutions to the problem and to decide which solutions are most likely to be effective.

Define problem	What is the problem?
Brainstorm solutions	What are the potential solutions to the problem?
	What are the potential consequences to the problem?
Evaluate consequences	What is likely to be the best solution?
Implement plan	How can I put the plan into action?
Evaluate plan	Is my solution working?
Amend plan	What might work better?

To help children develop problem-solving abilities it is important to provide lots of examples that they can learn from. Get into the habit of modelling problem-solving. Be explicit about your own problem-solving processes; explain to your child how you are thinking about a problem and coming up with a solution. You can then help your child to practise problem-solving. Think of a goal and help her to think about different ways to reach the goal. You might use role-play, stories and puppets to help her to find a solution.

When your child has a real-life problem encourage her to put this practice into use. The temptation is to offer solutions to children, but it can be more helpful to guide them through the problem-solving process. Support your child to try out the solution even if it is not the one that you would have chosen. Help her to evaluate how successful the solution has been.

You can also help your child to notice the problem-solving that is going on around her. Television, stories and real-life situations can provide opportunities to see how other people solve problems.

Luke has very poor problem-solving abilities. He tends to react to situations rather than thinking through the consequences. His impulsivity in particular gets in the way of planned action. In his teenage years this is becoming even more of a problem. The learning and emotional difficulties that Luke experiences means that he stands out in his peer group. As he grows older the gap between himself and his peers has widened. Luke finds this difficult to understand. He wants to do the same things that the other children are doing, and to be allowed the same degree of freedom, but his vulnerability makes it difficult for Jackie to allow this.

Difficulties in problem-solving mean that Luke finds it difficult to adapt to circumstances that have not been rehearsed; he is easily led by the suggestions of the other children and he is not able to stop and think before doing. Luke's very neglectful early experience has meant that he has certain cognitive deficits that contribute to a lack of problem-solving. He has a very poor understanding of cause and effect. He therefore finds it difficult to foresee consequences; or to understand how what he is doing can link to things that happen around him. He also finds it difficult to generalize learning. He can be taught to cross the road safely outside his home, for example, but also needs to be taught how to do this outside school. He does not apply what he has learnt in one setting to a similar but different setting.

One day Jackie allows Luke to go to the cinema with a friend, Robert. She is concerned about this but he has been asking and asking to be allowed to do something unsupervised by her. She carefully plans this, dropping him off at the cinema and arranging to pick him up again as soon as the film finishes.

Unfortunately part way through the film Robert becomes bored and decides to leave early. This was an eventuality that had not been considered. Not wanting to stay by himself Luke follows him. Robert suggests going to the park and Luke willingly goes along. He does not think about contacting Jackie, and cannot envisage how worried she will be when he doesn't come out of the cinema.

As they are wandering through the park a man approaches them, and asks them if they want an ice-cream. Robert starts to feel uncomfortable; he urges his friend on. Luke however is tempted. He likes ice-cream and is willing to follow the man. He has been taught about strangers and he knows that he must not go with anyone he doesn't know when walking home from school but now he is in the park. Fortunately for Luke at that moment a neighbour sees him and is suspicious. She comes over and the man makes a hasty retreat. She asks Luke where Jackie is and he tells her she is picking him up from the cinema. They walk back to the cinema together much to the relief of a frantic Jackie.

Jackie tries to help Luke develop problem-solving skills through the use of games, stories and explicit teaching, but Luke is likely to remain vulnerable and will need a continuing high level of supervision.

17

Thinking, Feeling and Behavioural Choices

Rewards, praise and logical consequences can all be helpful in supporting children to make good behavioural choices. The effectiveness of these approaches can be increased by understanding the ways that thinking, feeling and behaving link together (see Figure 17.1). Helping the child to improve his behaviour will be aided if you know what thoughts and feelings are influencing it.

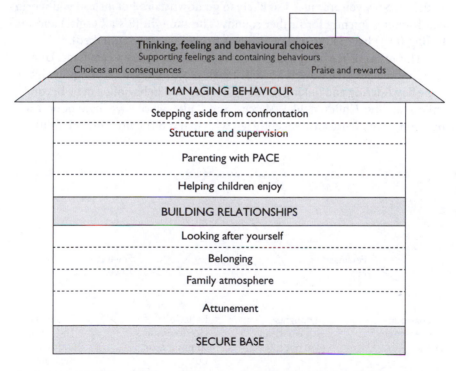

Figure 17.1 Thinking, feeling and behavioural choices (Adapted from 'The House Model of Parenting' in Golding et al. *(2006). Copyright © John Wiley & Sons Ltd. Reproduced with kind permission.)*

Thinking, feeling and behaving

Thinking, feeling and behaving are connected. Behaviours are determined not by the situation per se but by the appraisal the person makes and the feelings aroused by the situation. How the person thinks and feels determines how they behave. This in turn is influenced by early childhood experiences leading to the development of core beliefs and habitual ways of feeling. Thus children who experience early abuse and subsequent placement with foster parents may develop core beliefs that they are unloveable with the related assumption that if they get close to a parent they will be rejected. The experience of getting close to the parent triggers feelings of fear and anxiety. Their subsequent behaviour can be understood as a strategy to ensure that they do not get close.

To understand this link between thinking, feeling and behaviour imagine a simple event as in Figure 17.2. You are upstairs in bed when you hear a loud crash downstairs. What is your first reaction to this? Maybe you feel angry, imagining that the cat has knocked over the vase once again. You go downstairs to put the cat outside. In this case the thought (it's the cat) and the feeling (anger) influences your behaviour (going downstairs). But what if you don't think about the cat? Imagine instead that your first reaction is fear. You think that it might be a burglar. Now you are much less likely to go downstairs, but instead you stay in bed listening intently for further sounds. The thought (it's a burglar) and the feeling (fear) have led to a very different behaviour (staying in bed).

This example is a fairly straightforward one that is easy to envisage. Understanding the children however can be much more complex. Feelings are likely to be bewildering and linking thinking, feeling and behaviour can be beyond a child's ability. Children like Marcus and Luke who have had poor early parenting experience are frequently left with major difficulties in both thinking

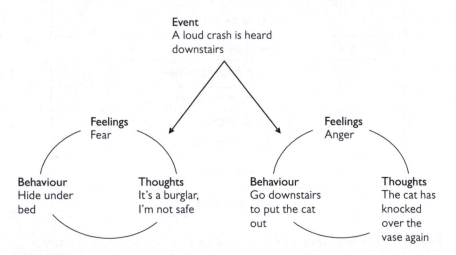

Figure 17.2 Thinking, feeling and behaving

and feeling and with very inflexible and reactive ways of behaving. *Emotional regulation* and *reflective function* can be underdeveloped. Thus the children may experience difficulty regulating and integrating emotional states. Rage, for example, can emerge suddenly and intensely. A lack of impulse control may mean that impulses determine behaviour. Additionally the capacity for *reflective function*, the ability to interpret the behaviour of self and others through an understanding of mental states, is poorly developed. Marcus and Luke are very poor at making sense of their own behaviour; it just happens or it happens because they are 'bad'. They are equally poor at understanding the behaviour of others. This makes it very difficult for them to understand the link between their own behaviour and that of others, to understand cause and effect.

At 14 years of age friendship is important for Luke and Marcus. Difficulties in managing relationships however mean that it is difficult for each of them to form and maintain friendships. On separate occasions these boys have both arrived home from school announcing that they have made arrangements to go out later with friends. This presents a dilemma for Jackie, Rita and Frank.

Jackie wants Luke to have friendships, but she is not happy with him being out unsupervised. She also isn't sure who these friends are that Luke has arranged to go out with. He mentions a couple of names but she has not heard him talk about these particular boys before. Luke is also not sure where they are going or what they will be doing. Gently Jackie tries to tell Luke that maybe going out is not a good idea. Luke does not want to hear any explanation; he just hears the 'no' and erupts in a torrent of anger. It is hours before he is calm again.

Rita and Frank are not happy with Marcus making plans without consulting them. They tell him that they are pleased that he wants to see his friends but that he must get their permission before he arranges to go out. Marcus is furious. He shouts at them that they have no right to stop him and he might just go anyway. Whilst he threatens to go out without permission he doesn't actually follow this through but Rita and Frank too have a very difficult evening as Marcus simmers in his bedroom.

Both these boys have demonstrated their distress through angry behaviour, but their underlying feeling and thinking are quite different.

Luke has always found it difficult to make friends. The chronic early neglect he experienced has left its mark despite the years he has spent with Jackie. He tries to become involved in what his peers are doing, but he does this in a clumsy way, which can be very irritating to the other children. A degree of learning difficulty also means that he is slower than they are and not very quick to pick up on what they are doing or the social cues they provide. They will tolerate him for a while but quickly tire of trying to include him. Luke is left to drift off and find someone else to play with. Recently a group of older boys have taken him 'under their wing'. They are part of a delinquent group and have seen in Luke an opportunity for some fun. He will do whatever they ask of him. For example, when they told him to roll in the mud he did, much to their amusement. They have asked him to meet them later as they are hoping they can get him to steal sweets for them. Luke is delighted to be included in their plans. He believes that other children don't like him; this belief leads him to assume that if he doesn't do what other children want he will have no friends. He therefore tries to fit in with what the other children tell him to do. When Jackie tells him that he can't go out he becomes very anxious. He fears that his new-found friends will not like him again. It is this combination of beliefs, fears and anxiety that underlie the angry outburst.

Marcus also struggles with friendships. He tends to organize his relationships around his perception of power and strength. He therefore approaches his peers aggressively, demonstrating his own strength. When he is involved in games his need to stay in control and to win can be a source of frustration to others. Marcus lacks the ability to resolve conflict and therefore his interactions often end in fights. Marcus does not find friendships very satisfying. Marcus therefore is not too concerned about meeting his friends as arranged, but it is important to be the one in charge. His experience with his father has taught him that people more powerful than you hurt you. His belief that people in control hurt you has led to an assumption that if he stays in control then he won't get hurt. Marcus doesn't want to be told what to do. Thus when Rita and Frank tell him he can't go out he feels that they are trying to control him. He becomes afraid and angry with them.

Thus although both Marcus and Luke are faced with a similar situation – they are being told that they can't go out – and although they both react similarly in that they get angry, the thinking and feeling that underlies their reactions are quite different. Of course the children do not understand any of this. They experience and they react. Rita, Frank and Jackie are left to pick up the pieces. They have to manage the challenging behaviour that the children present.

However, there is also a larger task to do here. If they can help the children to recognize the fear and anxiety that underlies their angry behaviour they will move forward in helping the children to develop the capacity to regulate their emotional arousal and to be able to reflect on their own behaviour and that of those they interact with.

Luke needs to experience empathy for how sad it is not to be liked by other children, and how worried he is that if he doesn't meet the boys tonight he might lose these new friends also. As he experiences this level of understanding he may be more ready to think with Jackie that perhaps these boys are not good friends, and maybe he will agree to invite Matthew over instead.

Marcus needs to experience empathy for how scary it is not to be in charge. As his fear of being hurt by them is understood he may be able to calm a little. Maybe he will then be able to co-operate with a compromise, which allows Rita and Frank to set the main boundary whilst Marcus has some control over what happens within this.

Thus behaviour management needs to go beyond the use of behavioural strategies to help children make better behavioural choices. Children need help to recognize feelings and beliefs that they may not be aware of, to regulate and manage emotional arousal and to interpret their own and others' behaviour. Only when they are not overwhelmed by the way they feel, and have some capacity for *reflective function* will the children be able to get maximum benefit from the behavioural strategies that you can use. Helping children with thinking, feeling and behaviour moves beyond containing and managing behaviour to helping the children develop emotional maturity and improved *cognitive* ability so that they are able to behave in ways that are more flexible and provide them with more choices.

The ABC of behaviour

Behaviour is learnt because of the consequence that follows it. This is sometimes called the ABC of behaviour (see Figure 17.3). Consequences, including rewards and sanctions, represent the behaviour that the parent has control over. By linking these consistently and predictably to the children's behaviour the children learn that they have a choice that can lead to a reward or a sanction.

A = Antecedent – this represents a cue or signal and acts as a trigger for behaviour.

B = Behaviour.

C = Consequence.

The model suggests that behaviour will be strengthened (i.e. more likely to occur again) if this behaviour is followed by something pleasurable (a reward or *positive reinforcement*) or stops something unpleasant happening (*negative reinforcement*). Behaviour will be weakened (i.e. less likely to occur in the future) if it is followed by something unpleasant (called a *punishment*). *Punishment* is used here as a technical term, an unpleasant consequence rather than something inflicted on the child in anger or to cause pain.

Rewards and punishments represent what children find pleasant and unpleasant rather than what we think they should like or not like. For example, a child might find being shouted at rewarding whilst having a treat punishing. Understanding this can help us to understand why his behaviour might be increasing when we think we are providing consequences that will lead to its reduction.

Understanding this pattern of rewards and punishers can be helpful in deciding what consequences to use. We can pick consequences that are acceptable to us and rewarding for the child (e.g. we would not shout at a child to reward him but would use something that we both find rewarding). Similarly we can pick acceptable consequences to follow behaviour we would like to see reduce. A child does not eat a meal therefore he does not get dessert.

The behaviours children display represent a choice. Parents don't control this behaviour. If they try to they will find themselves quickly caught up in

Antecedent	**B**ehaviour	**C**onsequence
Cues, e.g. when, where, who, what		
	Positive event Rewarding = Positive reinforcer	⟶ Behaviour increases
	Negative event Punishing	⟶ Behaviour decreases
	Ends negative event Rewarding = Negative reinforcer	⟶ Behaviour increases

Figure 17.3 The ABC of behaviour

control battles. Parents can however tell the children what choices they have and then control the consequences to the behaviours. These choices and consequences are explained calmly, and without stressing one choice over another. The children can make either choice. The parent does not get cross but simply implements the consequence.

- 'You can eat your dinner and then you will have dessert or you can leave your dinner and then you will leave the table.'

- 'If you put your shoes on we will go to the park; if you don't put your shoes on then you can help me tidy the kitchen.'

If one choice is not acceptable do not offer that choice. If the shoes have to go on, because you have to pick up another child from school, do not give the choice of not putting shoes on. The choices might be to put his shoes on himself or to have you put them on for him.

As we will explore later the best choice–consequence sequences involve natural or logical consequences. The consequence is connected to the choice. The children need to see the consequences as linked to their behaviour rather than as arbitrary so that they learn that they can control consequences through their behaviour.

A choice is not the same as a command. Commands have to be obeyed and often meet with anger when they are disobeyed. Choices and consequences help the parents to stay calm and in control rather than being pulled in to control battles that they rarely win.

When children become angry because of the consequences that they meet, the parents have an opportunity to provide *empathy* and support. They accept the anger and empathize with how difficult this is. The consequence still occurs for the behaviour but the feelings the children are expressing are validated.

Zoë has always struggled to link her behaviour to the consequence that follows. She reacts to how she feels rather than to what has happened. When she steals Catherine's make-up Catherine is angry with her. Zoë cannot easily follow the logic that taking the make-up makes Catherine angry. She complains to Jenny that Catherine is mean and horrid, and she hates her. When Jenny suggests that maybe Zoë should replace the missing make-up Zoë feels got at. Now it feels like the whole world hates her, and deep inside is the fear that this is because she really is a 'bad kid'. Zoë is overwhelmed by this fear and so she blames everyone else instead. It is all Catherine's fault; she made her take the make-up by teasing her about her spots. It is all Jenny's fault because she did not give her some extra pocket money this week. By blaming everyone else the fear that maybe she isn't good enough recedes a little.

Zoë needs predictable, calm and empathic responses that recognize her feelings of not being good enough whilst also helping her to begin to see the link between her behaviour and what follows. Empathy for her feelings combined with choices and clear consequences around her behaviour will gradually help her to feel better about herself and thus to be able to regulate her own behaviour more easily.

In the next part we will consider how to use rewards as a consequence for positive behaviour. Rewards are a powerful way to encourage prosocial behaviour but, as we will see, rewards for children with difficulties in attachment can be quite complex.

Rewards

Positive reinforcers or rewards strengthen behaviour because the child wants the consequence. When children have experienced a history of abuse, neglect and loss, the things they find rewarding can be very unexpected. Children may find a range of behaviours rewarding that we anticipate would be uncomfortable for them. Causing emotional and physical pain to others, saying 'no', engaging in and winning power struggles, and avoiding emotional engagement are examples of surprising but common rewards for the children. Their early life has taught them not to get close because others can't be trusted. The children therefore use their behaviour to ensure that closeness doesn't happen.

Similarly the rewards we want to offer the children can lead them to feel anxious and unworthy. Commonly children will sabotage planned rewards and treats as they demonstrate that they are not worthy of such attention. Alternatively they might behave well to get a particularly attractive reward, but as soon as the treat is attained they revert to their former behaviour. You are left feeling manipulated and ineffectual.

Behavioural strategies work because ultimately children want and value a relationship with the parents. They will try hard to earn rewards and treats, but most importantly they want to please you. For children who have learnt not to trust parents this can be very different. They may both fear and long for such relationships. This can lead to very complex and puzzling behaviours. This is why working on the child's behaviour alone without paying attention to the relationship will not be effective. Developing a positive relationship with you, feeling accepted by you and receiving *empathy* for the feelings being displayed are important to help your child begin to get used to and enjoy the typical range of rewards and treats parents provide for their children.

Catherine has always struggled to believe that her parents can provide her with security and comfort. Throughout childhood she has clung to self-reliance in order to avoid needing Jenny and Martin. Need and fear are too closely linked for her. As she experiences a need, anxiety builds up; by taking care of herself, the anxiety is contained. Although in many ways she has developed a more positive view of what parents can offer, and has allowed some level of parenting from them, the negative view that parents hurt you for being emotionally needing of them has also persisted. This means that Catherine has to cope with late adolescence, with its demands for increased independence and autonomy, without ever having learnt to be fully dependent. To successfully explore the outside world of friendship, boyfriends and independence she needs to be able to come back in, to touch base with Jenny and Martin, to let them contain her anxiety about her growing maturity and to use them as a secure base from which she can again venture out. As she feels secure at home she will be able to venture out more widely.

This process is very complex for Catherine; developing independence provokes anxiety and fear of not being up to the task. Catherine needs the security offered by Jenny and Martin, but whereas they should be a source of safety and comfort, her very need of them re-awakens the fear of her early years. Catherine is left oscillating between rejecting their support whilst falling back on her own fragile self-reliance and being fretful and demanding of them. Once again relationships are a source of difficulty rather than being rewarding to her.

Catherine becomes moody and difficult. She behaves in a way that is certain to annoy Jenny and Martin; she refuses to take showers; she comes down late for meals; she leaves dirty washing all over her room. Through these behaviours she is creating a distance between herself and her parents. As she experiences an increased need of them she works hard to put a space between herself and them. This however only reduces her anxiety temporarily because she does need the security they can offer her and so she will switch to being helpful and loving. She will offer to wash the dishes; she will spend the evening with Jenny trying out different hairstyles or watching a film with her. This starts to develop closeness between them, which again increases Catherine's anxiety, and so the cycle starts again. Jenny and Martin are left feeling manipulated and ineffectual. They fear Catherine's moods and can't believe in her friendliness. Catherine senses the confusion in them and her own fear that needing them will end in pain increases. Small signs of rejection, a refusal of her offer of help or a look of annoyance on their faces, trigger angry outbursts from her. Catherine needs to believe that Jenny and Martin will be reliably there for her whatever her mood or need. Jenny and Martin need to believe that Catherine's confusion and fear will reduce and her oscillating behaviour will calm if they hang on in there. Belief hangs by a thread on both sides through these difficult years.

The use of choices and logical consequences

When children behave in a certain way they are demonstrating a choice. This choice will lead to a consequence. When children understand the link between their choice and the consequence they can choose behaviour that leads to certain consequences and reject behaviour that leads to other consequences.

Children with early experience of inconsistent and insensitive parenting have often failed to learn the link between behaviour and consequences. Their behaviour had no relationship to the actions of their parents. They therefore have poor understanding of cause and effect. They perceive the consequences as just things that happen to them, as the other person being 'mean to them', or as 'the way it is'. They therefore have little motivation to reflect on their behaviour or to make different choices about how to behave, in order to make certain consequences happen. Thus their behaviour becomes *impulsive* or *compulsive*.

It is also common for behaviour to be organized around power struggles. The children demonstrate a need to control the relationship, to express their lack of trust in the parent, and their fear in their own badness and vulnerability. Engaging and winning power struggles means that they gain a sense of control, providing a superficial feeling of safety. The children can't trust the parent so they trust in themselves. Each time the parent is drawn into these power struggles it confirms for the children that they are unsafe with the parent, thus reinforcing their need to stay in control

In these situations behaviour is habitual, requiring little thought, but is also inflexible. Children are poor at adapting to changing circumstances. They need a period of highly consistent and predictable parenting in order to start to trust the parent, to feel safe and to make the links between behaviour and consequence. As was explored in Chapter 15 it may be beneficial to provide an increased level of supervision and structure. The children are helped to reduce their feelings of fear and to learn to trust in the parent.

As a parent experiencing these struggles with your child it can be helpful to remember that whilst you are not in charge of your child's behaviour neither is he in charge of your behaviour. He cannot make you behave in a particular way. You have choices about how to respond. First it is important that you stay calm; anger and frustration will only pull you into the struggle. Additionally try and maintain a high level of *empathy* and warmth; this demonstrates your care for your child and your desire to help and support him. Within this context there is a range of things that you could do. This represents a choice of consequences.

Whilst boundaries, limits and structure need to be consistent, consequences can be less predictable and sometimes unexpected. It is important that you follow through on consequences that you have given, but the choice of consequence can vary.

For example, you have asked your child to bring his dirty washing down, but he refuses.

- You could provide a logical consequence: 'When you bring the washing down I can put it into the machine and then we will have some time to play that new game you have got.' Or 'If you bring the washing down in the next five minutes then there will be time to go to the park and play football.' Logical consequences are explored further below.

- You could let the action, not bringing the washing down, lead to its natural consequence, no clean clothes to wear. After reminding the child of this likely consequence to his refusal you can calmly get on with your day leaving events to unfold. Of course you will also need to stay calm when your child discovers the lack of clothes. Remind him that when the washing appears downstairs it will be washed for him, and he will have clothes to wear again.

- You might take a different approach. Offer to do the task but let him know that you will take the cost of your services out of the weekly pocket money. Remember this is not a punishment but a consequence, stay calm and reasonable, and avoid making this sound like a threat.

- Sometimes it is difficult to come up with a quick but reasonable response. You can give yourself some extra time – 'That's an interesting choice you have made; I'll think about what is going to happen as a consequence. Don't worry, I'll let you know when I have thought of something.'

- You might decide to focus on the way your child is feeling and thinking, rather than directly focus on the behaviour. Use *empathy* and curiosity. 'I can see you have had a hard day; maybe we need to figure out together why you feel the need to be difficult right now.'

- Offer nurturing: 'It looks to me like you are having a hard time today; maybe you need a hug, and some quiet time with me.'

- Be playful. 'Let's see who can do this quickest; bet I beat you.' Or 'Looks like you want to make me mad. Let's see who can get most cross. Can you shout this loud?'

- Be surprising. 'It looks like you are having a hard time today; let's leave it for now and have a drink and snack.'

When you decide to link the child's behaviour with consistent consequences it is helpful if the consequences are logically connected to the behaviour itself.

- If you spill a drink you wipe it up.

- If you spend all your pocket money you will not be able to buy sweets on the way home.

- If you don't come home on time and I have to look for you then you will owe me the time back. You will help me with the jobs I have not yet done.

Over time these consistent and logical consequences will help the children to learn that their behaviour represents a choice. This in turn will lead to more thoughtful behaving as the children develop new and more flexible behaviour patterns.

At first the children will struggle to understand the link between choice and consequences. When negative consequences occur they will judge the world as arbitrary, mean and unpredictable. With continued consistency however the children will gradually come to realize that their behaviour and the consequence is linked, that the consequence can be controlled through choices in behaving. If they do not like a consequence they have the option of rethinking their behaviour and making alternative choices that lead to more pleasant consequences.

We have looked in this chapter at how you might support your child's ability to manage feelings, develop thinking and to become more flexible in behaviour. Through highly empathic, warm and nurturing parenting, which provides appropriate structure and supervision and calm and measured responses to behaviour, your child will start to feel safer. This will lead to a greater capacity to trust in his relationship with you and to develop a more secure attachment to you.

18

Managing Special Difficulties: Lying, Stealing and Self-harm

In this chapter we are going to move away from the house model to give some special attention to relatively common problems for children with difficulties in attachment. Of course many elements of the house model will be apparent as we explore how to manage these difficulties.

Children and young people who self-harm

Self-harming behaviours are perhaps amongst the most distressing behaviours that children and young people demonstrate. Watching a young person deliberately hurt herself can provoke fear, anxiety and anger as we feel excluded and unable to help.

Self-harm, sometimes called self-injurious behaviour, is the deliberate act of causing harm to the self. Self-harm is the expression of and temporary relief from overwhelming, unbearable and often conflicting emotions and feelings. There are clearly parallels with suicidal behaviour although the link between suicide and self-harm can be very blurred. The young person will engage in this behaviour with or without an intention to die. The act of suicide represents a serious attempt to die. Sometimes a young person comes close to death because of self-harming behaviour, although this hasn't been the intention. This is described as parasuicide.

Whilst self-harming behaviours are typically associated with teenagers, these behaviours can also be seen in children as young as toddlers. Young children, when distressed or very frustrated, might for instance bang their head against a hard surface, or bite themselves.

Why do young people self-harm?

Self-harming behaviours can be interpersonal or intrapersonal.

At the interpersonal level self-harm may be an attempt to obtain something from someone else. In this sense it can be seen as 'attention-seeking' or manipulative behaviour. However, it must be recognized that such behaviour stems from a deep-seated need to receive attention from another person, possibly to access nurturing, and care; desperate attention-needing rather than attention-seeking.

At the intrapersonal level acts of self-harm are private, hidden from others. Self-harm, in this instance, is a coping mechanism to change or control the self or to silently express frustration.

Thus self-harm can serve a number of different functions, which are not always easy to distinguish or separate. In addition self-harm can have multiple meanings for the same individual, making it even more complicated to understand.

Self-harm as a coping mechanism

There is a range of reasons why a young person may use self-harm as a way to cope. For example, it might help the person to avoid something, a difficult situation or painful and preoccupying memories, thoughts and worries. In this way she might be able to avoid unwanted and distressing feelings and emotions. When emotional pain is difficult to bear, physical pain can feel more tangible and manageable. Self-harm can also provide a release for anger and frustration thus providing relief. In all these ways self-harming behaviour can help the young person gain comfort and security. The very familiarity and routine the behaviour provides can feel reassuring.

Self-harm can alternatively be used as a punishment against the self or towards others. One way young people make sense of their difficult experience is to blame themselves. If they see themselves as bad somehow all the bad things that have happened to them make sense. Unfortunately this also leaves the young people with a pervasive sense of *shame* and anger. They may wish to punish themselves as a way of releasing the sense of badness being experienced. Self-harming behaviour becomes a way of coping with these difficult feelings and experiencing at least a temporary sense of redemption.

Alternatively the behaviour may be used to get back at abusers. These young people may be very clear that it is others who are to blame for the trauma they have experienced. It is safer however to redirect feelings of anger on to the self than at someone else. The self-harm provides an expression of rebellion and resistance. At the same time it gives the young people a sense of control, when their early experience has often left them feeling powerless, under the control of others. The self-harming behaviour provides young people with a way of achieving control that does not rely on anyone else. In this way they express their independence, *autonomy* and personal freedom when few other alternatives are available. This can lead to a sense of achievement and accomplishment, compensating for low feelings of *self-esteem*.

The self-harm can therefore help the young person to retain a sense of self, but the very strangeness of this behaviour also reinforces the feelings of being an outsider and alone. The consequences of self-harm can be very complex. The young person may feel a sense of relief in the short-term, but the guilt, *shame* and embarrassment will then start to overwhelm her, reinforcing feelings of being bad. This then leads to a further build-up of difficult feelings and the urge to self-harm increases again. Self-harm becomes increasingly dangerous over time as the young person finds that she needs to increase the degree of self-harm in order to achieve the same function. In this way the self-harming behaviour becomes compulsive. The young person experiences a sense of urgency, and need. At some time the self-harm can become addictive, at which point it becomes an end in itself rather than being used to achieve other aims.

Helping the young person who self-harms

Young people do want to be understood and helped but it is difficult and frightening to give up the behaviour that has become a part of their identity. The more others try to stop them, the more they cling to it. Suggestions for alternatives made by other people are unlikely to be helpful as it takes control away. Young people need to find an alternative for themselves. It is also important that interventions don't reinforce or perpetuate feelings of badness and the need for punishment.

This can be very difficult for those trying to help the young person as they try to get a balance between under- and over-reacting. Ignoring or minimizing the behaviour assumes that the behaviour is 'attention-seeking'. This approach tends to reinforce feelings of being worthless. The young person feels neither understood nor listened to.

As a parent this can all be very difficult. You will need to manage the behaviour, but you can't view this in isolation. Whilst you will need to provide increased supervision, and decrease access to objects for self-harm, it is important that this is done within the context of a supportive and accepting relationship.

Helping a young person who is self-harming begins with building a relationship. This requires a large amount of acceptance and *empathy*. Whilst you will not like the behaviour your young person is engaging in, it is important that you are non-judgemental and that you do accept the feelings and perceptions underlying the behaviour. Try to adopt a non-judgemental approach, which accepts and works with the negative feelings of the young person.

Young people need a trusting relationship, which can help them to explore their self-harm and look at different ways of experiencing a sense of control. They will be helped if they feel respected and accepted. It can be difficult but your young person will find it helpful if you allow her to talk about the self-harm without being made to feel bad or guilty. Often young people fear the behaviour will be taken away from them and they will be left without a coping mechanism. They need help to feel that they have a sense of control, which is not being undermined. If your young person trusts you not to make her feel bad she will be able to work with you to understand what the self-harm means. Thus you will be providing help and support without the expectation that the self-harm has to stop. With this approach your young person may be able to limit the behaviour and stay safe. Together, within a trusting relationship, you can both challenge the behaviour, which is now seen as separate from either of you.

Provide opportunities to talk but avoid pressurizing. Offer space to talk but don't mind silence. Young people need access to space where they can retreat to, either to rage or to be quiet. Supervision therefore needs to be balanced with personal space.

Young people need help to find other ways to feel strong. Self-harm will reduce when they have another involvement in which they can get absorbed. Finding activities, hobbies or other ways in which your young person can gain a sense of competence and satisfaction can gradually help to reduce her need to self-harm.

Helping the young child who self-harms

It can be very upsetting to care for young children who deliberately hurt themselves, especially when the children resist being comforted by the parent. Helping these children again begins with the relationship. The children are often dealing with their distress in this way because they haven't learnt to rely on a parent for comfort and support. Alternatively they may engage in the behaviour to ensure the parent's attention. They do not expect the parent to be available to comfort them and so they work hard to maintain this availability. Either way the child needs prolonged experience of a dependable, nurturing and sensitive relationship.

When your child is engaged in self-harming behaviour it is important that you do not express anger or shock. Either of these is likely to increase her distress. Instead gently distract and divert her. She may need some nurturing time with you, an opportunity for a cuddle, a comforting drink, etc. Provide *empathy* for the underlying feelings your child is experiencing. If she rejects this *empathy* more indirect methods may be needed. For instance you might talk to the family dog, within her hearing, about how sad/scared/lonely she is feeling, how she is frightened that you might not be there when needed.

Children will often respond to stories. A story about a bear who was too frightened to turn to others for comfort, and who tried to manage by himself, or a duckling who couldn't find his mother might help the child to explore the fears or sadness underlying her distress. Ending with the bear or duckling being helped by a friendly adult bear or duck can also give the indirect message that the child can be helped by the parent. An adopted child might be helped by a story in which the animal is adopted and helped by his new family. children can also help to create the narratives with the parent guiding ther resolved ending.

Managing risk of suicide

Caring for a young person who is suicidal can be very stressful. It is important to seek professional help and support. Sharing concerns and agreeing action that needs to be taken with another person can be helpful to reduce your feelings of isolation and fear of 'getting it wrong'.

Safety plans

You can help your young person to draw up a safety plan. This will help her to identify triggers that lead to self-harm and to consider a range of coping strategies that could be used instead. For example, she might feel that she can talk to someone, use a relaxation exercise or engage in an activity. If the young person finds it hard to talk to you when feeling anxious or upset she may be able to use a signal to communicate this in a way that you both understand. When developing a safety plan it is important that you remain non-judgemental whilst conveying the hope that the young person will stay alive. An example of a safety plan that you could help your young person to write is included at the end of this chapter. This can be accompanied by a similar plan detailing how the parent or supportive adult will also help to keep the young person safe.

Risk assessment of suicidal behaviour
Ask about suicidal thinking.

- Have you felt lately that you would like to go to sleep and not wake up?
- Have you just wanted to get away from it all?
- Have things been so bad that you thought you would be better off dead?
- Have you thought about hurting yourself or killing yourself?
- Have you ever tried to kill yourself?

If the young person admits to suicidal thoughts ask:

- Do you think you can keep yourself safe?
- How have you thought about killing yourself?
- Have you made any plans?
- What has stopped you attempting suicide so far?

There is a hierarchy of concerns ranging from suicidal ideas to the very worrying worked-out strategies (see Figure 18.1). The most worrying is the young person with fully formed and systematic plans who is rejecting any help.

Most concern

↑

Child displays repeated, potentially lethal actions

Child displays impulsive and partial actions

Child forms persistent, more systematized,
and comprehensive plans

Child forms fleeting, poorly thought-out plans

Child reports persistent and intrusive ideas

Child reports fleeting ideas

Moderate concern

*Figure 18.1 Hierarchy of concerns (Adapted from Sprague (1997). 'Clinical
Management of Suicidal Behaviour in Children and Adolescents.' p.117.
Copyright © Sage Publications Ltd. Reproduced with kind permission.)*

Exercise 18.1: Creating a safety plan

My safety plan

My name is

This is a little bit about myself
(Include things you like about yourself, what you are good at, what your hopes
and dreams are, as well as things that you find more difficult about yourself)

Why I feel I need a plan to keep myself safe

This is about the self-harm that I engage in

What is happening in my life that is so difficult that I hurt myself?	What emotions do I find so hard to manage that I hurt myself?

What triggers can I identify that lead to my hurting myself?
(e.g. when alone or with someone, in a particular place, when I have certain
thoughts, memories, feelings)

How do I feel after I have hurt myself?

Good feelings	Difficult feelings

Here are some ideas for keeping myself safe

Different, safer things I can do that help me feel good

Different things I can do that will distract me from hurting myself

Safe people
(People I can talk to when I am feeling anxious or upset; you could also write
down what you have agreed that they will do when you tell them how you are
feeling)

Safe places
(Places I can go to when I am feeling anxious or upset)

Phone numbers of people that I can ring when I am feeling anxious or upset
(These can be friends, family, social worker, therapist, ChildLine, etc.)

This is how I can keep the physical environment safe
(e.g. who looks after your tablets, sharp objects, what don't you leave lying
around)

Helping the child who lies and steals

Lying and stealing are two frequently observed behaviour problems in children who have been abused or neglected early in life. Children steal without apparent guilt or concern for others. This stealing can serve a number of purposes.

- Children steal because they want something. Having weak *empathy* they are unconcerned about the impact this will have on the owner of the item.

- Children may feel that they deserve the things they steal, perhaps linked to a past experience of not getting what they needed.

- Children may steal for trade. They may want items to trade for friendship or to sell in order to buy the food and drink that they are craving. Children who have experience of extensive neglect will often compulsively want to fill themselves up with the things they didn't get when they were little.

- Children may steal compulsively as a defence against anxiety. Often the children steal property of little worth. Rubbers and pencils may constantly go missing from school or the children may collect common household items such as batteries. They may steal and hoard food, showing little inclination to eat it. The child experiences pervasive anxiety and gets some short-term relief through this compulsive acquisition of things.

Lying and stealing are often closely linked. Children may lie to deny that they have taken something or to deflect blame for an event away from themselves. Often the child lies with audacity and is extremely convincing. The child is able to look the parent straight in the eye whilst lying. In fact it is not uncommon for this to be the only time that the child appears comfortable with eye-contact. The child may provide long and incredible explanations of what really happened, frequently pushing the blame onto someone else.

These behaviours can relate to developmental delays based on poor early experience of relationships. This can leave children with a weakly formed sense of conscience, the usual inhibitor of morally unacceptable behaviour. In addition a poor ability to think about cause and effect, a tendency towards concrete thinking and difficulty with abstract thinking contribute to the difficulties for children in thinking through what they are doing and what the likely consequences will be. A poor ability at knowing how we are thinking or what we are feeling makes it difficult for children to understand the impact of their actions on others. Not being able to understand that we would feel let down, or upset, they carry on and follow their impulses. Our reaction is then a surprise or puzzle to them. These *cognitive* difficulties therefore combine to make it difficult for children to enter into reciprocal relationships. Without this sense of mutuality, I am nice to you and you are nice to me, the usual inhibitions on lying and stealing are absent.

Why do children lie and steal?

There is a range of reasons why children lie and steal. They may want to cover their tracks, perhaps to avoid a feared punishment. Alternatively it may help to build themselves up in others' and their own eyes, and to re-invent their history. Children will tell tall stories or fantasy accounts of past and present experience. They may tell a story of some daring deed or clever feat, or they may invent experiences with a parent, sibling or friend. This type of self-deceit, which denies unpleasant or even painful realities, can feel very real to the children. They can become convinced that fantasies are true. The children might find it difficult to experience a parent challenging their account but may cope better if the parent provides *empathy* and support. 'Wouldn't it be nice to go fishing with your dad. I bet you would be able to catch a fish for supper.'

Lying can also disconnect the child from what really happened. This is a coping strategy to avoid feelings of *shame* and guilt. The child believes that she is telling the truth and thus avoids feeling that she has done something wrong. In trying to cope with intense feelings of badness and low self-worth she denies all mistakes, weakness or transgressions. The more strenuously and consistently children blame others and deny it was them, the more we can assume they are struggling with and trying to deny feelings of low self-worth, of not feeling good enough.

Lying and stealing can also provide a means of self-protection; by lying and stealing, the parent is kept at a distance. Feeling uncomfortable with closeness the children may prefer to have their parents angry with them because of their behaviour. Additionally when the children experience anger they may struggle to openly show this anger. Stealing and lying can both be subtle, *passive-aggressive* acts. These are behind-your-back behaviours that allow the child some sense of having got back against a world that has hurt her or a parent who she perceives as being mean to her. Alternatively more overt acts of stealing and lying can provoke the parent into being angry, providing the child with an outlet for the anger that has been building up within her.

Children may also find it difficult to trust their parents enough to tell the truth or to assume that they will be given what they need. They may lie and steal automatically through an unconscious need to conceal themselves, to protect the privacy of their thoughts, feelings and actions. This will also help children to feel a sense of control. A compulsive need to control in response to the anxiety of being dependent upon others is common in children who are struggling with relationships. Lying and stealing are both ways of exercising this control. Children experience the fooling of others satisfying and rewarding in itself.

This is linked with enjoying the conflict as they get into an argument over whether they did or didn't lie or steal.

Over time the lying and stealing become habitual, perhaps following experience in a family where the difference between lying and truthfulness was not clear, and when the child was regularly exposed to parents who took what they wanted. Having been brought up in a secret world of fantasy, guilt or blame, the child can develop a distorted view of the world, based upon lies, dishonesty and mistrust. Having learnt about lying and stealing from her own family she tries to cope with the world in the same way.

What can you do to help the child who lies or steals?

It is important to model honest behaviour. Your child needs experience of a family where honesty and dishonesty are clearly separated, and where honesty is valued. Your child can be given *empathy* and support to help adopt these same values.

You may find it helpful to avoid confrontation. Discussions about 'did you or didn't you lie or steal?' rarely have a positive outcome. Your child can continue to deny or distort the truth and you are left powerless to do anything about it. When you know that your child has transgressed you will find it helpful to avoid getting pulled into a discussion; instead calmly provide a consequence. By insisting that she tell the truth she is backed into a corner. Backing down once a lie has been told is difficult. It is better if you don't ask your child to admit to something that is already known between you. You can proceed on the assumption that this is known, e.g. 'I see from your homework diary that you do have some homework after all. Why don't we sit down now and I will help you with it and then we can have some supper?' Or, as one carer described to me when her foster son had helped himself to her small change before going on a school trip, 'Well done for remembering to take some money with you. You don't need to worry about it; I have deducted it from this week's pocket money.' In this way you provide a calm consequence without irritation or anger. Natural consequences provided with *empathy* and support can help your child to manage more honesty in the future.

At some point you will want to talk to your child about the lying or stealing. This will be easier when she is feeling calm. It is better to avoid a time when she has just been caught out. You will be feeling cross or irritated, and your child is likely to be experiencing a sense of *shame* and defensiveness. At a later time you will be more able to show *empathy* for the struggle she is having with being honest. You can let her know that you will support her and that you believe that she can be honest.

Sometimes children can tolerate parents commenting on their non-verbal communication. Your child can be helped to be honest because a part of them already is. Calmly or humorously comment on the signs she is giving out that she is lying either through her eyes or in her body.

Unfortunately living with a child who habitually steals can put a strain on the whole family. Everyone has to be more aware of their own possessions and things of value need to be hidden away. It is difficult when you feel that you can't relax in your own home. You will also need to provide a level of supervision that is burdensome. Checking bags on leaving and returning to the house can be onerous and feels intrusive. Until children are able to manage this aspect of their life however, this level of supervision provided with *empathy* and support can help them to feel safe and cared about.

It is also difficult when a child shows no remorse. The 'so what' attitude on top of the lying or stealing can feel like a double assault. You may also fear for your child's future, anticipating the trouble she will get into. Unfortunately trying to get a child to own up and accept responsibility often fails. The stealing and lying are being used as a dysfunctional way of getting deeper needs met. The child's feelings of *shame* will be buried deep. As you adopt a stance of *empathy* and support you will over time help her face this *shame* without becoming overwhelmed. Only then will she be able to accept responsibility for her behaviour.

19

Conclusion

The house complete

Children with difficulties in attachment find it difficult to trust and to feel secure with foster carers or adoptive parents. We have now worked through the house

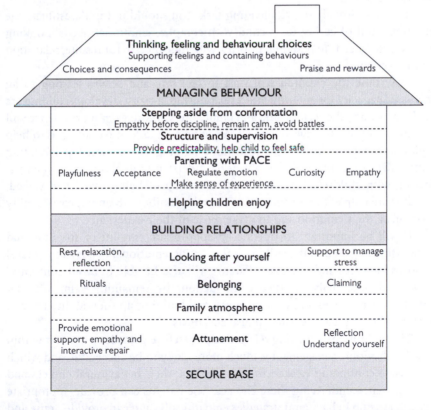

Figure 19.1 The house model of parenting (Adapted from 'The House Model of Parenting' in Golding et al. (2006). Copyright © John Wiley & Sons Ltd. Reproduced with kind permission.)

model of parenting, a model that builds trust, and security, allowing children to develop satisfying relationships (see Figure 19.1).

The foundation of this model is the provision of a *secure base* for the children. Parents provide parenting experiences that help the children to feel safe and secure, thus fostering attachment. This is a complex task as parents attempt to meet the need for nurturance and care despite the distorted way children express and hide their needs. Children experience living in a family that is very different from previous experience. The models of families and of self that they hold are gently challenged and children are helped to develop alternative models to sit alongside previous ones. *Attunement* and relationship repair support children in managing complex emotion, helping them to experience a sense of belonging to the family.

A *secure base* is achieved by parents taking control of the emotional atmosphere of the house. Parents accept the child, and demonstrate this acceptance through their commitment to him. By providing *empathy* and sensitive, responsive care the child is helped to understand and manage his emotional life. He will be able to enter into family life more fully, gaining a sense of belonging to this family.

This is a difficult and challenging task. You should not underestimate the emotional toll of caring for a child with complex emotional needs. Looking after yourself needs to be a high priority, with time built in for respite, relaxation and reflection.

Over time the children will start to feel safe and secure leading to an increased capacity for entering into a relationship. As trust develops children are enabled to enjoy the relationship and family life. Children's past experience will however continue to have an impact. An important task of parenting is to help children manage feelings of *shame* without harming the relationship. Parenting with PACE is recommended as a way of understanding, accepting and empathizing with children. Combined with a feeling of being loved and valued, children are helped to take their PLACE in the family, with an improved ability to regulate their emotion and to make sense of their experience.

It will be important to provide an appropriate amount of structure and supervision adjusted to the children's fluctuating emotional needs as their level of stress increases and decreases. Parents will also be able to avoid confrontational and potentially destructive interactions by remaining calm, offering children clear choices and consequences, and building up their ability to cope with and benefit from rewards, praise and treats.

The building of a trusting relationship therefore provides a context within which behaviour management is much more likely to be successful, and which can ensure continuing *empathy* for the children, their behavioural choices and the experience underlying these choices. The parents can provide appropriate discipline using behavioural strategies empathically; and can provide praise and rewards that are accepted by the children.

It is difficult to predict the impact of this approach to parenting on individual children. Offering the children experience of a more secure attachment will build resilience. This does not mean that all difficult behaviours will go away or that development will proceed without a hitch. There are many reasons for behavioural or developmental difficulties in addition to attachment experience. However, experiencing trusting relationships will go some way to help children cope with current or future adversity.

Some children will be able to learn to enter fully into reciprocal and mutually rewarding relationships. They will develop the capacity for appropriate self-reliance and for trust in others. The impact of early life does not disappear but coming to terms with this becomes growth enhancing as the child develops resilience and strength.

Other children will come part way in developing trust in self and others, providing them with an increased chance of a successful and rewarding adult life, although they may remain fragile with a vulnerability to further stress or adversity.

There are other children who will need life-long support. They will benefit from attachment-focused parenting, but will not grow into full independence. Often these are the children who are born more vulnerable. They may have been born prematurely, with pre-existing genetic difficulties or already damaged by the substance abuse or extreme stress experienced during development prenatally.

The degree to which children develop an ability for *emotional regulation* and a capacity for *reflective function* are amongst the most important factors in determining how far they can benefit from the alternative care they are receiving. These core abilities mean that they can cope with stress and further difficulties and can make sense of the behaviour of themselves and others. This in turn means that they can develop *empathy* for others and for themselves, can make sense of their experience both past and present, and can in consequence respond flexibly in the future. In understanding their past experience their future opens up, providing options and opportunities that they will be able to grasp with both hands.

And what about the children described throughout this book?

Catherine, Zoë, Marcus and Luke are all approaching adulthood. Their path through childhood has not been straightforward and parenting them has felt like a roller-coaster ride.

Catherine struggled through adolescence; with frequent angry outbursts and a desire to be far more independent than Jenny or Martin were comfortable with, arguments raged. However, whilst home could be tempestuous, Catherine was calmer at school. She worked hard and achieved GCSEs and two A-levels. She is now planning to go to art college. Leaving school and focusing on the future has provided Catherine with some goals. She is now calmer at

home and has a much-improved relationship with Jenny and Martin. She is looking forward to leaving home, but teases them that she will be home regularly to
get her washing done.

Zoë, in contrast to Catherine, is calmer at home but struggling more at
school. She has a very close relationship to Jenny and Martin and is beginning to
cope when their attention is not on her. She is due to sit her GCSEs next year,
but will struggle to get five A–Cs. She finds it difficult following in Catherine's
footsteps and perceives herself as 'stupid'. Jenny is encouraging Zoë to find a
vocational path, in the hope that this will help her to feel more successful. Zoë is
wondering about hairdressing and has just secured a Saturday job at the local
salon.

Marcus has continued to be very difficult to care for. His school career has
been erratic with a pattern of suspensions and exclusions. However, he has
now become involved in a local apprenticeship scheme that has been set up to
help disaffected young people. Marcus has been taken under the wing of a local
garage owner and he is enjoying working on the cars. Whilst he can still be quick
to anger the worst of his aggressive behaviour has subsided. His time in care is
drawing to a close but Rita and Frank have applied for Marcus to continue to
live with them in supported lodgings. They are concerned that he has recently
become involved at the fringes of a local gang of lads and has been in some trouble for stealing. More encouragingly he has made contact with his grandfather.
Rita and Frank are planning a trip to Jamaica next year. They are hopeful that by
becoming more involved in Afro-Caribbean culture Marcus will be diverted
from a path that they worry could end in prison.

Luke remains a very vulnerable young man whose neurodevelopmental
difficulties have become even more apparent as he has grown. He is close to
Jackie, and enjoys being helpful, making cups of teas and helping her with
household and gardening tasks. He continues to struggle with empathy, or
seeing things from another's viewpoint. When a neighbour collapsed outside
the house he was more interested in the ambulance than how she was. He has
no idea of money and has to be watched carefully or he would swap his CDs
and DVDs for sweets. He also continues to struggle to understand cause and
effect. He still does not understand why Jackie is cross when he has done something wrong. He has learnt to say sorry and they enjoy a cuddle to make up, but
Jackie suspects that he does not really understand what he is saying sorry for.
He likes to play with the younger children on the estate but Jackie keeps a close
eye on him, never letting him go far. She worries about Luke's future envisaging
that he will always need a high degree of supervision and care. Currently there
are plans to enrol him into a college specifically designed for young people with
learning difficulties.

References

Ainsworth, M. D. S., Blehar, M. C., Waters, E. and Wall, S. (1978) *Patterns of Attachment: A Psychological Study of the Strange Situation.* Hillsdale, NJ: Erlbaum.

Archer, C. and Gordon, C. (2006) *New Families, Old Scripts.* London: Jessica Kingsley Publishers.

Bowlby, J. (1973) *Attachment and Loss, Vol. II Separation: Anxiety and Anger.* New York, NY: Basic Books.

Bowlby, J. (1980) *Attachment and Loss, Vol. III Loss: Sadness and Depression.* New York, NY: Basic Books.

Bowlby, J. (1982) *Attachment and Loss, Vol. 1 Attachment.* London: Hogarth Press; New York, NY: Basic Books.

Bowlby, J. (1998) *A Secure Base. Clinical Applications of Attachment Theory.* London: Routledge.

Brodzinsky, D. M., Schechter, M. D. and Henig, R. M. (1993) *Being Adopted: The Lifelong Search for Self.* New York, NY: Anchor Books.

Cairns, K. and Stanway, C. (2004) *Learn the Child: Helping Looked After Children to Learn – A Good Practice Guide for Social Workers, Carers and Teachers.* London: BAAF.

Crittenden, P. M., Landini, A. and Claussen, A. H. (2001) 'A Dynamic-Maturational Approach to Treatment of Maltreated Children.' In J. N. Hughes, A. M. La Greca and J. C. Conoley (eds) *Handbook of Psychological Services for Children and Adolescents.* Oxford: Oxford University Press.

Davis, N. (1996) *Therapeutic Stories That Teach and Heal.* Published by Nancy Davis.

Dozier, M. (2003) 'Attachment-Based Treatment for Vulnerable Children.' *Attachment and Human Development 5,* 3, 253–257.

Dozier, M., Stovall, K. C., Albus, K. E. and Bates, B. (2001) 'Attachment for Infants in Foster Care: The Role of Caregiver State of Mind.' *Child Development 72,* 1467–77.

Fahlberg, V. I. (1994) *A Child's Journey Through Placement.* London: BAAF.

Fonagy, P., Gergely, G., Jurist, E. L. and Target, M. (2002) *Affect Regulation, Mentalization, and the Development of the Self.* New York, NY: Other Press.

Golding, K. S., Dent, H. R., Nissim, R. and Stott, L. (2006) *Thinking Psychologically About Children Who Are Looked After and Adopted: Space for Reflection.* Chichester: John Wiley and Sons Ltd.

Hobday, A. (2001) 'Timeholes: A Useful Metaphor When Explaining Unusual or Bizarre Behaviour in Children Who Have Moved Families.' *Clinical Child Psychology and Psychiatry 6,* 1, 41–47.

Hodges, J., Steele, M., Hillman, S., Henderson, K. and Kaniuk, J. (2003) 'Changes in Attachment Representations over the First Year of Adoptive Placement: Narratives of Maltreated Children.' *Journal of Clinical Child Psychology and Psychiatry 8,* 3 July, 351–367.

Howe, D. (2005) *Child Abuse and Neglect: Attachment, Development and Intervention.* Basingstoke: Palgrave Macmillan.

Hughes, D. A. (2006) *Building the Bonds of Attachment: Awakening Love in Deeply Troubled Children.* Northvale, NJ: Aronson.

James, B. (1994) *Handbook for Treatment of Attachment-Trauma Problems in Children.* New York, NY: Free Press.

Jernberg, A. and Booth, P. B. (2001) *Theraplay: Helping Parents and Children Build Better Relationships Through Attachment-based Play.* San Francisco, CA: Jossey-Bass.

Lacher, D. B., Nichols, T. and May, J. C. (2005) *Connecting with Kids Through Stories: Using Narratives to Facilitate Attachment in Adopted Children.* London: Jessica Kingsley Publishers.

Main, M. and Solomon, J. (1986) 'Discovery of a New, Insecure Disorganized/Disorientated Attachment Pattern.' In T. B. Brazelton and M. Yogman (eds) *Affective Development in Infancy.* Norwood, NJ: Ablex.

Meins, E., Ferneyhough, C., Wainwright, R., Das Gupta, M., Fradley, E. and Tuckey, M. (2002) 'Maternal Mind-Mindedness and Attachment Security as Predictors of Theory of Mind Understanding.' *Child Development 73,* 6, 1715–26.

Rutter, M., Colvert, E., Kreppner, J., Beckett, C. *et al.* (2007) 'Early Adolescent Outcomes for Institutionally-Deprived and Non-Deprived Adoptees. 1: Disinhibited Attachment.' *Journal of Child Psychology and Psychiatry 48,* 1, 12–30.

Schore, A. N. (1994) *Affect Regulation and the Origin of Self: The Neurobiology of Emotional Development.* Mahwah, NJ: Erlbaum.

Siegel, D. J. and Hartzell, M. (2003) *Parenting From the Inside Out.* New York, NY: Tarcher/Putnam.

Sprague, T. (1997) 'Clinical Management of Suicidal Behaviour in Children and Adolescents.' *Clinical Child Psychology and Psychiatry 2,* 1, 113–123.

Stern, D. N. (1985) *The Interpersonal World of the Infant.* New York, NY: Basic Books.

Sunderland, M. (2006) *The Science of Parenting: Practical Guidance on Sleep, Crying, Play and Building Emotional Well Being for Life.* London: Dorling Kindersley.

Trevarthen, C. (2001) 'Intrinsic Motives for Companionship in Understanding: Their Origin, Development, and Significance for Infant Mental Health.' *Infant Mental Health Journal 22,* 1–2, 95–131.

van der Kolk, B. A. (2005) 'Editorial: Child Abuse and Victimisation.' *Psychiatric Annals 35,* 5, 374–378.

Verrier, N. N. (1993) *The Primal Wound: Understanding the Adopted Child.* Baltimore, MD: Gateway Press Inc.

Webster-Stratton, C. (2001) *Incredible Years: The Parents, Teachers and Children Training Series.* Seattle, WA: Carolyn Webster-Stratton.

Further Reading

Archer, C. (1997) *First Steps in Parenting the Child Who Hurts: Tiddlers and Toddlers.* London: Jessica Kingsley Publishers.

Archer, C. (1999) *Next Steps in Parenting the Child Who Hurts: Tykes and Teens.* London: Jessica Kingsley Publishers.

Archer, C. and Burnell, A. (2003) *Trauma, Attachment and Family Permanence: Fear Can Stop You Loving.* London: Jessica Kingsley Publishers.

Archer, C. and Gordon, C. (2006) *New Families, Old Scripts.* London: Jessica Kingsley Publishers.

Bowlby, J. (1998) *A Secure Base: Clinical Applications of Attachment Theory.* London: Routledge.

Cairns, K. (2002) *Attachment, Trauma and Resilience.* London: BAAF.

Delaney, R. J. (1998a) *Fostering Changes: Treating Attachment-Disordered Foster Children.* Oklahoma City, OK: Wood and Barnes Publishing.

Delaney, R. J. (1998b) *Raising Cain: Caring for Troubled Youngsters/Repairing Our Troubled System.* Oklahoma City, OK: Wood and Barnes Publishing.

Fahlberg, V. (1994) *A Child's Journey Through Placement.* London: BAAF.

Geddes, H. (2006) *Attachment in the Classroom: The Links Between Children's Early Experience, Emotional Well-Being and Performance in School.* London: Worth Publishing.

Gilligan, R. (2001) *Promoting Resilience: A Resource Guide on Working with Children in the Care System.* London: BAAF.

Golding, K. S., Dent, H. R., Nissim, R. and Stott, L. (2006) *Thinking Psychologically About Children Who Are Looked After and Adopted. Space for Reflection.* Chichester: John Wiley and Sons Ltd.

Hart, A. and Luckock, B. (2004) *Developing Adoption Support and Therapy: New Approaches for Practice.* London: Jessica Kingsley Publishers.

Hobday, A., Kirby, A. and Ollier, K. (2002) *Creative Therapy for Children in New Families.* Oxford: BPS Blackwell.

Howe, D. (2005) *Child Abuse and Neglect: Attachment, Development and Intervention.* Hampshire: Palgrave Macmillan.

Hughes, D. A. (1997) *Facilitating Developmental Attachment: The Road to Emotional Recovery and Behavioural Change in Foster and Adopted Children.* Northvale, NJ: Aronson.

Hughes, D. A. (2006) *Building the Bonds of Attachment: Awakening Love in Deeply Troubled Children.* Northvale, NJ: Aronson.

James, B. (1994) *Handbook for Treatment of Attachment-Trauma Problems in Children.* New York, NY: Free Press.

Jennings, S. (2004) *Creative Storytelling with Children at Risk.* Brackley: Speechmark Publishing Ltd.

Jernberg, A. and Booth, P. B. (2001) *Theraplay: Helping Parents and Children Build Better Relationships Through Attachment-Based Play.* San Fransisco, CA: Jossey-Bass.

Keck, G. C. and Kupecky, R. M. (2002) *Parenting the Hurt Child: Helping Adoptive Families Heal and Grow.* Colorado Springs, CO: Pinon Press.

Lacher, D. B., Nichols, T. and May, J. C. (2005) *Connecting with Kids Through Stories: Using Narratives to Facilitate Attachment in Adopted Children.* London: Jessica Kingsley Publishers.

Salans, M. (2004) *Storytelling with Children in Crisis.* London: Jessica Kingsley Publishers.

Schofield, G. and Beek, M. (2006) *Attachment Handbook for Foster Care and Adoption.* London: BAAF.

Siegel, D. J. and Hartzell, M. (2003) *Parenting from the Inside Out.* New York, NY: Tarcher/Putnam.

Solomon, M. F. and Siegel, D. J. (2003) *Healing Trauma: Attachment, Mind, Body and Brain.* London: W. W. Norton and Co.

Stern, D. N. (1998) *Diary of a Baby.* New York, NY: Basic Books.

Sunderland, M. (2006) *The Science of Parenting: Practical Guidance on Sleep, Crying, Play and Building Emotional Well Being for Life.* London: Dorling Kindersley.

Sunderland, M. and Armstrong, N. (2003) *Helping Children with Fear: A Guidebook.* Brackley: Speechmark Publishing Ltd.

Glossary

Affectional bonds A bond or tie that exists between two people when they feel affection for each other.

Affect mirroring A process whereby the parent interprets what a child is feeling from observation of her behaviour. This interpretation is reflected back to the child to help her develop a deeper understanding of her feelings.

Ambivalent-resistant attachment The attachment that the child develops when a parent is experienced as inconsistent and unpredictable. The child learns to maximize displays of emotion in order to maintain the parent's availability.

Attachment A special type of relationship that develops when one person experiences security and comfort from another. A **selective attachment** occurs when the child relates to a **primary attachment** figure and a few intimate adults in this way.

Attachment behavioural system This represents the way that behaviour is organized in order to elicit care and comfort from the parent.

Attunement An emotional connection between two people in which one person mirrors or matches the vitality and affect (externally displayed mood) of the other.

Autonomy This represents the degree of an individual's personal independence.

Avoidant attachment The attachment that the child develops when a parent is experienced as rejecting. The child learns to minimize displays of emotion in order to maintain parent availability.

Coercive behaviour Behaviour displayed in order to ensure a particular reaction from others. The behaviour compels others to behave in a particular way.

Cognitive The conscious thinking processes. These take place in the cortex of the brain.

Coherent narrative Healthy individuals have a sense of themselves and their experiences. They form a coherent narrative of their life experiences. These are explicit memories held in a consistent and organized manner. Traumatic experience makes the holding of such memories and the development of such a narrative more difficult.

Compulsive behaviour Behaviour that is governed by an impulse to do something in order to maintain feelings of safety.

Developmental pathway This is a biological term that suggests that development can occur along one of a range of possible pathways. The pathway used depends upon an interaction between the child and environment. As development proceeds the number of potential pathways diminish.

Disinhibited behaviour Indiscriminately friendly but superficial behaviours, usually relating to an inability to engage in mutually satisfying relationships.

Disorganized-controlling attachment The attachment that the child develops when a parent is experienced as frightening or frightened. The child experiences difficulty organizing her behaviour at times of stress. As she grows older she learns to control relationships to force predictability.

Dissociation This is a psychoanalytic term to describe the process by which a person defends against overwhelming stress by cutting off from conscious awareness what is being sensed or felt. At its extreme the person cuts off from contact with others or the world, becoming numb, unfeeling or unaware. Dissociation reduces the ability to make sense of self or others.

Emotional co-regulation The capacity to regulate emotion is influenced by the experience of co-regulation whereby the parent interacts with the child to help her to manage her emotion and emotional arousal.

Emotional Dysregulation Dysregulation represents a lack of regulatory capacity. It occurs when an individual fails to control and modulate emotions and emotional arousal. The emotion overwhelms the individual and controls him rather than him being in control of the emotion.

Emotional regulation The capacity to control and modulate emotions and emotional arousal.

Emotional scaffolding A parent can help a child develop new abilities by starting where the child is and helping her step-by-step to learn a new ability. This type of help is known as scaffolding.

Empathy The ability to imagine and share what another is experiencing.

Experience dependent Development within the brain, which forms the neural pathways that determine how the brain will function, is dependent upon the person having certain experiences. Genes and experience interact to shape development. Thus if an infant is raised in the dark at a certain stage of development they will not learn to see. Nurturing experiences are also important for healthy brain development.

Exploratory behavioural system This represents the way that behaviour is organized in order to promote exploration of novelty within the environment.

Impulsive behaviour Behaviour that occurs without thinking. A person behaves without first thinking about the consequences that might occur following the behaviour.

Inhibited behaviour The child is fearful of others and is reluctant to engage with them in any way.

Interactive repair This is a psychological term used to describe the process whereby a parent re-establishes a positive emotional connection between themselves and a child (**attunement**) following a time when the relationship was ruptured, either because of the behaviour of the child or of the parent.

Internal working model (IWM) A cognitive model of the relationship that the child has experienced. This model influences how the child will respond to future relationships.

Locus of control This is a psychological term to describe the amount of control a person feels he has over situations in his life. An external locus of control suggests that a person feels that he has little control and that other people or the environment has this control. An internal locus of control suggests that a person feels that he has a lot of control over situations.

Mentalization The ability to predict responses of others based on an understanding of the feelings of others. This is dependent on the ability to take the perspective of the other person (**perspective-taking**).

Mind-minded Being aware of the mental state of the other. Understanding mental states (thoughts, feelings, beliefs and desires) helps us make sense of behaviour and therefore to understand the social world within which we live.

Negative reinforcement In behavioural psychology negative reinforcement refers to a consequence to a behaviour that is experienced as unpleasant. The person behaves in a certain way in order to avoid the negative consequence. Thus the behaviour is negatively reinforced. For example, a parent buys a child sweets in order to stop her crying. The sweet-buying behaviour in the parent has been negatively reinforced.

Obsessive behaviour Behaviour that is governed by a preoccupation with certain ideas or needs.

Passive-aggressive Expressing aggression towards others through indirect and unassertive acts. For example, a child might break something behind someone's back, not for any end in itself, but as a way of expressing anger.

Perspective-taking This is a psychological term to describe the process whereby an individual can imagine a situation or experience from the perspective of another person.

Positive reinforcement In behavioural psychology positive reinforcement refers to a consequence to a behaviour that is experienced as pleasant and thus rewarding. The person behaves in a certain way in order to gain the pleasant consequence. For example, the child cries because the crying has been rewarded by sweets. The child's crying behaviour has been positively reinforced.

Primary intersubjectivity This describes the early relationship between an infant and parent when each discover the other and learn more about the self in the process.

Projection This is a psychoanalytic term to describe the process by which a person transfers or projects feelings onto another.

Proximity-seeking Behaviour that is displayed in order to achieve closeness to an attachment figure. This increases feelings of safety and security for the child.

Pseudomaturity The child behaves in a way that is more mature than she is emotionally ready for.

Punishment In behavioural psychology punishment refers to a consequence to a behaviour that is experienced as unpleasant. The person stops behaving in this way to avoid the unpleasant consequence. For example, if a child was smacked when crying for sweets her crying behaviour would be punished leading her to stop crying. As punishment also leads to shame, to feelings of low self-worth and doesn't teach the child what behaviour is acceptable, it is generally considered to be a poor parenting technique. Parents are advised to reward good behaviour rather than punish bad behaviour.

Reflective function The ability to think about our own mind and the mind of others. This leads to the ability to understand why things happen and why people behave as they do.

Regression This is a psychoanalytic term to describe the process whereby a person who is experiencing high levels of stress reverts to behaviour representative of an earlier stage of development.

Secondary intersubjectivity This describes the infant–parent relationship and their joint attention to people, objects and events in the world. The child learns about the world and the impact of the world on herself and her parent.

Secure attachment The attachment that a child develops when a parent is experienced as sensitive and responsive to her emotional needs. The child learns trust in others and appropriate self-reliance.

Secure base A secure base occurs when a child is able to feel secure with a parent and is therefore able to engage in confident exploration.

Self-efficacy This is a psychological term used to describe the belief an individual holds about his own ability. High self-efficacy suggests that the individual is confident in his abilities whilst low self-efficacy suggests that the individual lacks confidence in his abilities.

Self-esteem This describes how a person perceives himself, his sense of his own worth. Thus a person's opinion about himself leads to his self-esteem. High self-esteem suggests that an individual perceives himself positively whilst low self-esteem represents a low opinion of himself and his worth to others.

Separation protest The protest that the child displays when accessibility to an attachment figure is threatened.

Shame A complex emotional state when a person experiences negative feelings about himself. A feeling of being not good enough.

Social understanding Understanding social relationships and social situations. Social understanding is important for getting on with people and for making and maintaining friendships.

Splitting This is a psychoanalytic term used to describe the process whereby when someone can't cope with ambivalent feelings about others they compartmentalize those people as all good or all bad.

Theory of mind This is the understanding that what another person thinks, feels or believes might be different from what I think, feel or believe, and that what another person thinks, feels and believes is a good predictor of behaviour. Theory of mind typically develops between three and four years of age.

Subject Index

233

Author Index